THINK
LEAD
DISRUPT

THINK
LEAD
DISRUPT

How Innovative Minds
Connect Strategy to Execution

Peter B. Nichol

For information about permissions to reproduce selections from the book, or about special discounts for bulk purchases, please contact: booksales@datasciencecio.com

Publisher's Catalog-in-Publication Data
Library of Congress Catalog Card LCCN No. 2020922775

ISBN: 978-0-578-78738-1

Printed in the United States of America.

For Ann

CONTACTING PETER B. NICHOL

Sharing ideas makes me happy. I enjoy leading, motivating and coaching executives on how to perform and think at their best.

The motivation for the development of this book, arose from my passion to share my best ideas. We are taught to ride a bike. We are taught to speak a language. We are taught to read. We aren't taught how to think of ideas. As a 4x author and contributor to *CIO*, I wanted to share approaches to generate world class ideas, while connecting strategy to execution. After all it all comes down to execution.

Think Lead Disrupt is the culmination, across decades, of the best sources for ideas, visions and inspirations I have discovered. It captures how innovative leaders continually generate unique ideas.

I welcome your stories, insights, and any useful tools and techniques you have to improve how to create unique ideas and deliver with excellence. I guarantee I'll read all the letters and email I receive. However, due to the pure volume, I'm not able to respond to every request for information.

For leaders, teams, and organizations interested in engaging me for board advisory, consulting, or speaking please contact me at OROCA Innovations:

Peter B. Nichol
Chief Technology Officer, OROCA Innovations
145 Barkledge Drive
Newington, CT 06111
E-mail: peter.nichol@datasciencecio.com
Twitter: @peterbnichol

For additional information on the book, Think Lead Disrupt, please visit the website:
www.datasciencecio.com/thinkleaddisrupt

For additional information on the book, Leading With Value, please visit the website:
www.datasciencecio.com/leadingwithvalue

For additional information on the book, The Power of Blockchain for Healthcare, please visit the website:
www.datasciencecio.com/blockchainbook

For additional information on the book, Learning Intelligence, please visit the website:
www.datasciencecio.com/li

ABOUT THE AUTHOR

PETER B. NICHOL (@peterbnichol) is a technology executive with 19 years of experience who's dedicated to driving innovation, digital transformation, leadership, and data in business. He helps organizations connect strategy to execution to maximize company performance.

Peter has led businesses through complex changes including the adoption of data-first approaches for portfolio management, Lean Six Sigma for operational excellence, departmental transformations, process improvements, maximizing team performance, designing new IT operating models, digitizing platforms, leading large-scale mission-critical technology deployments, product management, and agile methodologies, and building high-performance teams.

Peter has been recognized for Digital Innovation by CIO 100, MIT Sloan, Computerworld, BRM Institute, and the Project Management Institute. As Managing Director at OROCA Innovations, Peter leads the CXO advisory-services practice that drives digital strategies.

Peter was honored as an MIT Sloan CIO Leadership Award Finalist in 2015 and is a regular contributor to CIO. com on innovation. As Head of Information Technology, Peter was responsible for Connecticut's Health Insurance Exchange's (HIX) industry-leading digital platform, which has transformed consumerism and retail-oriented services for the health-insurance industry. Peter championed the Connecticut marketplace digital implementation with a transformational, cloud-based, SaaS platform and mobile application. He was recognized as a 2014 PMI Project of the Year Award finalist, CIO 100, and received awards for best digital services, API, and platform. He also received a lifetime achievement award for leadership and digital transformation and was honored as a 2016 Computerworld Premier 100 IT Leader.

Peter has a Bachelor of Science in Computer Information Systems from Bentley University and a Master in Business Administration from Quinnipiac University, where he graduated Summa Cum Laude. He earned his PMP® in 2001 and is a certified Six Sigma Master Black Belt, Certified SAFe® Agilist, Certified SAFe® Practitioner (SP), Certified ScrumMaster®, Business Relationship Management Professional (BRMP®), Certified Business Relationship Manager (CBRM®), and the first globally credentialled Master of Business Relationship Management (MBRM®) by the BRM Institute. Together we can change the world!

For more details, please visit
https://datasciencecio.com/about/

ACCLAIM FOR PETER NICHOL'S BUSINESS BOOKS

THINK LEAD DISRUPT

"Think Lead Disrupt presents unique insights on how innovators can continually evolve ideas for digital transformation. Nichol, a respected writer for CIO, has shared the secrets to move from strategy to execution. A must-read!"

— AMRESH MATHUR
DIGITAL TRANSFORMATION EXECUTIVE,
SAMSUNG ELECTRONICS AMERICA

"Think Lead Disrupt will illuminate how brilliant leaders identify new ideas to transform their businesses. Nichol presents the practical impacts of how ideas lead to disruptive business transformations. A refreshing look at how evolutionary and revolutionary ideas fuel business transformation. A must-read for every innovator!"

— QAMAR ZIA
SENIOR DIRECTOR OF TECHNICAL SERVICES,
KÖRBER SUPPLY CHAIN

"A prolific writer in a Zen master fashion strikes again. Building on his CIO experience, Peter dissects the anatomy of innovative ideas and creativity once again in his upcoming book. *Think Lead Disrupt* is riveting, addictive, and disruptive. How leaders think, innovate, and grow from the ashes? If you are looking for the food for thought, the meal has been served."

— MINHAAJ REHMAN
CEO AND FOUNDER, PSYDA

"*Think Lead Disrupt* is a fantastic book for leaders that want to develop innovative ideas that can be translated into world-class business products, services, and interactions. Nichol's voice as a CIO and global thought leader is simple to understand and easy to apply. This is a must-read for innovators leading teams, departments, or organizations that must be on the cutting edge!"

— AARON S. BARNES
CEO AND CO-FOUNDER, BUSINESS RELATIONSHIP MANAGEMENT
(BRM) INSTITUTE

"A wise man—my 100-year old grandfather—once told me, when faced with a complex problem, always go back to first principles. From there, assumptions can be questioned, and the status quo can be challenged. *Think Lead Disrupt* embodies this philosophy and presents unique insights into how innovators can continually evolve digital transformation ideas. Nichol, a respected writer for CIO, has shared the secrets to move from strategy to execution. A must-read!"

— ERIC ACTON
HEAD OF INNOVATION ECOSYSTEMS, ROLLS-ROYCE

"A must-read. Everyone wants to think like an innovator. Every day we're immersed in a world that is lightning fast. In this world only the best ideas are funding, implemented and adopted. Nichol has captured why innovative executives are able to continually discover earth-shattering ideas."

— MATHIAS GOYEN, MD
CHIEF MEDICAL OFFICER EUROPE, MIDDLE EAST AND AFRICA,
GE HEALTHCARE

"The innovation mindset is fundamental to source new solutions. Without this you will not have the right foundations to really achieve true innovation. Peter clearly articulates how having the right innovation mindset provides a path to harness disruptive strategies and approach new ways to solve old problems!"

— STEVE SUAREZ
GLOBAL HEAD OF INNOVATION, FINANCE AND RISK, HSBC

"A great book for leaders looking to create an organizational culture and the capacity to accelerate innovation. A must-read book that explores the art and science of innovation!"

— KRISHNA CHERIATH,
VP, HEAD OF DIGITAL, DATA AND ANALYTICS, ZOETIS INC.

LEADING WITH VALUE

"We all know that traditional PMOs are broken and don't provide the value executives expect. *Leading with Value* is the first book to systematically break down the concept of value into pieces that every leader can take advantage of for their organizations' benefit. If you want to do a better job of quantifying the impact and value of your team, this book should be your first read!"

— TRUSHAR SHAH
HEAD OF ENGINEERING, GEP WORLDWIDE

"Learn how to speak the language of business value! *Leading with Value* is the solution that every business relationship partner has been looking for—the complete guide to effectively communicating business value!"

— GLENN REMORERAS
CHIEF INFORMATION OFFICER, MARK ANTHONY GROUP

"CIOs expect their leaders to understand how to quantify value. Nichol takes the mysterious and complex topic of value and simplifies it to the essential nuggets we all need to understand. Struggling to quantify the value of your team? Pick up a copy of *Leading with Value* and stand out from your peers with your understanding of how to effectively communicate value!"

— HATEM ELMANAWY
DIRECTOR OF PROJECT MANAGEMENT, OCEAN CAPITAL

"Value is, perhaps, the most misused word in the corporate lexicon. Identifying and aligning on what value must be captured is itself a challenge, and companies rarely follow-through during and post capability acquisition to ensure anticipated value is, indeed, captured as planned with little to no erosion. Quite admirably, Peter has taken on and delivered on this challenge to explain a complex topic in straightforward terms. *Leading with Value* provides a holistic take on value - Identification, Stewardship, and Realization - that brings us back to the basics while challenging our thinking."

— RAM MADRAS
EXECUTIVE DIRECTOR OF IT STRATEGY & PLANNING,
BLUE CROSS AND BLUE SHIELD

"Nichol finally wrote the business book for all levels from the CIO to the manager. Every leader is charged with creating and capturing business value. *Leading with Value* takes the time to elaborate on how specifically to take abstract concepts and turn them into concrete and quantifiable examples of value. Change how you look at business problems forever with Leading with Value!"

— ISAAK GEORGIADIS
HEAD OF VALUE COST MANAGEMENT, BEI DRÄXLMAIER GROUP

"*Leading with Value* provides several methods and the essential nuggets that allow companies to transform Project-Management Offices into Value-Management Offices. Nichol's new book is a must-read for Senior Executives, PMO leaders and project managers that want to expand their knowledge on discovering, realizing and optimizing the value of their project, teams and portfolios!"

— JEAN BINDER
HEAD OF LIFE SCIENCES PROGRAM MANAGEMENT OFFICE,
PHILIP MORRIS INTERNATIONAL

"*Leading with Value* offers insightful examples of how to capture and communicate value to your business partners. Do your leaders understand your value? Can your peers describe the services you provide? As a CIO and 4x author, Nichol harnesses his experience to empower leaders to maximize business value!"

— KRIS SPRAGUE
HEAD OF PROJECT PLANNING & SCHEDULING,
REGENERON PHARMACEUTICALS, INC.

"*Leading with Value* provides several methods and the essential nuggets that allow companies to transform Project-Management Offices into Value-Management Offices. Nichol's new book is a must-read for Senior Executives, PMO leaders and project managers that want to expand their knowledge on discovering, realizing and optimizing the value of their project, teams and portfolios!"

— JEAN BINDER
HEAD OF LIFE SCIENCES PROGRAM MANAGEMENT OFFICE, PHIL-
IP MORRIS INTERNATIONAL

"*Leading with Value* presents a unique formula that helps leaders maximize business value. If you're a leader looking for methods, approaches, and solutions to quantify business value, this book will be your best guide!"

— NANJI CHANDRASEKHAR
VP OF IT INFRASTRUCTURE & CLOUD OPERATIONS,
ASPEN DENTAL MANAGEMENT, INC.

"*Leading with Value* offers CDOs and CIOs concrete ways to capture and communicate the business value of their data, analytics and technology investments. Nichol makes the case for why traditional budget and PMO measures are outdated and offers more relevant approaches for a rapidly changing digital world. A must-read!"

— CINDI HOWSON
CHIEF DATA STRATEGY OFFICE THOUGHTSPOT &
HOST OF THE DATA CHIEF PODCAST

THE POWER OF BLOCKCHAIN FOR HEALTHCARE

"The Power of Blockchain for Healthcare presents a crisp and fresh perspective of blockchain tailored to healthcare. Nichol focuses on how blockchain will enhance the patient and provider experience and the technology we use to interaction with patients. A must-read!"

— RAJA RAMACHANDRAN
FOUNDER, RIPE.IO AND FORMER MANAGING DIRECTOR, R3CEV

"The Power of Blockchain for Healthcare is an essential read for any seasoned leader, and with Peter's unique perspectives it's no wonder he is one of the most influential innovation voices on healthcare innovation. A must read."

— GUILHERME STOCCO
HEAD OF STRATEGY AND INNOVATION, BANCO ORIGINAL

"Peter offers a new voice presenting fresh perspectives on how blockchain will transform the healthcare experience. *The Power of Blockchain for Healthcare* presents the unconventional potential utilization of blockchain beyond the financial sector and within an industry that is on the verge of a disruption."

— EMILIA POPOSKA
CO-FOUNDER AND CEO, BRONTECH

xvii

"Blockchain technology will fundamentally transform, disrupt and change our world much like the internet has done. All industry segments will be affected, and it will allow for fundamental shifts in business models. Nichol magnificently articulates the implications for the healthcare industry. A must read for every senior executive who wants to be prepared for the future."

— JACK SMIES
VICE PRESIDENT & BUSINESS HEAD MIDDLE EAST, WIPRO

"Peter accelerates past the typical explanation of blockchain, and immediately carves out blockchain's value for healthcare. If you're already familiar with blockchain but truly want to understand how blockchain will disrupt healthcare, then *The Power of Blockchain for Healthcare* is the book for you."

— ERAN ORR
FOUNDER & CEO, VRPHYSIO INC.

"The Power of Blockchain for Healthcare provides a compelling argument for the transformative impact that blockchain will have on the patience experience. Nichol magnificently articulates a future vision of health, a vision every executive should experience."

— SAN BANERJEE
HEAD OF CONSUMER DIGITAL SOLUTIONS, HUMANA

"Peter dives into unexplored, valuable territory in *Learning Intelligence*. A must-read for any leader wanting to compete in the innovation-powered landscape of today."

— MARSHALL GOLDSMITH
THE AUTHOR OF THE #1 NEW YORK TIMES BESTSELLER,
TRIGGERS

"An important book for the new digital economy which requires fundamental skills that can adapt to a dynamic and fast moving environment. Peter has captured the quintessential element for preparing organizations to meet and exploit these digital capabilities."

— DALE DANILEWITZ
CHIEF INFORMATION OFFICER, AMERISOURCEBERGEN

"This is a great book, offering much wise advice. I most appreciated Nichol's insight around the value of data, information, knowledge and wisdom. *Learning Intelligence* is the new currency for exponential thinking."

— DAVID M. JOHNSON
SVP & GLOBAL HEAD OF PUBLIC SECTOR GROUP, COGNIZANT

"The ability to unlearn and learn is vital, as business leaders constantly navigate through change. *Learning Intelligence* is the tool they have been waiting for!"

— GURMEET CHAHAL
SVP AND HEAD HEALTHCARE, HCL TECHNOLOGIES

"Nichol is an insightful innovator and partner in driving transformation change within organizations. This book is a must read for business leaders charged with transforming their organization's ability to learn."

— LENNOX BROWN
CHIEF INFORMATION OFFICER, ANALOGIC

"Using well-presented research, Nichol makes a convincing argument for corporate leaders to grow their knowledge in this area. This book is a useful tool in recognizing the strategic impact of *Learning Intelligence.*"

— KARL PANSEWICZ
CEO, SNAPCODR, INC.

"Peter has identified the "secret sauce" for organizations to evolve their culture of innovation and learning. *Learning intelligence* is the missing link most organizations seek but rarely find."

— CHRISTOPHER CORNUE
CHIEF STRATEGY & INNOVATION OFFICER, NAVICENT HEALTH

"*Learning Intelligence* identifies a phenomenon that has defined this and future generations potential to advance and succeed – the ability to learn. We observe more and more that multidisciplinary approaches are key to finding new innovative solutions to challenging problems – and this requires all stakeholders to possess the learning agility necessary to make breakthroughs. I applaud Peter Nichol for capturing this in an easy-to-understand book."

— GEORGE T MATHEW, MD
CHIEF MEDICAL OFFICER, HEWLETT PACKARD ENTERPRISE

"Peter B. Nichol does an excellent job taking the important and complex, learning intelligence concepts and giving every individual advice to put into action to improve their ability to learn. *Learning Intelligence* is a great combination of strategy and practical approaches, sure to help anyone improve their ability to learn and innovate successfully."

— NICOLAS BRAGARD
CHIEF INFORMATION OFFICER, ESKER

"Peter is an expert at taking organizations from Information Strategy to Implementation to Value Realization. In *Learning Intelligence*, he applies this expertise to help individuals and organizations raise their Human Capital to new heights!"

— RICHARD SINGERMAN, PHD
ADJUNCT ASSISTANT PROFESSOR, JOHNS HOPKINS SCHOOL OF
MEDICINE

"Peter's new book *Learning Intelligence* captures the essence of the "ability to learn" – the foundation for success. A must read, for all leaders who want to be successful in life!"

— BALU MV
CHIEF INFORMATION & INNOVATION OFFICER,
AVA INTERNATIONAL

"A highly accessible book for all business executives that demand the best talent to meet operational objectives. *Learning Intelligence* provides a broad understanding of the ability to learn in a model that works brilliantly for both industry, government, and academic settings."

— SAFDAR ZAMAN
HEAD OF IT STRATEGY AND GOVERNANCE, NAKHEEL PJSC

"In *Learning Intelligence*, Peter B. Nichol launches a fascinating new concept with the potential to help business leaders significantly advance product and process innovation in every industry... The book clearly describes how leaders can acquire these valuable skills by accurately improving their *Learning Intelligence* and then continually working to measure their LQ."

— ROBERT COLI, MD
FOUNDER & CHAIRMAN,
DIAGNOSTIC INFORMATION SYSTEM COMPANY

"Peter extends the current view on personal maturity by introducing LQ – Learning Quotient – a complement of intelligence and emotional intelligence quotients by focusing on our ability to change, grow and live. A fascinating view and an area which every leader must explore."

— THOMAS WALENTA
BOARD OF DIRECTORS AND FELLOW, PMI

"It has been said that 'minding your P's and Q's is applicable to life and business. Peter Nichol's extraordinary new book enhances complete understanding of the Q's which is half the battle in successful startups and corporate enterprises. This is a game-changer."

— EDWARD BUKSTEL
CEO, CLINICAL BLOCKCHAIN

"An important read for all leaders as we move towards a future, where speed, adaptability, knowledge, and sound decision making are the currency for success."

— STEVE LAWLER
SVP REGIONAL GROUP, CAROLINAS HEALTHCARE SYSTEM

Innovation Mindset (n): a group of individuals with an innate curiosity to challenge conventions in search of new ideas for the advancement of individuals, teams, and organizations.

PREFACE

Innovative thinkers approach problems uniquely. They think differently and, therefore, solve problems differently. Discovering where original ideas grow, how to discover new value, and how to enable organizational innovation is the key to building sustainable competitive advantages.

Everyone has the ability to be innovative. It's true some folks are more naturally curious than others. However, innovation can be learned. It's not only special people in special places that build unique products, services, and interactions. The image of innovation growing in secret labs from elite minds has transformed to one of warm coffee houses and engaging, late-night discussions in parking lots. Innovative minds are curious.

Are you trying to spot innovative thinkers? They don't jump out from a crowd—they blend in. As they mix into the flow of the daily grind, one interesting characteristic becomes more pervasive: They bend convention, hoping to find new value. They don't do what everyone else does.

For example, let's take waiting in line at a grocery store. Think about that for a minute. Recall the last time you waited in line at a grocery store. It might have been during a busy Saturday morning at Costco or the day before a holiday where everyone was out shopping. When you found yourself in a long line, you undoubtedly quickly got into one of the shorter lines. Why? Well, that's what we're trained to do. After you were in line, if you paused to look around, someone else also got into that line.

Then they left. They left to explore. They lost their spot in line, hoping to find a line that was shorter. They fully understood that they might have to return and wait in the same line—a line that, five minutes later, would be even longer. Innovative thinkers aren't storms that enter a room; they're a series of small waves—waves of innovation.

In every part of my career—my work advising leaders, coaching teams, and leading organizations—I repeatedly hear the same question: How do we build an innovation mindset?

Organizations that ask for guidance are often the most successful. The pillars of these organizations once ensured profitability, stability, and value. I've discovered that these foundations of growth have become less pronounced as I speak with organizations or walk their halls. What's changed? The leaders.

In this book, I explore the elements that make up the innovation mindset. The book has three parts:

Part I, The Growth of Original Ideas, explores where innovative ideas originate. Chapter 1, The Science of Ideas, is the staple of the book and pokes at the different types of thinking to uncover the value of first-principle thinking—the value of original thinking. Chapter 2, Breaking Limits, touches on the benefits of breakthrough innovations and why exponential innovation is so powerful. Chapter 3, Mental Models and Divergent Thinking, spotlights sources of inspiration and methods to frame the velocity of innovation you're experiencing today. Chapter 4, Predicting Innovation, opens the discussion to a connected world—a world of collaboration, platforms, and prediction markets.

Part 2, Inspiration from Outside, shifts our focus from looking inside our organization to observing life around us—outside our comfort zone. Chapter 5, Innovation's Boundaries in a Boundless World, addresses the guardrails of innovation and shows us how we can break barriers. Chapter 6, The Art of Prediction, tackles the gray areas of innovation and how understanding prediction markets can influence your idea revolution. Chapter 7, Inspiration from Nature, peers into the wild world of Nature to gain insights and unique perspectives. Chapter 8, Innovation Platforms and Economic Shifts, is the more obvious side of innovation, exploring how collaborative consumption, co-creation, and platform ecosystems drive disruption.

Part 3, Enabling Organizational Innovation, provides the pieces to put everything together: how to create ideas that lead to new creations, where technology is driving change, and when to enter the frontier when others wait. Chapter 9, Discovering Innovation, frames models of discovery and describes how to manage innovation and watch innovation from the outside. Chapter 10, The Idea Revolution, discusses emerging technology trends and how to identify technology that's invisible to others. Chapter 11, Embracing the Threat of Innovation, acknowledges that there are technologies ahead of others that truly have the power to disrupt your business today; we'll touch on a couple briefly. Chapter 12, Innovation as a Strategy, emphasizes that innovation occurs as part of a deliberate plan—rather than being a random act—and therefore requires planning. Chapter 13, Innovation on a Data Playground, dials into the significant impact that big data, data science, and data analytics have made on business, which they'll continue to heavily influence. Lastly, Chapter 14, The Humor of Innovation, touches on individual development, major innovation competencies, and smiles at our ability to predict the next innovation.

These are the hotbeds of innovation: how innovative minds work, what they explore, and how they think. Set your pace, and enjoy the journey. Innovators are believers. Innovative minds think differently.

Today, we step out of line.

Peter Benton Nichol
Connecticut, USA

TABLE OF CONTENTS

"It's easy to come up with new ideas; the hard part is letting go of what worked for you two years ago, but will soon be out of date."

– ROGER VON OECH

PART I

THE GROWTH OF ORIGINAL IDEAS

The ability to generate unique ideas that either inch innovation forward, break through existing paradigms, or result in radical revelations stems from your mindset.

In the following chapters, we'll wander through the pillars of an innovation mindset and open the door to new markets, the science of ideas, and how removing middlemen opens markets to unlimited growth. These markets begin with ideas but eventually manifest in the physical world—in your environment. Design thinking shapes the process of design, connecting those great ideas to address business and social issues. By using creative strategies and applying design thinking, we can approach problems from a human-centered mindset to integrate ourselves into a more desirable future.

Design-thinking principles flow nicely into the cycles of inspiration. Nature, laws of innovation, and hype play hidden roles in the discovery of new ideas, concepts, and applications that can be combined with existing uses for new benefits—in a word, taking what's old and combining ideas together to form totally original premises.

There's no silver bullet for generating a new mindset. There are, however, new concepts and ways of thinking that, when combined, do generate new and unique ideas.

CHAPTER 1

THE SCIENCE OF IDEAS

*"To accomplish great things
we must dream as well as act."*

— ANATOLE FRANCE

Chapter Objectives

After reading this chapter, readers will be able to:

- Appreciate how brilliant minds think differently
- See how first-principle thinking can be used to break down complex topics
- Know how intelligent people solve "unsolvable" problems
- Know the benefits of arguing from first principles
- Explain the concept of ideonomy

Introduction

In the pages that follow, what you won't find is a picture book on innovation. There won't be graphics attempting to offer your mind a false belief that, if you see a few dozen pictures, you'll start to think differently.

What you will find as you're guided through this book are idea igniters—an outline from which you can create new ideas.

This is the advanced version of the picture book. Pictures are prescriptive and provide detailed illustrations of concepts. My intent over the next several hundred pages is to fire your imagination with new frameworks, constructs, methods, ways, reasons, and other useful approaches to enable you to change your thinking.

This book is a guided tour of how innovators think, what they use to extend their knowledge, and why they're able to think differently for different results.

You can set your own pace. You're welcome to walk, jog, or run through the concepts presented in this book.

The Innovation Mindset provides the foundation for how to think differently. How you use this information is up to you.

First-Principle Thinking

Original ideas aren't born of assumptions from the past. They're spawned from the strategic and calculated alignment of ideas into seemingly abnormal combinations, creating new causes.

Ab initio, the Latin term for 'from the beginning,' is used in the sciences, especially in physics. For example, if a theoretical work is said to start directly at the level of established science and doesn't make assumptions—for example, positing empirical models and fitting parameters—this is first-principle thinking. We know that empirical models are based entirely on data. Data is often extrapolated or estimated into

4

calibrated models. Then, of course, we have to make sense of this, so we shove the data into a fitted model using regressions including linear, quadratic, cubic, quartic, exponential, logarithmic, logistic, power, or sine models.

These all expand on old thinking, stretching the old into 'new information.' (Hint: it's not new.)

Truly great minds don't think this way. They use first-principle thinking. These are foundational propositions or assumptions that can't be deduced from any other proposition or assumption. In short, you can't just read and connect the lines because there are no lines to connect.

In philosophy, first-principle thinking often uses a priori terms and arguments as opposed to a posteriori terms or reasoned arguments. For philosophers, epistemology is the home of first-principle thinking.

Aristotle saw first principles as "the first basis from which a thing is known" (Met. 1013a14–15).

Descartes described the concept of a first principle in the following excerpt from the preface to the *Principles of Philosophy* (1644): "But a perfect knowledge of all that man can know, as well for the conduct of his life as for the preservation of his health and the discovery of all the arts, and that knowledge to observe these ends must necessarily be deduced from first causes; so that in order to study the acquisition of it (which is properly called philosophizing), we must commence with the investigation of those first causes which are called Principles."

Quantum mechanics took a leap from Schrödinger's equation to calculate electronic structure. In this case, innovation or first principles didn't fit any existing models based on experimental data. There was no line to connect. Schrödinger was a first-principle thinker.

Pioneers Use First-Principle Thinking

Where will the next big invention come from? What will be the next object, thing, or experience that transforms how we interact, with whom we collaborate, and how society spends its time?

We all know customer experience is changing, and consumers are demanding more. What if the next big thing isn't linear? It can't be deduced from the information we have using logical analysis. The assumptions that guide your organizational security decisions, the assumptions that inspire your teams, and the assumptions about how the best companies innovate are old. They won't bring us 10x results. All that information—while interesting, like finding a shiny new penny—won't be a game changer.

The concept of first principles is the most powerful method for breaking down complex topics. First, we can think about problems using analogues. An example of this could be building a new online business system based on your prior experience or an experience you've seen in other industries. This thinking rarely is innovative or disruptive and is generally ineffective, resulting in low customer satisfaction. Why? "Oh, I saw that already. Yes, it works okay."

The second approach to thinking through a problem uses first principles. This decomposes an idea into the most fundamental components. For example, if you're trying to understand culture or patterns of consumer behavior, you don't start by reading recently published works on the topic. You go back—way back—to the beginning. You understand how humans evolved and why patterns of behavior existed 2000 years ago, and then you work your way forward.[1] So, your deductions about consumer behavior are original and rooted in your research. Find the intersection of value—the value you see that others don't. Why? They're not looking.

Look around your work environment. Seriously, get up and look. What do you see? Do you see first principles at

6

work? I doubt it. What you see is people falling behind, using thinking that's old.

The CIO leaders and innovators, the folks in your organization that push and are open to change, don't think the same as everyone else. They're different. Their minds simply don't operate the same. This is how transformational change begins—from new causes or first principles.

The Science of New Ideas

Physiology is the study of life science. Economics is concerned with the transfer of wealth. Ideonomy is the science of ideas.

Patrick Gunkle created this new field called ideonomy, which he describes as "the science of the laws of ideas and of the application of such laws to the generation of all possible ideas in connection with any subject, idea, or thing." [2]

Ideonomy is "preoccupied with the discovery, classification, and systematic characterization of universal ideas, with facilitating the human use of ideas, and with automating the creation of ideas." [3] There isn't a more expansive subject than ideonomy, which encapsulates 200 categories that "include the study of analogies and differences, shapes, causes and effects, processes, actions, appearances, questions and answers, properties and relations, languages, generalizations, errors, metaphors, functions and values, networks and hierarchies, interactions, cognitive and heuristic principles, and future possibilities."

Ideonomy attempts to capture the science of laws—similar to nature's impact on subjects, ideas, and things.

The concept is complex, and we'll digest it in chunks. Each scientific law was originally born from weaker or rather less-than-scientific presumptions—experiments, beliefs, or hypotheses. The embryonic development of accepted science can be used to better grasp how innovation—and, correspondingly, the innovation mindset—grows to the point where ideas are more readily accepted.

There are 12 ways in which ideonomy creates value. Ideonomy:

1. Shows how things are alike
2. Suggests alternatives or improves analysis of situations
3. Uncovers anomalies
4. Structures arguments
5. Explores assumptions
6. Characterizes behavior
7. Analyzes the nature of beliefs
8. Identifies the causes of things
9. Clarifies chains of events
10. Characterizes the role of chance
11. Shows how things can be usefully combined
12. Augments creativity

SHOWS HOW THINGS ARE ALIKE

To uncover hidden beauty—whether you're scanning an amazing mountaintop from the comfort of your chair or observing artificial-intelligence robotic mechanisms—we must show how things are alike. This approach seems too simple, almost dumb, really. Yet, there's a hidden, raw brilliance in the approach. The ability to study unrelated things and then identify how these superficially unrelated things are similar comprises much of the essence of innovation. We could combine the strategy of an energy company with the need to innovate legacy equipment with the desire to redesign business processes. Or we might observe a colony of ants and their plight in trying to lift almost 20 times their body weight (if a second grader could do this, they'd be able to lift a car) and compare that to how business-social interaction (human colonies) interact for better business outcomes. These so-called "super-organisms," a term identified by biologist William

Morton Wheeler in the 1920s, can help identify similarities that otherwise would have gone unobserved.

SUGGESTS ALTERNATIVES OR IMPROVES ANALYSIS OF SITUATIONS

The processing of information within a meeting or during a conference call isn't efficient. This manner of information presentation, discussion, debate, and consensus usually results in an unclear semi-agreement. The final decision is often either polarized to an extreme position by those of influence or is mutilated to the extent that the best ideas are weakened on arrival at the median decision point. For example, should we advance into a new market? Yes, this is the future of the gig economy. No, this is an unproven revenue stream for the company. The result? A marginally insignificant investment, which arguably will have no positive or negative effect on revenue or earnings. Gunkel suggests that similar mistakes are forgotten and opportunities are foregone in a repetitive cycle. Ideonomy can help connect the dots into a rational structure—a structure that previously didn't exist.

UNCOVERS ANOMALIES

Every few months, your car doesn't start up. Traffic is slow on the ride to work now and then. Your team misses deadlines infrequently, but the event repeats every so often. Anomalies are difficult to uncover. They can't be avoided, and they're tough to spot. That is, until you have data. Indications and small clues start to surface within large data sets. Data can lead innovators to reach new insights, whether leveraging mobile-usage data from enterprise email apps to physically building access-card data sets from corporate locations. Anomalies are easy to ignore, and we often miss them—well, we used to miss them until computers came to the table with a helpful assist.

Think of how you can classify these anomalies into types. How can you predict when they occur? Why do these events emerge within your environment? The study of ideonomy, as it relates to innovation, can help to uncover many of these answers.

STRUCTURES ARGUMENTS
To present—and, more importantly, to sell—innovative ideas, you must be able to structure an argument. Sadly, most arguments are a poor attempt to glue together strings of unrelated concepts that individually might be useful but collectively don't add much value. The result is a badly structured argument.

Alternatively, consider a good argument, which is nothing less than a chain of ideas—whether the prior ideas are linked through a concept, value, or intent to the next idea in the chain. This chain creates the "chain of innovation." The properties of this chain also mirror that of a physical chain: the collective chain is no stronger than the weakest link. In our case, the weakest idea (argument or counter-argument) thereby defines the strength of your argument. Creative ideas that are unique are great. Ideating on concepts that might transform experiences has enormous value. However, if these concepts, theories, and applications aren't communicated through a strong chain, every successive statement loses power and, ultimately, will fail at persuading behavior change.

EXPLORES ASSUMPTIONS
Every time a statement is made or an idea is presented, there's a set of underlying assumptions that often go untold. Hyper-set (over) and hypo-set (under) assumptions are inherently molded into statements and beliefs as they're presented.

A curious mind quickly separates these ad infinitum assumptions from the real criteria that must be filtered to make a reasonable decision or set of decisions. When you ideate on the concept with yourself or your team, start by identifying the existence of assumptions that should be more clearly defined and the nonexistence of other assumptions that should also be more clearly defined. The action of thinking through these assumptions will result in the maturation of your idea and ultimately help the delivery of your design. As questions are thrown about, as is always the case, your prior narrowing of ambiguities through the clarification of assumptions (existent and non-existent) will add rigidity to the argument for your innovative idea.

CHARACTERIZES BEHAVIOR

There are behavioral traits that promote innovation and those that detract from an innovative atmosphere. One must observe this language as we would listen to understand the patterns in spoken Spanish, Italian, or French. Innovation has its own language to communicate, systematize, and predict behavior that's favorable. Whether we're observing primal animal instincts and sounds or the interactions of humans (our teams and organizations), there's a language. For us, this is the language of innovation.

As you design your innovation program, consider the reasons why some methodologies, languages, and behavior-adaptation programs are successful. The Agile SAFe framework? The Project Management Institute's program and project PMBOK methodology? Each of these systems has defined its "laws of science." These laws combine significant regularities with general patterns including phraseology to enable more effective communication. Like most new languages, there's a learning curve; however, once you're over the curve, the productivity accelerates. Do you have phrases that pull your team together? Do goals, milestones, and landmarks sound as foreign as the words of an African tribe? Your team is its own tribe. You, as the innovation leader, must define the new language and accepted behavior—the language of innovation.

ANALYZES THE NATURE OF BELIEFS

Ideonomy can help us uncover our beliefs. Mastery, purpose, and autonomy drive motivation in ourselves and our teams.

How do we, as innovators, get at the heart of our teams—the raw essence of their motivation, beliefs, and values?

Every human holds bias and grasps ever so tightly to the premise that each decision is unique, calculated, and is meant to be acted upon. History tells a different story.

That our daily interactions are driven by deep, internal beliefs can be explained by "sociological, historical, psychological, anthropological, biological, physical, mathematical, or even logical laws" or phenomena.[4] To this end, we arrive at epistemology—the universal science of beliefs.

How long do we hold on to a belief? How do we deconstruct it when that belief is formed out of thousands of years of arbitrary experiments? When do we substitute old beliefs with new ones? With our team, is this mechanism formal, or do we just hope it's done—now and again?

The value of holding on to beliefs is the knowledge that, at some point, we need to let them go. But how is this done? Consider how you explicitly reset your beliefs and the beliefs of your team. Which beliefs require the support and delivery structure of the sciences (mathematical, biological, physical, or psychological)? Good innovation considers one or more of the sciences. However, great innovation merges the physical and psychological world to connect actions to behaviors—physical, biological, and digital. This is a world that can transcend from physical spaces to virtual spaces while still comfortably sitting in the living rooms of our mind.

IDENTIFIES THE CAUSES OF THINGS

We're talking about the taxonomy of innovation. Taxonomy is a rarely used word and simply references a method or way to group things together—how we group these items, which are called terms. We see these examples every day, all around us, but we don't acknowledge them as taxonomies.

A collection of a certain kind of animal might be called "birds." Your digital music library might be organized by genre. A group of foods most of us should eat more of are "vegetables." Each of these examples is considered a taxonomy. These groupings aid in our classification of categories of interest. By defining categories, we enable a greater level of comparison as it relates to interrelationships, effects, and the diagnoses of root causes. New relationships that weren't evident previously provide a fresh perspective on the challenge at hand. How do we determine the best time to launch? Which teams are in the best positions to mature their innovation pilot? These and other questions can be understood by defining the taxonomy of innovation. Secret: it's different at every company.

CLARIFIES CHAINS OF EVENTS

Whether we're talking about how millionaires are made, how businesses take off, or how accidents occur, there's always a chain of events. If we're lucky, these are positive, but, inevitably, there are times when luck runs out and these chains have negative outcomes.

The news headlines every morning shout about chains of events such as "Five Steps to Get Super Rich" or "12 Habits to Ensure your Business Happiness" or "How to Build a Culture of Innovation in Eight Days." It's true there are probably thousands of steps to becoming super rich, but we know telling people this wouldn't sell. Even in a simple, five-step process, we can see patterns. These patterns, if we pay attention, are linked by a "chain of events." If our team is a powerhouse of innovation, we're building a certain type of chain. Inversely, if the team is dysfunctional—with few ideas maturing—we've developed a different and less efficient chain.

What type of chain are you building personally and professionally? Is that chain of events helping or hurting your ability to innovate? We don't reflect on these aspects of innovation often enough. This is where thoughtful and deep innovation occurs. Deep inside our DNA and that of our teams and our organizations is where the answers lie dormant and waiting to be unearthed. You, as an innovator, must be the one to discover them. Build an association of awareness of the chain of events not an ignorance submerged in present-day knowledge.

What's the biggest chain you're seeing? Have these trends emerged as a result of your analysis and reflection? In your introspection, have you discovered micro-chains—small, faint indications that that chain of events might be shifting? These micro-chains aren't scientific—they're theoretical: "I believe it might occur. My gut tells me a shift is occurring." Most of these micro-chains can't be supported or connected to practical or physical events, but they do set the pillars of your hypothesis. They're a prediction of change to come.

Now that you've thought about the chains of events that may be active within your environment or industry, it's time to look outside for reciprocities. What are the trigger events that could impact your chain? Think about the branchings and counter-flows of actual and potential events. Innovators are always looking forward while at the same time making decisions, armed with a perspective that most don't find the time to build.

Let your mind wander. Start to write down the networks that may impact your chains of events. Explore the structures or archetypes that have formed to support these chains of events. Are they positive structures or negative structures? As an innovator, you're solidifying the positive structures and slowly dismantling the less-than-constructive ones—before the team even knows they've been adjusted. Innovators tune chains of events to be favorable. Everyone gets lucky, but innovators—those with an innovative mindset—get lucky more often.

CHARACTERIZES THE ROLE OF CHANCE

You get to the check-out counter only to find that lane is now closed. You get into your car, which didn't start yesterday, and, this morning, the engine turns over. You race to the Post Office to mail a letter but arrive five minutes after it closes;

yet, the door is still open, and the nice lady helps you out. Happenstance. Chance. Luck.

What's the role of chance in innovation? Do the toughest master innovators of the day like Elon Musk (CEO, Tesla Motors) or Jeff Bezos (founder and CEO of Amazon) have some magical DNA the rest of us don't possess? I'd offer they don't. I'm also not a huge believer in luck, but I'm often reminded of the famous quote from Samuel Goldwyn (1879-1974), the American film producer: "The harder I work, the luckier I get." Innovation requires hard work—with some luck attached.

Being lucky is a tough and stressful way to drift through a career. You'll be better served to work your butt off and smile at the luck you experience along the way. We can't predict chance. It can't be empirically proven. What we can do is identify indications that define or interrelate potential outcomes to present more than a delusion. Using ideonomy, we can build sets of phenomena that carve out experiments and inquire into the possibilities of chance. It won't be controlled, but it can be monitored. What mechanisms do you have in place that act as guidelines for experimentation?

SHOWS HOW THINGS CAN BE USEFULLY COMBINED

Have you ever been thinking about a problem and, after days, you still don't have a lot of good options for solving it? These aren't the simple problems like a technical fix or solution. Nope, these often are more organizational. These problems have solutions that won't be identified as working or not working for weeks or even months. The tail that drags on the solution to these problems is much longer. However, when you feel most at a loss, you draw the ideas, shapes, and theories on a whiteboard and, somehow, a pattern emerges. This situation has happened to each of us—and, to many, more than once.

The process of combining and separating goes back to our childhood—connecting blocks and then separating them, over and over. Yet, as we did this, we saw different patterns. Maybe a new shape emerged, or the colors of the blocks suggested a new form. Innovation is a study of combinations. Innovation takes old blocks and combines them into new combinations that previously went undiscovered.

Natural combinations occur all around us. Rock formations on a mountaintop. The funnel of city folk descending into the subway. The quiet buzz around your paved driveway as a new ant castle is being formed in the corner. Innovation is uncovered by looking at old combinations and creating new ones, not by finding new things. But, as we can combine old items to form new ones, we also can separate old items in different ways to create new value.

AUGMENTS CREATIVITY

There are myriad techniques to look differently at problems. You can read a book (excellent choice). You can create a list of seemingly unrelated areas. The assumptions could be challenged. You could use first-principle thinking.

To solve the unsolvable problem, you have to abandon the approaches others took who failed. Let go of your old experiences—they won't help. To truly innovate requires running down a trail that today doesn't exist. You might not even know when you're on the trail or off it until the end. Yes, in the middle of this plight, you'll seem a bit crazy. The core concept is relaxing so you can restructure or augment your creativity.

Geniuses produce. They create. They list. They ideate. They discover. They're not afraid to wonder. The result of a massive volume of work will, in essence, produce a few golden nuggets. One or two ideas that are sound. Guess how they did this. It wasn't because they're amazing. The success didn't occur as a result of natural brilliance. Nope, they used volume. A vat of ideas that was stirred daily and eventually produced a few grams of gold. What? That makes no sense. You're right. But even you and I can get our head around the fact that after "x" amount of volume is accumulated, eventually there will be something of value.

Adjust your methods and tactics to create a volume-based system of ideation. Use your imagination. Push the possibilities to the edge. This creativity is also bound by a time dimension. This isn't to say that creating a single idea for five years won't result in something stellar. It could. However, if you were able to create the volume of ideas in, say, one intense month, there's a greater likelihood you'd be able to identify those gold grams earlier.

Conclusion

Have you ever read an article and immediately had a great thought about something seemingly unrelated? If you have, you've experienced the application of one of the most simplistic mental models: applying context. We covered how to create original thoughts with original assumptions and first-principle thinking. Before you race through the next chapter, take a minute to think about how you can apply first-principle thinking to something you're doing this day, week, or month. Don't build off someone's belief that wearables are the next big thing. Go back in history. Step back in time. Research the mid-'90s and the Defense Advanced Research Project Agency (DARPA) and the progressive "Wearables in 2005" workshop hosted in 1996. Or head into the 1980s with Steve Mann, a researcher in electronic photography, and his EyeTap project. Eventually make your way back to "GoPigeon," an attempt by Julius Neubronner in 1907 to outfit pigeons with cameras—arguably the first application of GoPro with a drone.

By using first-principle thinking and mental models, your mind will crack open and you'll discover renewed inspiration—with an innovative mindset.

CHAPTER 2

BREAKING LIMITS

*"In every work of genius, we recognize
our once rejected thoughts."*

— RALPH WALDO EMERSON

Chapter Objectives

After reading this chapter, readers will be able to:

- Explore exponential and breakthough innovation
- Describe five methods of discovering breakthrough ideas
- Identify how to discover their innovation mindset
- Understand exponential trust in a trustless world

Exponential and Breakthrough Innovation

The terms "invention" and "Innovation" are frequently interchanged. The two terms are quite different, and I'll explain why. Invention is about creation, and innovation is about change. An invention is the creation of a new product, service, or interaction (including processes). Also, an invention can be both autonomous and induced and may not be associated with a commercialized product. For example, a product could be built but not launched into a market. The motives behind invention may be economic but often include a non-economic rationale. Invention usually is restricted to R&D-type activities and precedes innovation. Another way to look at invention is to see it as innovation minus the commercial exploitation.

Innovation, on the other hand, is the introduction of a new product, service, or interaction into the marketplace. Innovation is less about creation and more about an introduction for commercialization. Economic drivers propel innovation, and it's usually induced.

An invention may involve change. However, innovation almost always involves organizational change and therefore succeeds or follows invention. Innovation is invention plus the commercial exploitation. As we explore ways to innovate, we ultimately end up exploring models of innovation. Models are defined by three dimensions: concretely (an equation, a figure), abstractly (a theory, an approach), and functionally (a heuristic, an ideal-type).[5]

Exponential innovation assists us to enter a new world. Several popular books have helped us capture what exponential innovation means. Klaus Schwab, a German engineer and economist who's best known as the founder and executive chairman of the World Economic Forum, supports this thinking.[6] Schwab defined this new world thus: "In the new world, it's not the big fish that eats the small fish. It's the fast fish that east the slow fish."[7] Fast wins and slow losses. Exponential innovation is non-linear growth. When considering innovation approaches, we tend to think of an event that happened yesterday or today. We look for the flash in today's newspaper, a topic that applies to concepts that are fresh and hot. What we miss is the reflective perspective of models that helps us get to transformative innovation—models that have been in place longer than the latest headline. Innovation is everywhere. It was also everywhere a day ago and 100 years ago. Reset your mind.

Exponential innovation and 10x growth lean on the realization that exponential innovation is non-linear. It's not something that evolves; exponential innovation jumps.

There are five, non-linear innovation models:

- Stephen Kline's Chain-linked Model
- Ralph Gomory's Circle Model
- Alic-Branscomb's model
- OECD's Oslo Manual
- John Ziman's Neural Net model

STEPHEN KLINE'S CHAIN-LINKED MODEL

Let's briefly explore these models and why they can tell us useful information. The Chain-Linked Model is a popular, non-linear innovation model. This model asserts that information isn't the source of innovation.[8] There are three primary elements of the Chain-Linked Model. First is the foundational layer. In this layer are elements such the potential market, invention and production of analytical design, intricate detail and tests, redesign and procedures, distribution, and marketing. This foundational layer is linked to a second layer comprising the existing body of knowledge (the knowledge foundation). This knowledge foundation is linked to the third layer—research.

Combined with this model are the socio-technical systems (STS) within an organization or the organizational development. "Organizational development is an approach to complex organizational work design that recognizes the interaction between people and technology in workplaces." The Chain-Linked Model is the recognition of the importance of the interaction between people and technology in workspaces for innovation.

CHAIN-LINKED MODEL STEPS:

- Identification of new, unfilled markets needs
- Design, production, and distribution of new innovation
- Tapping existing research and new research

RALPH GOMORY'S CIRCLE MODEL

Born in Brooklyn Heights, New York, Ralph E. Gomory invented what he called the cyclic model or, as some refer to it, the Circle Model of innovation, which he coined the Ladder Model. Dr. Gomory has a long and distinguished career, earning his Ph.D. in mathematics at Princeton University, later serving as IBM Senior Vice President for Science and Technology, and, finally, retiring in 1989. Dr. Gomory has written several articles articulating the transition from the ladder of science to a development cycle for products.[9] Dr. Gomory argues that "the Ladder [Model] is characteristic of the early stages of an industry and the Circle [model of innovation] is characteristic of later stages."[10] Dr. Gomory presents the Ladder as the reasonable perception of the relationship of innovation to production. The theory states that this process slowly moves in the direction of progress. It's not radical, but it's a more progressive than incremental innovation in that there are breakthroughs. Often, this step-by-step process manifests as inching toward practicality and is driven by engineers or scientists.

The alternative, a more "cyclic development" process, is governed by the product cycle. "Cyclic development is a competition among ordinary engineers in bringing established products to market."[11]

It's worth noting that Gomory believes this model is evolutionary and involves continuous improvement. The model is clearly a state of business and is, at its core, incremental. However, I propose that, by shortening the cycles from years to months and from months to weeks, this model can lead to exponential growth.

CYCLIC INNOVATION MODEL STEPS :

- Work is completed one step ahead (not two) of manufacturing or development.
- New product launches are linked to existing product sunsets.
- Design specialists and manufacturing people work side by side.[12]

ALIC-BRANSCOMB'S MODEL

This model resulted from the combined thinking of Dr. John Alic, a senior associate of the Office of Technology Assessment of the US Congress, and Dr. Lewis Branscomb, a professor from Harvard University, both of whom were interested in US technology policy after World War II. They weren't pioneers of innovation models. However, they did conduct important work around the evolution of linear models.[13] [14] For our application, their thinking and framework will be useful.

What if innovation wasn't about products or services? What if it had nothing to do with company-to-customer interactions? Alic believed that innovation was an outcome of a social process. The result of inputs, combined with products and insights into new markets such as the derivative of merging what's known (declarative knowledge) with what can be done (procedural knowledge), constitutes a commercialized innovation.[15]

23

ALIC-BRANSCOMB'S MODEL STEPS:

- Innovation is a social process—outside people must be involved.
- The combination of knowledge (old and new) provides new value or innovative value.
- Innovation depends on R&D. It's important to understand embryonic technologies that could impact technologies (people, process, outcomes) that are commonplace today.

OECD'S OSLO MODEL

The Organization for Economic Co-operation and Development (OECD) is a unique forum where the governments of 30 democracies work together to address the economic, social, and environmental challenges of globalization. The OECD first published the Oslo Manual in 1992. The Manual was updated twice, first in 1997 and, more recently, in 2005. The Manual introduced the premise that "it's widely accepted that innovation is central to the growth of output and productivity."[16] The Manual illustrated how to develop and capitalize on the process of innovation. The use of the Manual highlights the evaluation of linkages to connect knowledge flow among firms to enhance the development of innovation. Our application will concentrate on the general institutional environments within which firms operate:

- The basic educational system for the general population, which determines minimum educational standards in the workforce and the domestic consumer market.
- The university system.
- The specialized technical-training system.
- The science and research base.

- Common pools of codified knowledge such as publications and also technical, environmental, and management standards.
- Innovation policies and other government policies that influence innovation by firms.
- Legislative and macroeconomic settings such as patent law, taxation, corporate-governance rules, and policies relating to interest and exchange rates, tariffs, and competition.
- Communications infrastructure including roads and telecommunication networks.
- Financial institutions that determine, for example, the ease of access to venture capital.
- Market accessibility including possibilities for the establishment of close relations with customers as well as matters such as size and ease of access.
- Industry structure and the competitive environment including the existence of supplier firms in complementary sectors."

These environments are the methods within which companies operate; they're also necessary for the emergence of innovative ideas. The Oslo Manual has a heavy emphasis on technological product-and-process (TPP) innovation commonly found in manufacturing. However, identifying how your organization operates is essential to discovering where innovation can begin.

OECD'S OSLO MANUAL STEPS:

- Establish a dynamic process to measure innovation.
- Identify the factors that influence innovation activities.
- Understand the novelty (boredom vs. curiosity balance) and the degree of diffusion (extent to which innovations spread) within your organization.

JOHN ZIMAN'S NEURAL NET MODEL

John Ziman, a theoretical physicist, suggested a map that connects theoretical knowledge and reality. Neural networks or connectionist systems are a computational approach to how the biological brain solves problems. These large constellations of neurons connected by axons seem apparently unrelated when, in fact, each unit is connected to many other units.[17] These systems work in harmony. They also are self-learning and self-training; they aren't explicitly programmed. Ziman was before his time in suggesting innovation models for the cognitive space. What's unique here is the "unpacking" and interconnection of different domains (in our case, departments of organizations). His thinking was that by using a net of ideas, new patterns can be formed and existing patterns can be transformed, thereby creating new value.

JOHN ZIMAN'S NEURAL NET MODEL STEPS:

- Acknowledge that linear models of innovation are oversimplified and don't work.
- Hold the course: innovators end experimentation too early, giving way to overhasty rejection.
- Build strategies to test theories. Predictability in an evolutionary process is impossible, and general predictability of phenomena is extremely limited.[18]

The search for innovation is never-ending. It's everywhere and nowhere. You find it when you're not looking and, during the more exhaustive searches, it's elusive. Leverage these models and experiment with the steps to tilt your thinking about how innovation emerges and how to capture it.

Conclusion

When you think of innovation, ideas like the television, radio, and the first iPhone may come immediately to mind. Yes, these are all innovations and largely breakthrough innovations. These are important to revolutionize a business, industry, or segments.

Alternatively, incremental innovation can be just as powerful. The progression of the indoor light has improved substantially over the last 10 years. Lime and Bird just improved on the concept of the two-wheel bike. However, by adding electricity, that incremental innovation had a huge societal impact. Innovation can be breakthrough or incremental. The next time you're trying to think of a breakthrough innovation, start with a basic product, service, or interaction you use today. Then explore ways to extend that capability to add functionality for a specific market.

CHAPTER 3

MENTAL MODELS AND DIVERGENT THINKING

*"Usually the first problems you solve with
the new paradigm are the ones that were
unsolvable with the old paradigm."*

— JOEL A. BARKER

Chapter Objectives

After reading this chapter, readers will be able to:

- Appreciate how intelligent people solve "unsolvable" problems using mental models
- Identify tools to improve their everyday thinking
- Explore the Heisenberg Uncertainty Principle
- Understand when paradigm shifts are detectable
- Rationalize the Pygmalion Effect
- Understand Dunbar's Number
- Remember Cialdini's Six Principles of Influence on innovation
- Drift from flypaper theory to swatting flies

Mental Models

In the mid-1990, there was a speech titled, "The Psychology of Human Misjudgment," which Charlie Munger gave at Harvard University. Munger was an American businessman, lawyer, investor, and philanthropist. He also served as vice chairman of Berkshire Hathaway, the conglomerate controlled by Warren Buffett. Before heading off to explore mental models and new ways of reframing existing knowledge, it's valuable to understand elements of the human response. Each idea, creative solution, and approach your team generates will depend on other stakeholders' adoption. And, frequently, this judgment is flawed. It's useful to identify these flaws before you deliver the new idea.

Munger identified 24 cognitive biases within the psychology of human misjudgment (he subsequently added one more, which we'll also include):[19]

Bias 1 – Reward and Punishment Super-Response Tendency: Others aren't incentivized or disincentivized the same as you or your team. Behavior won't be changed unless incentives align.

Bias 2 – Liking/Loving Tendency: With products, services, and interactions that we love or admire, we tend to ignore their faults. We focus instead on their strengths and even create fallacies that don't balance with reality.

Bias 3 – Disliking/Hating Tendency: We tend to ignore things we despise. Alternatively, this manifests as dislike toward a person or individual, not a product or action. Refocusing energy on the activity helps diminish the bias.

Bias 4 – Doubt-Avoidance Tendency: When unsure of a future decision, the tendency is to add information (often not relevant) in the hope of enabling a quick decision.

Bias 5 – Inconsistency-Avoidance Tendency: Change isn't fun. As a result, humans resist change. This is a form of inconsistency avoidance.

Bias 6 – Curiosity Tendency: This occurs when there's not enough curiosity to learn and eliminates what Munger calls, "the man with a hammer."

Bias 7 – Kantian Fairness Tendency: Unfair for some is acceptable when there's greater fairness for all. Many can't accept this and will explore unethical means to attempt to find balance. "Give to get" is the thinking here, but not all play with this in mind.

Bias 8 – Envy/Jealousy Tendency: This is self-explanatory; however, this occurs when discontent or resentment builds over responsibility, accountability, and just pure luck of success. This isn't loud but rather quiet and can be very dangerous if not monitored carefully.

Bias 9 – Reciprocation Tendency: A favor is reciprocated, but so is harm.

Bias 10 – Influence-from-Mere-Association Tendency: If you associate with success, you're perceived as successful, and the inverse is true. Identify the group you associate with wisely.

Bias 11 – Simple, Pain-Avoiding, Psychological Denial: This tendency manipulates or distorts the facts until they're bearable. Often the end product looks nothing like the starting point.

Bias 12 – Excessive Self-Regard Tendency: Is everyone above average or no one? This is overconfidence resulting from downstream complexity that isn't anticipated.

Bias 13 – Over-Optimism Tendency: This is the abundance of optimism arising from not weighting the most likely or worst-case scenarios with the best-case scenarios. Resources are incorrectly allocated, which limits innovation growth.

Bias 14 – Deprival-Super-Reaction Tendency: People prefer to avoid loss rather than to acquire gains; e.g., cut costs rather than invest in an idea that could save 5x the cost.

Bias 15 – Social-Proof Tendency: Similar to group think, this natural tendency is to think as others think and act as others act.

Bias 16 – Contrast-Misreaction Tendency: The magnitude of the decision is missed, and decisions are made at the people or object level and not as they relate to the combined value of the advantage or disadvantage.

Bias 17 – Stress-Influence Tendency: The greater the stress, the faster the reaction. Often these decisions are dysfunctional.

Bias 18 – Availability-Misweighing Tendency: Overweighting what's in front of us is easy. This results in an incorrect perception of progress. Thoughtful checklists can help.

Bias 19 – Use-it-or-Lose-It Tendency: This is acquiring a skill and immediately using it (when it often doesn't apply). A classic example is reading about a new concept in a book or being applied by a competitor and rolling it out the next day department-wide. Context is critical for growth.

Bias 20 – Drug-Misinfluence Tendency: This is the human tendency to avoid pain. It's unpleasant and, therefore, we, as society, avoid it. Sometimes the pain needs to be removed.

Bias 21 – Senescence-Misinfluence Tendency: As we age, certain skills erode. The once-experts are no longer experts. As technology transforms, keep a pulse on who's transforming and who's not.

Bias 22 – Authority-Misinfluence Tendency: Most want to follow within an organization, but very few want to lead (regardless of role). Pay attention to who's truly leading.

Bias 23 – Twaddle Tendency: This tendency is spending time on worthless or nonsense activities. Employees are busy but, holistically, no progress is made.

Bias 24 – Reason-Respecting Tendency: Not everyone wants to understand (similar to memorizing information for an exam). Some just want answers, not the reasoning.

Bias 25 – Lollapalooza Tendency: This tendency persists when groups with extreme tendencies act together for one outcome. Often this outcome is extreme.

Every innovation requires working with others—even if it's only to hand over or commercialize a product, service, or interaction. Understanding how human bias affects decisions and acceptance or rejection of the innovation is at the center of understanding influence.[20] Imagine how this has affected your past ideas and how these biases will affect your future ideas. Influence is an important part of the overall framework of mental models.[21]

During a commencement speech for USC School of Law, Charles Munger addressed why having mental models and a curiosity to learn is vital for success. Here's part of his address:

> "Marcus Cicero is famous for saying that the man who doesn't know what happened before he was born goes through life like a child. That is a very correct idea. If you generalize Cicero, as I think one should, there are all these other things that you should know in addition to history. And those other things are the big ideas in all the other disciplines. It doesn't help just to know them enough so you can [repeat] them back on an exam and get an A. You have to learn these things in such a way that they're in a mental latticework in your head and you automatically use them for the rest of your life. If you do that I solemnly promise you that one day you'll be walking down the street and you'll look to your right and left and you'll think 'my heavenly days, I'm now one of the few most competent people in my whole age cohort.' If you don't do it, many of the brightest of you will live in the middle ranks or in the shallows."[22]

Mental models help explain how and why things work. No mental exercises could be more important for building an innovative mindset than how you see problems—and, more specifically, why you see them differently than your office neighbor. Thousands of mental models exist. Many of these improve decision making, problem solving, and the quest for

33

truth, but they don't all work all the time. Use your curiosity to navigate through the maze of models to select models that help generate new ideas:

- Systems thinking
- Sensitivity analysis
- Critical mass
- Heisenberg Uncertainty Principle
- Divergent thinking vs. convergent thinking
- Paradigm shift
- Bayes' Theorem
- Simpson's Paradox
- Preserving optionality
- Pygmalion Effect
- Growth mindset vs. fixed mindset
- High-context vs. low-context culture
- Loyalists vs. mercenaries
- Dunbar's Number
- Minimum Viable Product (MVP)
- Cialdini's Six Principles of Influence
- Flypaper Theory
- Rumsfeld's Rule
- Hunting elephants vs. flies

Systems Thinking

Systems thinking is an approach to solving problems that examines the linkages and interactions among the individual components that dynamically define a system. If we define the boundaries of a system at the perimeter, it's difficult to understand the relationship and relevance of the individual components. Using a systems-thinking approach focuses on the policies, processes, practices, and people holistically and then later breaks these down into basic units. These basic units are easier to manage and have clear boundaries within the environment. Systems thinking prevents systemic failures of confused goals or a weak, system-wide understanding.

Developing a systems-thinking approach requires thinking of the system as one functional piece. Systems thinking is used to help collaboration across functional areas where leadership understanding must be achieved at the system—not the component—level. Additionally, this process acknowledges that, for each process that we deliberately build, there's a parallel or shadow system. Usually, we, as innovators, focus on the rational system. However, it's important also to consider the non-rational or shadow system in which issues of politics, trust, hopes, greed, favoritism, ambitions, and other power struggles exist.[23] Systems thinking helps innovators see the "big picture," especially with regard to problems whose solutions aren't obvious.

Sensitivity Analysis

Sensitivity analysis helps us understand the impact of a range of variables on a given outcome. A simple example would be to compare the relationship between innovation and firm performance. Concentrating on sensitivity analysis helps you to understand where your firm should invest or, in our case, what areas of our innovation are worth exploring further. A better understanding of variables like speed, location, and brand ultimately affects the outcome. Sensitivity analysis can also be used to conduct a systematic review of a sequence of decisions.

For example, if your innovation is targeting the older segment of a population, how would you determine the lower limit? That is to say, do you make the target group over 60, 65, 70, or 75 years of age? Sensitivity analysis can be used to determine if the findings are relevant to the decisions raised in the process of obtaining those findings. Don't allow sensitivity analysis to be confused with subgroup analysis. Higgens offers good advice on sensitivity analysis. "First, sensitivity analyses don't attempt to estimate the effect of the intervention in the group of studies removed from the analysis, whereas in subgroup analyses, estimates are produced for each subgroup. Second, in sensitivity analyses, informal comparisons are made between different ways of estimating the same thing, whereas, in subgroup analyses, formal statistical comparisons are made across the subgroups."[24]

Critical Mass

Critical mass is a term used in physics and means "the amount of fissile material needed to sustain nuclear fission."[25] However, our definition is a bit different. Critical mass is the minimum amount of something required to start or maintain any project or venture. Here, too, we're talking about energy in the form of the buy-in, resources, and support necessary to advance ideas forward. Done well, critical mass defines the point beyond which success is inevitable. At this point the market reaches critical mass. Products can reach critical mass by passing a certain percentage of market adoption. Businesses can reach critical mass. And innovative ideas can reach critical mass.

When you initially suggest an innovative idea or concept, it's unlikely people will love it and cheer for its adoption. More often than not, people will be skeptical and present reasons (many not valid) why the concept will fail. In the book, *Play Bigger*, the authors call this person a Zed: "the person who doesn't believe in the category and will work to sabotage it."[26] Understanding how to get around these people is vital for navigating the path to success effectively. Take the time to sit down and map out your ecosystem. This also has been called the "Chicken or Egg Problem." In a multi-sided market—as in the case of Airbnb—we have producers (hosts) and consumers (renters). If there's a surplus of producers and limited consumers, the producers won't be motivated to participate. Inversely, if there's an excess of consumers and limited producers, the consumers won't be motivated to participate. It requires a balance. Designing this balance is crucial to achieving critical mass.

Heisenberg Uncertainty Principle

The Heisenberg Uncertainty Principle, borrowed from quantum mechanics—where it's also known as the Uncertainty Principle or the Indeterminacy Principle—was discovered by German physicist Werner Heisenberg. The principle states that both the position of an object and its velocity can't be measured exactly at the same time, even in theory. As we gain more insight and knowledge, our focus narrows. We lose, in effect, our ability to act creatively. An excellent example of this process is thinking outside the square or thinking outside the box—the "nine-dot problem." The nine-dot puzzle introduced in 1959 by John Adair floated through consultancy circles. This puzzle is an intellectual challenge to connect nine dots by drawing a continuous line that passes through each of the nine dots, and never lifting the pen from the paper.

PUZZLE

Puzzles help us realize that we simplify paradigms to support our reasoning and, therefore, box in our conceptual frameworks. We add constraints that don't exist. We create barriers where there are none. Using uncertainty helps us to gain perspective and consider options that initially didn't seem feasible.

Divergent Thinking

Divergent Thinking is about developing in different directions. It's a method to open your mind into multiple directions, resulting in generating more options. What if your funding was cut, and you'd planned on securing funding from a particular cost center? You're now required to open your mind and consider possibilities that just a day earlier you didn't need to consider. Divergent thinking can be spontaneous or free-flowing—ideas generated at random. What's the effect of the innovative idea? What's important about the creative idea? Asking some of these questions helps stimulate divergent thinking among your teams. A few examples to encourage divergent thinking include brainstorming (generating ideas in an unstructured manner), keeping a journal (recording ideas spontaneously), free writing (non-stop writing for a set period), and mind mapping or subject mapping (brainstorming ideas in a visual map or picture form). Convergent thinking—thinking that brings things together—is the opposite of divergent thinking.

Paradigm Shift

A paradigm shift is a substantial change in an approach or in the underlying assumptions. Coined by Thomas Kuhn (1922-1996), paradigm shifts started with primary changes in concepts and experimental practices of a scientific discipline.[27] Kuhn believed that these shifts were a sign of a scientific revolution that stepped outside the normal perspective of a prevailing framework (or paradigm). Paradigm goes back to the original meaning of the word in Greek: "example." Paradigm shifts show, via a concrete example, that a change in direction has occurred.

There were two initial uses of the term paradigm. The first was to represent something in common with members of a specific community. These shared commonalities could include techniques, patents, and values. The second meaning was a single embodiment of a common model; e.g., Newton's *Principia,* which were used to develop physical theories and mathematical methods for the field of calculus.[28] What's relevant for us is the delineation between merely common values and real paradigm shifts. Ptolemaic cosmology to traditional cosmology (1543), Aristotelian mechanics to traditional mechanics (1687), the discovery of hyperbolic geometry (1826), the evolution from goal-directed change to Darwin's natural selection (1859), and the transition to Einstein's relativistic worldview (1920) each is a classic model of a paradigm shift. These are so monumental that their impact is clearly evident. Yet, ripples or small tremors start much earlier—before such broad adoption is visible. Inside your economic market, organization, or team, where are the tremors occurring that have the potential to shift the paradigm?

Bayes' Theorem

Bayes' Theorem is a classical application of conditional probabilities and describes the probability of an event with respect to conditions that may be associated with that event. The concept was first introduced by Thomas Bayes (1701-1761), who presented the equation that allows new evidence to update beliefs. Bayes' Theorem separates events from tests.

For example, there could be a test to determine if a patient has melanoma (skin cancer), but a positive result is different from the patient actually having melanoma. Just because you have a positive test doesn't mean you do, in fact, have melanoma caused by sun exposure. There's a high percentage of false positives. The frequency of false positives is increased when we're talking about less common diseases like pancreatic cancer as opposed to the common cold or a step throat.

Bayes' Theorem—more commonly called Bayes' Rule—is a simple formula used to calculate conditional probabilities. The Theorem uses three values: A (the probability that the hypothesis is true), B (the probability that the hypothesis is false), and P, what's called 'prior probability' or 'prior' (the probability that you would have attributed before you believed hypothesis A to be true).

$$P(A/B) = P(B|A)P(A) / P(B)$$

Where A represents the event and B represents the test.

A: could mean that the event, "patient has melanoma," tells you that 7 percent of patients entering a clinic for cancer testing likely have melanoma. $P(B) = 0.025$ (lifetime risk).[29]

B: could mean it was confirmed that the patient had excessive sun exposure. Fifty percent of the clinic's patients are exposed to extreme sun (more than 3 hours a day). $P(B) = 0.50$

You may also know that, among those patients diagnosed with melanoma, 86 percent of cases were largely attributed to sun exposure. $P(B) = 0.86$

Bayes' Theorem tells you:

$$P(A|B) = (0.86 * 0.025) / 0.50 = .043 \text{ (4.3 percent)} \text{ }^{30}$$

Therefore, if the patient had excessive sun exposure, their chance of being diagnosed with melanoma is 4.3 percent. This is a much larger increase than the 2.5 percent offered by the above method. It's also atypical that any specific patient will, in fact, have melanoma.

Bayes' Theorem helps innovators to negotiate the probabilities of conditional events and use that information to find out what's really going on. By using Bayesian reasoning, we can get close to a conclusion we can trust by incorporating additional evidence. What's important to note is that, according to Bayes' Theorem, new data and assumptions change probabilities.[31]

As innovation problems become increasingly complex, applying Bayesian and behavioral economic methods can be effective for addressing 21st-century organizations, where decisions are risky and markets are dynamic.

Simpson's Paradox

Simpson's Paradox, or the Yule-Simpson effect, is "a paradox in probability and statistics in which a trend appears in different groups of data but disappears or reverses when these groups are combined. It's sometimes given the descriptive title *reversal paradox* or *amalgamation paradox*.[32]

Simpson's Paradox was first introduced in 1903 by Udny Yule, a British statistician. The paradox is a special case of omitted-variable bias. This concept is significant, and we'll see how it parallels innovation as we run through a few examples.

There was a famous kidney-stone-treatment study that determined newer treatments were more effective than traditional surgery. However, it was later uncovered that the new treatments were being used primarily on smaller stones.

Another example was an elementary-school test that found minority students in Texas outperformed their peers in Wisconsin. However, it was later discovered that Wisconsin beat Texas in this test, due to the large number of Texan minority students. Should Texas spend money copying Wisconsin? No. Simpson's paradox could lead to effective teaching strategies.

There are three variables in every Simpson's paradox:

- The explained
- The observed explanatory
- The lurking explanatory[33]

Simpson's paradox was at work in 1973 when the University of California, Berkeley, was brought into litigation for sex discrimination. The graduate school had accepted 44 percent of male applications but only 35 percent of female applicants. After some detailed research, there was a statistically significant bias in favor of women. Yet, when properly pooled (broken down by department), science departments were receiving more male applicants and the humanities had more female applicants. Examining male and female acceptance

41

rates within individual departments tells a different story: department A (82 percent of women accepted, 62 percent of men accepted), department B (67 percent female, 63 percent male), department B (34 percent female, 36 percent male), department D (34 percent female, 33 percent male), department E (23 percent female, 26 percent male), and department F (6 percent female, 7 percent male). However, when these distributions were combined, there was a 30 percent acceptance among females and a 46 percent acceptance among males—a classic Simpson's paradox. In this example, if we only had two departments—one "hard" to get into and the other "easy" to get into—we'd expect varying results. Even if both departments preferred women, if too many women applied to the departments, their acceptance rate would drop below that of the men.

Preserving Optionality

Preserving optionality is a strategy to keep one's options open. During a state of indecision, leaders resist making decisions too early—ideally, not before all the uncertainties are resolved. In theory, this sounds like good advice. Who wouldn't want more options over less? However, the challenge presented isn't one of more decisions but rather missing opportunities that existed yesterday and are gone today. We've experienced optionality-based transactional exchanges such as the Lemon Law or the Consumer Bill of Rights. Even your ability as a consumer to return a given product is, in effect, your ability to preserve optionality. With consumer goods, we pay a premium to preserve our right to "send it back." The backbone of commerce is trust and, if a manufacturer trusts its product, we consumers tend to trust that company. Yet, this doesn't work as well when you're innovating and searching for unique strands of value amidst a wreckage of bad ideas.

Innovators are encouraged to experiment, and this, in a sense, is preserving your optionality. But every innovator and leader will reach a point where the ability to be decisive outweighs the benefit of preserving optionality.[34]

Pygmalion Effect

The Pygmalion Effect or the Rosenthal Effect is the phenomenon wherein higher expectations lead to an increase in performance.[35] The effect was named after the Greek myth of Pygmalion. Pygmalion, in Ovid's *Metamorphoses*, (Book X), is a sculptor who falls in love with an ivory statue he's made. The sculptor begs the gods to produce a wife in the likeness of the statue. His wish is granted, and the statue is brought to life.

The corollary is that low expectations lead to a drop in performance. A principle of this effect is to never forecast the failure of a new innovation, even if you believe the challenge to be insurmountable. While trust is respected, gripe sessions with subordinates could set up a framework for future failures. In most settings, high but achievable expectations create an effective method for teams to rally around a vision.

Growth Mindset vs. Fixed Mindset

Growth mindset vs. fixed mindset addresses the argument that abilities are accruable versus innate or fixed. If you believe your character, intelligence, and creative ability are static, you subscribe to the fixed-mindset club. On the other hand, if you believe that successes and failures aren't signs of intelligence but of how abilities are stretched, you, my persuadable friend, have adopted the growth mindset. The intent isn't to exert influence toward one model or away from the other. The value is understanding the benefits and pitfalls of whichever mindset you subscribe to. This additional self-awareness enables you to see over, through, and beyond your teams. This is a skill set that few have harnessed.

High-Context vs. Low-Context Culture

High-context vs. low-context culture has to do with how people within a culture relate to each other, how they treat space, how they treat time, and how they learn. High-context cultures are dependent on trust and build familiarity slowly with clear boundaries as to who's in one's inner and outer circles. Interaction in high-context cultures is heavily non-verbal and relies on facial expressions, gestures, or eye movement for conversational direction. Territoriality is communal, and space isn't respected. Temporality is vague, and keeping a set time for events, outings, or gatherings is difficult. Learning is embedded as part of a situation, and the first step to learning is observing. In high-context cultures, there's a strong preference toward learning in groups for decision making and problem solving. Examples of high-context cultures include Japanese, Chinese, Arabic, Greek, Mexican, Spanish, and Italian.

In contrast, low-context cultures have relationships that begin and end quickly and have unclear boundaries of who's in one's circle. Identity is defined by one's accomplishments, and interaction comprises communication via words more than by non-verbal means. Territoriality is owned, space is compartmentalized, and time is respected. Learning occurs by following directions, and the preference in problem solving is individualistic. How messages are delivered is directly related to how they're received. A few examples of low-context cultures include German Swiss, German, Scandinavian, American, and English Canadian. Inspiration needs to be generated from the inside. However, encouragement can come from the outside if the right context for the culture is addressed.

Loyalists vs. Mercenaries

Loyalists can withstand virtually any obstacle while mercenaries have no loyalty and will walk out on the team or the leader at the earliest sign of trouble. Employees are loyal to leaders they believe in. This is why a new leader can appear to dramatically turn team performance around. It's not that anything different occurred with the team or that the strategy is fundamentally different (although it could be); it's that the team believes in the leader. This is a value that authentic leaders carry and narcissistic posers don't. Maybe it's presence of mind, a sense of calm, or a fiery vision. Authentic leaders are leaders that employees and teams want to follow. To reach 10x growth, we need to become that authentic leader.

It's also been said that people aren't loyal to leaders but rather to a mission or aspirational goal. Innovators and leaders must first clearly establish that aspirational goal to ensure high-performance team members believe in what they're working on.

To create a house of loyalists, it's necessary to design a mission-driven culture. Daniel Pink presented motivation effectively framing it as mastery, purpose, and autonomy. We're talking here about the "why" or the purpose. Lead with a purpose. Build a vision with a mission. Create values and a culture of passion. Establish a culture that encourages loyalists and not mercenaries.

Dunbar's Number

Dunbar's Number suggests a cognitive limit to the number of relationships an individual can maintain in which the individual understands how each person knows and relates to the others. First proposed by Robin Dunbar, a British anthropologist, in the 1990s, he conducted a study of the correlation between primate brain size and the average social group size. After extrapolating the results, Dunbar proposed that humans could only maintain 150 stable relationships.[36] The example that Dunbar used to reinforce the concept was, "putting it another way, it's the number of people you would not feel embarrassed about joining uninvited for a drink if you happened to bump into them a in bar."[37] How many relationships can you successfully maintain? Which are being neglected? As you continue to innovate, grow, lead, and develop teams, keep in mind Dunbar's Number and how you're actively managing your relationship limit.

Minimum Viable Product (MVP)

Minimum Viable Product (MVP) is a product that contains the minimal set of features to validate your business hypothesis. MVP development is a technique for building features that collects the maximum amount of customer learning with the minimum amount of effort. This process considers the fact that many developed products fail to get anyone to care about them, and they target no audience. Once the cool factor is removed, there's no market, and the features don't address a need. One example would be: Instead of spending 3+ weeks building a new launch site for your innovative product, you build an MVP. This might be a WordPress blog that's registered, hosted, overlaid with a theme, and online within hours. This would be your MVP version 1.0.

Not every product is conducive to starting with an MVP. Legal, regulatory, and other market pressures require creating security and privacy controls before a launch can occur. However, there are cases where MVPs are a great starting point. Beginning with a clear view of your options helps to ensure the best path is set for the team and organization.

Cialdini's Six Principles of Influence

Cialdini's Six Principles of Influence references the 1994 book published by Robert Cialdini, *Influence*. Within this book are many useful methods. We'll focus on the widely known six principles of influence:

1. Reciprocity: A favor I do for you must be repaid to me.
2. Commitment/consistency: When you state your commitment, you'll likely act in a consistent manner.

3. Social proof: When decisions are unclear, we look to others to recommend actions.

4. Liking: If you're likable, others are more likely to do what you ask.

5. Authority: If your actions mirror those of someone in authority, others will often obey.

6. Scarcity: The harder it is to get, the more we want it (as in consumer retail products).[38]

Flypaper Theory

The flypaper theory or honeypot theory says that it's preferable to lure enemies into a single space where they're most vulnerable and where it's easier to kill them.[39] The flypaper theory is based on military strategy. A similar strategy was fought during the second US-Iraq War (2003-2011). The premise was that initiating the fighting in Iraq would keep the fight in Iraq, so a flypaper trap or terrorist magnet was designed to keep the war away from America. The objective was to create a target of opportunity—where Americans wanted to fight—to prevent future attacks on the United States.

A similar strategy, though softer, can be adopted for innovation teams and organizations. Consider the following: Where do you want to fight the battle for innovation? What are you protecting? To which arena do you want to draw in your competitors?

The challenge with this strategy is that, at some point, the competitor becomes aware they've been drawn into a new game where the odds might not be even. The desirability of this strategy is the ability to fight where your team and organization are strongest and keep the innovation battle away from your home court. Set the battle location. Define the game. Choose the engagement strategy.

Rumsfeld's Rule

Rumsfeld's Rule is a principle drafted by former defense secretary Donald Rumsfeld, who, while discussing military performance, stated, "You go to war with the army you have, not the army you might want or wish to have at a later time." In simple terms, we use the resources we have today, not the resources we hope to have tomorrow. This principle applies as much to innovation as to military strategy. Rarely do we have the staff, resources, time, or money to execute the ideal strategy. The ability to adapt and use limited or less-than-ideal resources is how great innovators are defined.

Bill Joy, Sun Microsystems co-founder, coined the term Joy's Law, which similarly states, "No matter who you are, most of the smartest people work for someone else." At the core of this principle is the belief that smart means capability, not the willingness to work for a particular company. The capability to work for one company doesn't necessarily translate into a willingness to work for another company. The single greatest challenge for innovators is finding ways to apply this knowledge.[40]

Hunting Elephants vs. Flies

Hunting elephants vs. flies is a humorous analogy for how to reach $100 million in annual revenue by targeting different customers. This comparison was envisioned by Christoph Janz, a micro VC investor.[41] Janz identifies five methods for building a $100-million business: flies, mice, rabbits, deer, and elephants. To build a $100-million business, it takes 10 million customers at $10 each (flies), 1 million customers at $100 each (mice), 100,000 customers at $1,000 each (rabbits), 10,000 customers at $10,000 each (deer), or 1,000 customers at $100,000 each (elephants).

Therefore, as you're thinking about growing revenue, consider which species you're hunting: 1,000 elephants, 10,000 deer, 100,000 rabbits, 1,000,000 mice, or 10,000,000 flies. It makes a difference in your strategy. If your chief innovation officer doesn't have a simple answer to, "What are you hunting?" it's probably because he or she is in the woods chasing anything and everything—not a good strategy. Be prepared, and have a plan before hunting for top-line revenue growth with innovation.

Each of these mental models is extremely useful in the right circumstances. None of them will work all the time. Use your experience and the wisdom you've earned as an innovative leader to determine which principle, rule, or technique is the most applicable for the challenges before you.

Conclusion

Mental models present a new way to envision a future. They place us mentally into a new space. The result of experiencing this new space is that new or original ideas are born that we otherwise might not have thought of.

Are you applying bias into your thinking? Have you considered how Heisenberg would look at the problem by disconnecting the dots? Is there a paradigm shift that's taking place and affecting product success? The fascinating thing about mental models is placing yourself in a new situation where you can understand the emotional and philosophical frame in which a person is operating. Use categories, concepts, identities, prototypes and worldviews of mental models to discover a new way of looking at something old.

Use mental models to see what others can't and to discover what others won't.

CHAPTER 4

PREDICTING INNOVATION

"Those who have knowledge, don't predict.
Those who predict, don't have knowledge."

— LAO TZU, 6TH CENTURY BC CHINESE POET

Chapter Objectives

After reading this chapter, readers will be able to:

- Appreciate the pace of incremental innovations
- View how pioneers think to inspire change
- Explain how intermediation and disintermediation occur and the role of trust
- Comprehend the origins of design thinking
- Understand the Stanford process for design thinking
- Appreciate the advantages of design thinking

Incremental Innovation

Innovation takes many forms. Every organization eventually reaches a crossroads where it must determine whether it's going to pursue an incremental or exponential innovation approach. If you've ever sat down and tried to think of breakthrough ideas quickly—as we all have—not many new ideas emerge at that particular time. This is when we turn to a method that's proven to generate results, even if they're limited in possibilities.

Incremental innovation is a series of small improvements or upgrades made to a company's existing products, services, processes, or methods.[42] The objective isn't to radically transform a process, product, or service but rather to improve something that your organization has already developed. Efficiency (energy, efforts, or money), productivity (rate of output), and competitive differentiation (strategic positioning to set the brand apart from competitors) each can be objectives of incremental innovation. When the topic of incremental improvements is raised, it's commonly skipped over to race into breakthrough ideas and revolutionary products with exponential growth potential. However, that's not how our teams and organizations traditionally operate. In fact, even the most highly capable teams need consistent improvement. It's also not a bad thing to constantly be improving.

Do you have a gmail account? Well, I think everyone does. This was an incremental improvement for Google. Started in the 1990s as web-based mail and kicked off by Paul Buchheit, gmail was eventually launched by Google. At the time this idea was ignited, many other—and, frankly, better—email solutions existed including Yahoo! Mail and Hotmail. Did we need another mail service? Buchheit found that, while these services did offer mail, a new need had emerged due to the high volume of Internet mail: the ability to search. Incremental improvements for mail storage led to new thinking that users' mail could be stored forever versus the 2MB to 4MB of storage that was standard. Traditional limits on mail storage were updated to 100MB and, quickly, to 1GB. Later, Buchheit was joined by Sanjeev Singh, an up-and-coming engineer, who left Google to start FriendFeed. Along with Brian Rakowski, they formed Google gmail interfaces and launched the product only to Google employees in 2004.

What if Buchheit only wanted to build ideas using exponential innovation? We likely wouldn't have gmail.[43]

Rarely do we notice incremental innovations. Things just work a little bit better. The redesign of a gas station's entrance. The flight path routing a commercial airliner. The intake forms at your local hospital. What do these innovations mean for business? "Everything is the same, but nicer."[44] Most consumer-consumption categories in growth economies aren't revolutionary transformations of products but alternative, low-tech improvements. Housing, utilities, personal care, telecom, and home furnishings each have made little progress over the last 10 years relative to other sectors such as financial services or insurance services. Incremental innovations have power.

Applying a transversal process to crank out incremental innovations creates an intersection of value resulting in exponential discoveries. However, these discoveries will be periodic in their emergence within your teams.

Incremental innovations are safe. There are several reasons why starting with sequential, controlled changes might be a wise decision for your team.

INCREMENTAL INNOVATION BENEFITS:

- Jump starts the movement toward a strategic vision, moves teams outside of institutional mindsets, and starts progress.
- Improves organizational value while falling within the existing structures, processes, and values of the organization.

- It's hard to argue with improving a service, product, or interaction incrementally; e.g., "ABC product engagement could improve by 5 percent."
- Small changes help to adjust an organization's spot within an existing marketplace.
- It allows some early wins. Incremental innovation presents a low-risk approach to early wins to engage stakeholders cross-functionally.
- Cumulative progress improves processes and can free up capital that can be reinvested into high-risk value propositions that otherwise wouldn't have been funded.
- It's not sufficient to only focus on exponential innovation existing within an organization's product range, which can have similar disruptive effects on the market.
- The risk associated with incremental R&D effects ensures that cost structures are contained and decreases financial uncertainty.
- Changing product attributes can alter how customers notice the product.
- Adjusting the throughput can increase production capacity and productivity and reduce costs.

INCREMENTAL INNOVATION RISKS:

- The improvements offered provide little incentive to convince customers to incur switching costs.
- Low financial returns.
- Technological uncertainty could make the time spent irrelevant.
- Low chance of transformational success when compared to more revolutionary or radical approaches.
- Evolutionary processes are time-consuming.
- Decreased probability of profitability.

- The extended duration increases the coordination within the company, increasing the complexity of political interference.
- Within a risk-adverse culture, the lack of qualified personnel and longer development times increase the probability that the initiative will be killed.
- It's easier to think about incremental ideas than it is to think about transformative ideas; it's difficult to select the right ideas.
- Measurement of incremental innovation is difficult, and rarely is adequate planning conducted to ensure adequate or accurate measures.[45]

Radical Innovation

We've entered the age of radical innovation. Steven Kotler and Peter Diamandis talk about the six D's of exponentials. Kotler, co-founder and director of research for the Flow Genome Project and author of several books, partnered with Diamandis, CEO of the X PRIZE Foundation and co-Founder and Chairman of the Singularity University, to develop "the Six D's."[46] [47] [48] These are a list of chain reactions that radical, innovative organizations utilize to develop new opportunities:

- Digitalization
- Deception
- Disruption
- Demonetization
- Dematerialization
- Democratization

Digitization is a state in which new technologies experience unprecedented growth. The central theme is the conversion of things into ones and zeros. A classic example is Moore's Law, which refers to an observation made in 1965 that the number of transistors per square inch on integrated circuits had doubled every year since their invention.[49]

Deception refers to the initial state of innovation. More specifically, in accordance with the Gartner Hype Cycle, this state would occur before the "Innovation Trigger" phase. During this state, adoption is growing; however, the growth is misdirected because it doesn't appear to build quickly at first. Kotler identifies this as the whole-number barrier, providing the example that 2 becomes 32 which becomes 32,000.[50]

Disruption is defined as what happens when existing models don't produce consistent outcomes—typically around effectiveness and cost. Classic examples are computer memory for efficiency or storage space as in the case of CDs. When it's possible to purchase books online in seconds, why drive to the local library for a book (although some of us still enjoy that experience)?

Demonetization is about removing cost obstacles from the equation. Typically, disruption drives down cost, which makes the cost of goods or services cheaper and thereby removes existing barriers to innovation. For example, if Microsoft no longer requires the production of MS Office in hard copies, the scale of distribution using cloud-based technology becomes crucial, where cost quickly approaches zero.

Dematerialization is the shift from owned to leased or rented. The material possession of physical products is removed from the mix. For example, a photographer once needed a separate camera for her work; today, of course, we all use our cell phones for photography. Similarly, traditional or physical GPS units are being replaced by map software such as Google Maps or MotionX mobile applications.

Finally, *democratization* is a state in which technology is widely accessible, and government or private industry no longer has exclusive access due to barriers of cost, access, and scale. Thomas Friedman, an American journalist, author, and three-time Pulitzer Prize winner, suggested that "our era of globalization has been characterized by the democratization of technology, the democratization of finance, and democratization of information."[51] Classic examples are the first movable printing press that Johannes Gutenberg invented in 1439. Characters were assembled manually, and a skilled compositor could assemble 2,000 characters or letters in an hour. It wasn't until 1970 that computers became a factor in the evolutionary process. Today, most hotels offer free printing to guests, and a good printer is under USD $100. Broad accessibility has democratized printing technology.

An excellent illustration of radical innovation and exponential growth was highlighted in a report from a consultancy in the Netherlands. The question posed was, "When a bacteria colony in a container is doubling in size every minute, and the container is filled in one hour, when is the container half full?"[52] The answer? After exactly 59 minutes: 59 minutes to fill the first half and 1 minute to fill the second half. Radical innovation is non-linear, and this unconventional thinking expands the mental gap between what we believe is possible and the heights to which virality and technology adoption can take us.

How Innovative Pioneers Think

To perform differently, it's necessary to start by thinking differently. It's no longer possible to develop innovative solutions in a silo. Why work in a silo when you can work with friends or business colleagues interested in similar outcomes? Business and technology executives are realizing that 100% of $0.00 is still zero, and 50% of something is still something. The focus is turning to channel margins with a concentration on selling price and cost-plus-margin opportunities. Leveraging intermediaries in the software development channel does, in fact, increase profit, not decrease it. Communication with customers declines, and so do the associated costs.

Partnerships don't have to be 50/50. More and more, these are focused on profit sharing. This is how innovative executives are expanding and growing their businesses—minimizing risk and maximizing exposure.

Lead by establishing unassuming partnerships. Challenge the norm to exceed normal margins. We've heard this before. This concept isn't new. What's the value of your company's social network? Did you know there are banks now that only lend based on the strength of a company's social network? That's right—someone with a minimal social presence and someone with a huge network of 10,000 won't get the same rates for their business loans. At what point does a credit check not even matter, and it's solely the strength of your social influence (the network effect) that will drive how close to a prime rate your business will get?

We must be social. This doesn't mean only doing speaking events, which we all do. It means having a following, sharing things you might not otherwise share, and being a part of the crowd you seek to lead. Developing a strong, visible, social presence and being a social engager is the definition of the new CIO.

Be social, share, communicate, and be involved in swirling ideas.

The past leads to the future, from the 1870 invention of the bulb-shaped glass-encasement for Thomas Edison's new incandescent lamp to the 1912 glass signal lanterns for America's railroads to TV picture tubes in 1947 to the development of the first optical fiber capable of maintaining the strength of laser-light signals over significant distances in 1970 to Gorilla® Glass in 2007.

Corning has constantly re-defined innovation. Why has Corning been so successful? A lone inventor alone in the lab? Youthful innovators? "Special people in special places?" Large corporate funding fueling innovation? No. They partner. They share. They grow bigger together—with help.

Take your biggest competitor and explore what opportunities you have together: to partner, to share, to grow bigger together.

Consolidation opens unassuming partnerships. Consolidation remains an effective strategic tool. Consolidation has long been used to achieve and sustain power in the marketplace. From Jay Gould's railroad-industry revolution post-1870 to Standard Oil achieving monopoly power through regional consolidation and vertical integration in the mid 1800s to the U.S. steel industry's aggressive consolidation and operational alignment. New consolidation opens competitive advantages in diverse industries. Throughout history, consolidations have led to faster consumer adoption. Why? Because the alternatives erode. However, in mainstream consolidation, unassuming opportunities crack the framework and enable niche opportunities to expand where before they were restrained. Design-for-value approaches and new market opportunities will unlock as consolidation constrains the mainstream.

Find the edge of value, and then find a partner to share the growth.

DISINTERMEDIATION AND INTERMEDIATION

By bringing back the middleman into digital innovation, disintermediation promotes disruption and intermediation fosters innovation.

Disintermediation removes the middleman from business transactions and, by doing so, improves the value of an existing product or service. Disintermediation is often accomplished by changing the perception of delivery.

Inversely, intermediation injects a middleman between distribution channels; e.g., between a customer and businesses that previously sold directly to consumers. Intermediation gains traction when the platform is so large that companies can't afford not to leverage that platform to reach customers.

COINING THE TERM

Let's start with the history of the word, disintermediation, to guide our journey to its real meaning. Jonathan B. Welch, in his 1980s article, "Explaining Disintermediation at Mutual Savings Banks," which was published in the *Financial Analysts Journal,* describes the disintermediation of the mortgage market and the homebuilding industry during the 1960s and 1970s, when the amounts withdrawn over a period exceeded the amounts deposited. A contributing factor was the interest-rate differential between savings deposits and Treasury bills. However, the term disintermediation was coined in the mid-1960s, when consumers started to see government-imposed limits on interest-bearing savings.

Consumers responded by quickly investing in government securities, private stocks, and bonds, which resulted in removing their prior investments from savings accounts. As a result, consumers began to explore borrowing capital from markets other than banks and thereby circumventing banks as the middleman. Disintermediation is about removing the middleman in the distribution chain.

DISINTERMEDIATION

A classic supply chain involves producers, wholesalers, retailers, and consumers. Disintermediation fractures the role of the middlemen between producers or avoids traditional distribution channels with intermediates such as distributors, brokers, or agents. In the case of disintermediation, one step is removed; e.g., a producer goes directly to the retailer, thereby eliminating the need for the wholesaler. In simple terms, business goes directly to the consumer—although this could mean the removal of any single point within the supply chain that makes the process more straightforward.

The disruption generated by disintermediation can be significant and reshape entire business models, as was the case with banking. The travel industry is another sector impacted by disintermediation. Travel agents were disintermediated by online travel websites such as kayak.com, expedia.com, hotwire.com, traveocity.com, and hipmunk.com. These online marketplaces unseated traditional travel agents, and the tourism industry was changed. Likewise, traditional publishing channels like Encyclopedia Britannica and Microsoft's Encarta were disintermediated by Wikipedia.

Disintermediation can take markets by surprise. Banking wasn't prepared and neither was the music industry. The theme of digital disintermediation is harnessed well in the plight of the music industry and its struggle to maintain active control over distribution in the era of CDs. Consumers briefly loved CDs until they hated them, when, during the 1990s, they were forced to buy CDs with songs they didn't want. Ultimately, the music industry failed and, eventually, it awoke to realize that Apple controlled its inventory. Newspaper publishers, the music industry, and real estate each has been on the receiving end of disintermediation with the likes of Craigslist, Apple iTunes, and Trulia. Disintermediators include Uber (freelance drivers and riders, removing cab companies), Airbnb (hosts and renters, removing hotels), and Apple iTunes (viewers and creators, removing the music store). Business can be a disintermediator or intermediator, and it can even hold characteristics of both.

Disintermediation is bound to happen in healthcare. Where will disintermediation start? The drug companies could directly reach consumers, bypassing hospitals. Hospitals may opt to cut out private insurers and generate robust, provider-sponsored plans offered straight to patients. Physicians may choose to circumvent hospitals and renegotiate compensation if they can provide new care alternatives and structures through tele-health options incorporating direct interaction with patients. Healthcare is on the cusp of disintermediation.

INTERMEDIATION

Almost more interesting than disintermediation—removing the middleman—is intermediation, which adds the middleman back into the mix. Intermediation occurs when digital platforms inject themselves between the customers and a company. These platforms are so large that businesses can't afford to ignore them. Intermediation creates a dependency, and disintermediation removes the dependency.

The *Digital Disruptive Intermediaries* report published through the University of Sydney Business School captures the heart of intermediaries extremely well. Digital disruptive intermediaries are disruptors and can be categorized into eight archetypes:

- **Digital stores** (online; e.g., amazon.com, expedia.com)
- **Content hubs** (consumer interaction; e.g., Apple's iTunes, Netflix)
- **Sharing hubs** (user-generated content; e.g., Pinterest, YouTube)
- **Promoter focus** (best price to consumers; e.g., Priceline.com, Groupon)
- **Aggregators** (comparisons in fragmented markets; e.g., Unimall.de, Pizza.de)
- **Discriminators** (customer reviews; e.g., reddit, Yelp)
- **Crowdsourcers** (customer-sourced services; e.g., Kickstarter, IndieGoGo)
- **Matchers** (linking supply and demand; e.g., Airbnb, Uber, e-Harmony).

Who's an intermediary? The real definition is hardly glamorous; every business is an intermediator. Many intermediaries have become icons within their industries due to their disruptive impact, their brand recognition amplified by the media, or word of mouth. Intermediaries include Facebook (between users and advertisers), Twitter (between companies and consumers), Apple Pay (between credit-card companies and cardholders), and Apple HealthKit (between payers and members or between providers and their patients).

The digital innovators of tomorrow will forego the disruption that disintermediation creates for the innovation that intermediation fosters. Digital platforms are welcoming back the middleman.

Design Thinking

Digital-technology designers and business-design architects have shifted from designing physical objects or services to designing our interactions with them.

Stanford University catapulted design thinking into the mainstream when it first introduced the concept as a formal method taught to engineering students in 2005. The organic roots of design thinking go back farther and lead us to Harold Van Doren, who wrote the book, *Industrial Design: A Practical Guide,* published in 1940. Van Doren describes the need for the design of industrial parts to lift off the paper and take the form of three-dimensional—not two-dimensional—clay models. He expands by saying that, when designers use clay, they gain more experience than designers who depend only on paper and pencil. Van Doren, of course, is talking about the value of interactions and experiences. It seems a bit comical that this concept was "discovered" 65 years later at Stanford.

Van Doren outlines five key steps in this process, which he calls an "integrated design program:"

- Understand the clay or wax studies (research)
- Draft a rough dimensioned layout
- Present the model
- A full-size dummy model or mock-up is prepared by the client from drawings supplied by the designer
- A full-size working model is prepared by the client and created in metal or other final materials

Several parallels exist between this initial model and the future Stanford design-thinking process, which will be evident as we cover the Stanford design-thinking approach.

THE STANFORD UNIVERSITY MODEL

Fast forwarding 70 years, the Institute of Design at Stanford, or d.school, uses a framework surprisingly similar to

63

Van Doren's. The d.school prepares future innovators to use design thinking to inspire multidisciplinary teams to foster radical collaboration. The central theme uses prototyping to discover new solutions. The theory behind design thinking is that "to create meaningful innovations, you need to know your users and care about their lives." This theory aligns well with the Doblin Innovation Model, described in the book *Ten Types of Innovation: The Discipline of Building Breakthroughs*, which outlines the 10 types of innovation: 1. Profit model, 2. Network, 3. Structure, 4. Process 5. Product performance, 6. Product system, 7. Service, 8. Channel, 9. Brand, and 10. Customer engagement. The Doblin Innovation Model explains that most companies look for innovation between "product performance" and the "product system," but the biggest opportunities are anchored in the "profit model" or within "customer engagement" innovation.

The Stanford process for design thinking defines design thinking for innovation as a discipline managed with the following action steps:

- Empathize
- Define
- Ideate
- Prototype
- Test

Stanford's five-step process uncovers the value of design thinking and finding simplicity within complexity.

EXPLAINING THE FIVE-STEP PROCESS

The first step of design thinking is **empathizing**, a focal point in design thinking where you observe, engage, watch, and listen. In the context of healthcare, this step solves "why" patients do things while more deeply understanding their physical and emotional needs. It's about discovering what's meaningful to them.

The second step is **defining** the problem clearly. The only way to create the right solution is by framing the right problem.

The third step is to **ideate,** which means going beyond obvious solutions and increasing the innovation potential by harnessing a collective perspective. Fresh team members and participants collaborate to uncover unexpected areas for exploration, driving teams beyond the present solutions.

The fourth step, **prototyping,** occurs after we've ideated on the problem and it's now clear; it's time to start the conversation with prototyping. This step begins by deconstructing large problems into smaller and more testable chunks. We've all heard the saying, "A picture is worth a thousand words." Well, if a picture is worth a thousand words, a prototype is worth a thousand pictures.

The fifth step, **testing,** is where we build the experience and play out the previously identified interactions.

THE LOW COST OF EXPERIMENTATION

Creation breeds ownership and, at this point, the team actively works through ideas. Failing quickly and cheaply is encouraged. Ultimately, the team comes together to determine if the experience initially envisioned is going to work. In a healthcare context, the last step, testing, gives the patient a chance to experience the interactions. Interactions allow designers to learn more about the patient. The prototypes and solutions are refined and form the basis of future prototype iterations. We ask users to compare their perspectives while being engaged in creating experiences. There's no more talk about the experience; the patient is experiencing it. How are they interacting? How do they feel? What questions do they have? When design thinking is applied to healthcare, it transforms innovative ideas into practical solutions that change how patients receive care.

For an uncomplicated view, the process has been described in a linear progression. In practice, these steps can be executed in various orders depending on your methods, style, and the patients involved.

Conclusion

How you generate ideas stems from how your mind designs and connects pieces of seemingly unrelated information into dynamic combinations.

Whether you're searching for anomalies or experimenting with trapping the creative nature of chance, combining old ideas and reassembling them into new constructions is the bedrock of all innovation.

Each process we adhere to has producers and consumers. Sometimes these are obvious, as in the case of Airbnb (hosts and renters) in a two-sided market. However, often the products and consumers are less clear, as in the case of a visit to the doctor (payers, providers, patients) in a multi-sided market. Regardless of interaction, you, as an innovator, have the ability to intermediate (inject) or disintermediate (remove) any single or multiple player from that game. Powerful players actively design the rules for the games in which they engage. Many times, these games of business have human factors involved with designing physical objects, services, or interactions that can be improved through design thinking: empathizing, defining, ideating, prototyping, and testing.

Each approach has benefits when used in the right context. You, as an innovator, need to determine which context offers the best opportunity.

PART II

INSPIRATION FROM OUTSIDE

Every day, new people enter our lives. Tomorrow, you'll have a new experience at work (or while working remotely). The day after, you'll meet someone for the first time. You'll share ideas and discover something you never knew. It might be as simple as a Netflix documentary or new concept introduced in a book you haven't yet read.

In these chapters, we'll explore how to experience these types of situations with greater frequency. What if you're not starting that new job or not meeting a ton of new people weekly? Where do you go for new ideas? How do you think differently? What can push you from your currently comfortable place on your mental couch to something a bit more adventurous?

We're going to start by looking outside our immediate circle—of things, of people, of our environment. We'll be looking at how innovation rules are created. That means, why it's okay to wear brown shoes with black pants—once you know the rules. We need to understand the rules, so we consciously know when we're breaking them. Nature will come into focus like never before. All these unique ideas. Guess what? They aren't really all that unique. We just didn't stop and observe.

Lastly, we'll look at platforms, how they change interactions, and how they'll take a larger role in the future.

CHAPTER 5

INNOVATION'S BOUNDARIES IN A BOUNDLESS WORLD

"The great accomplishments of man have resulted from the transmission of ideas of enthusiasm."

— THOMAS J. WATSON

Chapter Objectives

After reading this chapter, readers will be able to:

- Build a framework of the laws of innovation—so you can break them
- Explain the Law of Leadership, the Law of Patience, and the Law of Process
- Discuss the relevance of the Law of Culture (people, ideas, alignment, and communication)
- Recall concepts that affect your ability to influence and expand your social proof
- Have a basic understanding of the laws of innovation
- Understand the Law of Diffusion and Innovation
- Be familiar with the theory of innovation alignment
- Identify the consequences of innovation adoption: desirable vs. undesirable, direct vs. indirect, and anticipated vs. unanticipated

Laws Governing Innovation

Have you ever worn a brown belt and black shoes? How about boots with dress pants or a skirt? Every year in Miami, there's the Annual Breaking the Laws of Fashion show. Stumbling upon this event reminded me of when I first wore a brown belt with black shoes. Shockingly, it's much more recent than I care to admit. The event reminded me that while there are rules in fashion, if you understand what you're breaking, it's okay to break the rules. Innovation also has rules that can be broken. However, like with fashion, before you break the rules, it's wise to at least understand you're breaking them.

There are Seven Rules of Innovation:

1. Collaborate to Engage
2. Wonder for Discovery
3. Empower Creativity
4. Innovation as a Strategy
5. Open Innovation to All
6. Co-opetition to Grow
7. Share for Inspiration

Rule 1: Collaborate to Engage

Collaborate for greater value. One of the greatest challenges when doing business is communication. It's also the number-one reason most projects fail—the lack of effective communication—according to the Project Management Institute. Attitudes toward authority, concepts of time, adherence to rules, building relationships, level of English language ability, and communication styles are but a ripple in our ability to effectively communicate with business counterparts. Developing team structures is one of the most important factors to success when building effective innovation teams.

Understanding how communication increases in complexity as a team (number of internal or external partners) changes is essential to capturing the value of collaboration. For example, let's look at communication as a team grows and communication increases in complexity: three people is three lines of communication, four people is six lines, five people is 10 lines, six people is 15 lines, seven people is 21 lines, eight people is 28 lines, nine people is 36 lines, 10 people is 45 lines, 11 people is 55 lines, 12 people is 66 lines, 13 people is 78 lines, and 14 people is 91 lines. This is essential information when planning to assemble a "simple innovation team of 15." I can tell you from experience that if you're doing anything at all complex, the teams need to be small. I have a hard and fast rule I've used for almost two decades: no group shall ever be greater than eight people, including the leader. Overall, complex communication is the quickest route to failure. When planning to solve the communication challenge, reflect on how your team will work best and the ideal group size.

It's okay to break the rule of collaboration. There's an African proverb that says, "If you want to go fast, go alone. If you want to go far, go together." You, as a leader, need to determine where you are on your innovation journey and what pace is best for success.

Rule 2: Wonder for Discovery

Wondering encourages new value. Pikkel, Quinn, and Walters wrote a very practical book called *Ten Types of Innovation*. In this book, they outline the "Ten Types Framework"—the discipline of building breakthroughs. The framework breaks down the process of innovation into three models for analyzing and beating the competition:

1. Configuration (profit model, network, structure, process)
2. Offering (product performance, product system)
3. Experience (service, channel, brand, customer engagement)

The model is very useful when attempting to categorize innovations to identify why the innovation is unique.[53] This process can be hugely useful for teams both old and new. It's planned and procedural. This is a foundational understanding of the process of innovation that every innovative mind should grasp.

However, what if you don't plan and just let your team experiment for a period? We observed this trend starting in 2004 with the Google IPO letter inked by Larry Page and Sergey Bring: "We encourage our employees, in addition to their regular projects, to spend 20% of their time working on what they think will most benefit Google. This empowers them to be more creative and innovative. Many of our significant advances have happened in this manner. For example, AdSense for content and Google News were both prototyped in '20% time.' Most risky projects fizzle, often teaching us something. Others succeed and become attractive businesses." Whether or not Google still offers this option is up for debate. We know companies can be deliberate. They can also allow wondering. They knew the rules, and they broke them.

Have you ever just walked? I don't mean walk to somewhere. I mean, have you ever just walked? It could have been on vacation or while killing some alone time. You had no destination; you were just thinking and exploring. While in college, I rode motorcycles a lot to relax. It was my escape from the busy pace of life. I was juggling a heavy academic course load, working for the CEO of Arthur D. Little, and taking nighttime technical certification classes, so my schedule didn't afford me a lot of free time. However, usually between 11 pm and 1 am, I'd play a game. I called the game the "two lefts." The goal was to explore an area where I'd never been before on the motorcycle.

I would start about three to five miles from campus and then, for 45 minutes to an hour, I'd ride, taking the first two lefts and then the first right. It was unbelievable what I discovered during those trips. I found a fantastic late-night dinner one evening. Another time, I uncovered an incredible chicken wing joint. Innovation requires slack time—giving yourself permission to wander.

Rule 3: Empower Creativity

Have you ever met someone that was truly creative? These are the people that have a knack for generating ideas that are well outside conventional thinking. Your team might have been brainstorming ideas to improve the efficiency of a process or to design a new consumer interaction. Then, seemingly out of nowhere, this individual generates an idea that redirects the discussion. Basically, without this specific contribution to the group, the team would have gone in a totally different direction. This is empowered creativity. It's the ability to re-imagine the future by removing perceptions that limit your reasoning—idea limiters.

The ability to innovate is based on information transformed into knowledge that breaks free ideas that otherwise might incubate for hours, weeks, or even years. Empowering creativity within your teams isn't trying to have the team concentrate really hard to think of breakthrough ideas. We've all done this. We also all know that this approach doesn't work. What does work? The raw problem must be redefined.

If we simply solved the problem in front of us or our team, we wouldn't solve the problem we needed to solve. Have you ever heard the phrase, "Your problem is not your problem?" The concept here is that what you're solving is a symptom or an effect of the root-cause issue that you and the team should be solving. You'll feel great when you solve that surface problem, but nothing, ultimately, will change. This is exactly what we're trying avoid when we innovate. We want to solve that root problem so we'll need to only solve it once. Otherwise, another problem (or bottleneck) will emerge, and we'll solve that one, and so on.

Innovation isn't creativity. This was the conclusion of Vijay Govindarajan, a professor at Dartmouth College's Tuck School of Business and the Marvin Bower Fellow at Harvard Business School; and Chris Trimble, also a professor at Dartmouth College's Tuck School of Business. Their book, *The Other Side of Innovation: Solving the Execution Challenge*, challenged how innovation occurs and delineated the difference between innovation and creativity based on research and interviews with executives.[54]

When we empower creativity, we're generating new ideas or expanding on old ideas. What's relevant for us is that there's a disconnect between the front end of innovation (creativity) and the back end (execution). For example, early on, Kodak identified the need for the digital camera and the need for digital photography. Their creativity process, or how they empowered creativity, was working; however, there was no follow-through. Govindarajan and Trimble elaborate on where organizations have the most trouble. The biggest challenges, surprisingly, aren't generating good ideas. The challenge comes after there are some sparks of success. Politics, turf battles, and the like all factor into slowing the wave of innovation—the ability to execute.

As you empower creativity (ideas) and innovation (execution) with your teams, make a conscientious decision about where to focus your efforts. It might be better to execute on one great idea than to explore 20.[55]

Rule 4: Innovation as a Strategy

Your organization has a financial strategy, marketing strategy, operations strategy, human-capital strategy, and a maintenance and operations strategy. With the right level of access, these are all available to leaders. But where is your "innovation strategy?"

The innovation strategy is an organizational investment in research-and-development activities to encourage advancements in the technology of business capabilities including products, services, or interactions. Generating ideas is the start. However, by defining new market needs (not existing customer needs), your organization can develop an innovation process. This process leads to outcome-driven innovation (ODI).

While at IBM, Anthony W. Ulwick, the founder and Chief Executive Officer of Strategy LLC in San Fransisco, CA, developed this process. Ulwick communicated his ideas in a *Harvard Business Review* article on how companies should develop products to fulfill what their customers want to accomplish. Guess what. This wasn't determined by asking customers what they wanted. Asking customers only offers solutions that create order-takers; this approach doesn't stimulate new ideas. This is the danger of listening to customers too carefully.

The rationale that Ulwick presented was that customers only know what they've experienced. This results in a limited reference point and, therefore, a narrow scope of "new" ideas.

Ulwick's theory was that instead of asking customers "what they need" in terms of features, ask customers "what they want as outcomes." Thus, the ODI model acknowledges that the need-first approach is structurally flawed and presents alternative principles for how teams should approach innovation:[56]

1. When it comes to innovation, the job, not the product, must be the unit of analysis.
2. A job map provides the structure needed to ensure all customer needs are captured.
3. When the job is the unit of analysis, needs take the form of customer-defined metrics.
4. ODI's "jobs-to-be-done" principles apply equally well to design innovation.
5. The opportunity algorithm makes it possible to prioritize unmet needs.

6. Opportunities (unmet needs) dictate which growth strategy to pursue.
7. Scattershot brainstorming doesn't work; sequenced and focused idea generation does.
8. Concepts can be evaluated with precision against customer-defined metrics.[57]

Envato, headquartered in Australia and founded in 2006, provides creative assets for web designers, including themes, graphics, video, audio, photography, and 3D models. Envato has over 1.5 million active buyers and sellers and over 6 million community members. For their Envato Elements 2016 product launch, they used outcome-driven innovation to deliver this new product. The process was extremely effective and took less than six weeks of part-time effort. The book entitled, *What Customers Want,* elaborates on this implementation approach. Here's the short version:

1. Run interviews
2. Consolidate information
3. Design surveys
4. Process responses
5. Analyze the data
6. Present the outcome-based findings[58]

The value here is that the entire process is driven by outcomes not "me too" feature additions that never solve the underlying problems. By taking an outcome-driven innovation approach, your team will be able to dial into the real transformational changes that could leap-frog your organization forward to develop sustainable competitive advantages.

Rule 5: Unlock the Innovation

It's not surprising that the Massachusetts Institute of Technology is a hub of innovation. Companies that have taken flight out of MIT have a valuation over $1 trillion and, if combined into a country, would be considered the 17th largest economy in the world.[59][60] The bedrock of MIT's success is a network of entrepreneurs that continually unlock innovation's potential.

To discover breakthrough ideas, we first need to start with an understanding of the data or market landscape. Harnessing the power of big data is the next frontier for innovation, competition, and productivity. To creatively and effectively uncover value, we must first look for insights through research. Where's the market going? What industries are impacted? When will services be enabled by data to drive new outcomes?

Second, information can't be accessed unless it's transparent. Are you familiar with how supply-chain just-in-time (JIT) systems leverage transaction data to dynamically adjust product inventories to help leaders make better decisions? What data do you not have? What data would improve current divisions? Is high-frequency data being used to expose variability and boost performance?

Third, filter the data to make small molehills of the mountains of data accessible to your organization. These smaller piles of data are easier to mine, analyze, and make trend predictions against. Are you capturing the data you need? Has the team captured the right value, drawing from real-time processes? Are you competing with new entrants and playing the right game, driven by data?

Assessing how to unlock value requires every member of the team to be an entrepreneur. It's easy to suggest the team be creative and innovative. Reflect for a moment. How are you, as a leader, designing to empower your team with the best data, information, knowledge, and wisdom to generate those breakthrough ideas? Now you're thinking like a game changing innovator.

Rule 6: Co-Opetition to Grow

It's not enough to succeed. Others must fail. Is this how you lead, inspire, and motivate your teams? Move the game from win-lose to win-win.

Adam Brandenburger, professor at the Harvard Business School, and Barry Nalebuff, professor at the Yale School of Management, present an alternative approach in their book entitled, *Co-opetition.*

Co-opetition is a revolutionary mindset that combines competition and cooperation. It's a game-theory strategy that's changing the game of business. Competition is a game among sellers to reach objectives such as increasing profits, market share, and sales volume by varying the elements of the marketing mix: price, product, distribution, and promotion. The nature of this relationship is adversarial. Cooperation, alternatively, is the process of working together to the same end. Cooperation is a unification of people or businesses to meet common economic, social, and cultural needs and aspirations through a jointly owned and democratically controlled business. Often this utopian view is unachievable in its pure form.[61]

The idea of co-opetition integrates the natural competitive nature of business with the spirit of cooperation. It puts aside the notion that one organization must lose for the other to win. Co-opetition considers that the market is large enough for both organizations to combine resources (economic, human capital, physical, and knowledge) to jointly win.

What's new isn't this concept; it's where it's being applied. Do you believe you're leveraging principles of co-opetition? Answer a few questions:

1. Can you name three companies your team is working with to extend your innovation capability (your ability to execute)?
2. Which direct competitor are you working with for a joint outcome to benefit both organizations?

3. Is your team swapping resources with your competitor to share core knowledge of processes to grow and enhance both operations?

There's probably some room for opportunity to expand your team's innovation thinking. Maybe swapping staff is too progressive, but what can you do today? Your ability to reach exponential or breakthrough innovations requires you to do what others won't do. You want to innovate, and so do your competitors. Grow your innovation mindset by thinking how your team and organization could align with a competitor to grow and capture a new opportunity. Evaluate the game you're playing. Even if you play the game the best, you could still lose if you're playing the wrong game.

TWA, Nintendo, Minnetonka, and Alibaba are excellent examples of playing the game by redefining the game. TWA removed seats to give passengers more leg room. Nintendo sold games to a concentrated market. Minnetonka, seller of Softsoap (a liquid soap), locked up the two main plastic-pump manufacturers. Alibaba's core businesses (Alibaba, Taobao, and Tmall) are making it easy to do business anywhere.[62]

Rule 7: Share for Inspiration

Open-source technology and services used to be substandard. Then, one day we woke up, and open-source-grown systems represented the best in quality, durability, and security. WordPress (blogging platform), Mozilla Firefox (Web browser), GIMP (image editing), OpenOffice (used to create documents, spreadsheets, presentations, and databases), and Ubuntu (operating system for Linux) all fall under the Open Software License (OSL).

There's a single macro goal that open-source systems value—collaboration. These groups collaborate with various actors to ensure that the best ideas are considered, analyzed, and acted upon to build—in this case—software that's stable.

Yet, usually when we innovate, we don't collaborate as much as we should. The reason that your team should collaborate more isn't to include other members of the organization or external partners in the innovation journey—although collaboration does provide that useful benefit. The primary objective is to develop the best ideas and then innovate or execute on those ideas. It's implied that, in order to succeed, we'll need the best minds from a range of areas to ensure the product, service, or interactions are evaluated from all domains. This is only achievable if we have all domains represented, both inside and outside our organization.

The next time you hear the word collaboration and you think, "Sure, we'll include them when we need them," think about that again. We don't want those domain experts; we need them. They're essential to our innovation success and to ensure that awesome new ideas materialize into something tangible for our customers.

Challenge the prevailing model within your own organization and identify powerful industry examples where this approach has proved fruitful. Embrace collaboration to improve the odds of successful innovation initiatives. Assess whether what you're building could be used by others to build something even better.

Earn some innovation credit by contributing through collaboration to build more powerful models that have the potential to change your business's operating models.

Law of Leadership

This Law of Leadership is new. It's new thinking based on old standards. The Law of Leadership is about how leaders must adapt and change their style to align with the team and/or organization they lead.

As you build the capability to innovate within your team or organization, a realization will soon emerge: innovation is less about creating (building stuff with your team) and more about leading (listening to your team).

The Law of Leadership states that a leader's style should flex to absorb the leadership styles of the people they lead. This means that, on your team, different people need to be led by different styles of leadership. One style doesn't work for all. This took me years to fully understand. It isn't good enough to be you. Most likely, you'll need to change your approach depending on the team member you're leading and their needs. There are, broadly, 20 core leadership styles that every innovator should know. You won't be using them all at the same time. However, over your career, you'll use 90 percent of them—if you're leading correctly.

These are the 20 core leadership styles:

1. Autocratic
2. Bureaucratic
3. Leader who coaches
4. Cross-cultural
5. Emergent
6. Laissez-faire
7. Strategic
8. Team
9. Facilitative
10. Participative
11. Servant
12. Transformational
13. Charismatic
14. Visionary
15. Transactional
16. Level 5
17. Primal
18. Authentic
19. Innovative
20. Situational

The autocratic leadership style centers on the balance of control between the leader and the team. The bureaucratic leadership style relies on clear lines of authority. The leader-who-coaches leadership style uses the leader's ability to teach and train new leaders. The cross-cultural leadership style uses the knowledge of cultural similarities and differences to unify the team. The emergent leadership style grows team members who evolve into leadership roles (e.g., team leads). The laissez-faire leadership style—delegating leadership—is a hand-off approach that allows group team members to make decisions. The strategic leadership style enhances long-term success by influencing others to voluntarily make decisions. The team leadership style downplays the need for formal leaders and encourages "team leaders" to take more active leadership roles. The facilitative leadership style uses indirect communication patterns to guide the group to consensus versus overtly controlling the team. The participative leadership style is a balance between controlling and engaging with the team (active participation). The servant leadership style puts the needs of followers first; servant leaders focus on a great need to serve the organization over themselves. The transformational leadership style is used if significant changes are required—change that's usually widespread, mission-critical, and represents a monumental cultural shift. The charismatic leaderships style emphasizes the charm and persuasiveness of the leader. The visionary leadership style inspires action through a shared future vision or purpose. The transactional leadership style, or managerial leadership, is a reward-and-punishment approach focused on supervision, organization, and performance. The Level 5 leadership style is demonstrated through humility and an enormous professional will to succeed. The primal leadership style leads with an emotional message that's received well by a team's sense of purpose and emotional reality to move the team in a positive direction. The authentic leadership style builds a leader's legitimacy through honest relationships based on an ethical foundation. The innovative leadership style is a combination of leadership styles that influence the creation of products, services, and interactions. The situational leadership style requires leaders to adjust their leadership style based on the followers they're trying to influence.

Every style has a purpose and can be the best style in a specific set of events. Your role as an innovator means it's sometimes hard to figure out the best style for leading your team. It's unlikely it will be the innovative leadership style only. Leaders that are building their innovation mindset should be comfortable in a range of leadership styles, not just one.

Law of Patience

One of the first rules you learn when you fly airplanes is the Law of Patience. You wait for the lesson. You wait for the instructor. You wait at the plane for fuel. You wait to get the weather report for your destination. You wait and wait and wait. Interestingly, by the time you earn your pilot's license, you're quite comfortable waiting. In fact, that waiting is one of the enjoyable parts of flying. Preparing to fly can't be rushed; the process just flows.

It doesn't matter if we're talking about mowing the lawn, waiting for a flower to bloom, or leading innovation teams. These processes take time—often more time than you'd planned on. Innovation takes time and you, as an innovator, must have a long-term focus in mind. You could race over the lawn with the mower, skipping spots. But just mowing the lawn isn't the only goal; you want a good-looking yard. The single goal of innovation isn't only to create and deliver winning products or services. That would be great, of course; however, that's only a part of what we're looking for when we innovate. Innovation is about bringing together the team to create something amazing. This means that you, as an innovator, can't rush the process. You can't race through the preflight. You can't run the mower around the yard. You can't push your team faster than they should go. This is the softer side of building an innovation mindset. It's about thinking beyond your current flag and capturing the bigger picture.[63]

Don't force innovation. From the beginning, be clear about the business expectations and the length of time required to achieve them. Design a checklist to help you and the team measure if they're making progress toward the innovation objectives.

Law of Process

The Law of Process is the third law from John Maxwell's book entitled, *The 21 Irrefutable Laws of Leadership*. The Law of Lid (leadership's ability determines a person's level of effectiveness) and the Law of Influence (the true measure of leadership is influence—nothing more, nothing less are the first two laws. The Law of Process, the third law, suggests that leadership is evolutionary and develops daily, not in a day. The same can be said for "innovation as a process;" innovation develops daily, not in a day, minute, or second.

The core tenant of this law is you see leaders and innovators where they're visible taking on additional responsibility. The sexy part of leadership is amplified and the dirty part (hiring or reorganizations) is not discussed. Great leaders know this and plan accordingly.

There are many forms of recognition including: formal awards, company-service honors, and informal appreciation such as verbal appreciation or additional respect in meetings. This isn't where any of the leadership occurs. Similarly, evaluating a breakthrough product isn't where innovation is found, either. Innovation, like leadership, is found buried under the daily routines of those innovators and leaders.[64]

What's missing from the pictures of big smiles in front of the podium holding the innovation award is the hard work and sacrifice that resulted in achieving that objective. Innovators that evolve learn. Innovators adapt. As you're searching for the secret to innovation success, be mindful of your personal innovation-mindset evolution. What are you doing today to increase your ability to innovate? What are you planning to do tomorrow? Innovators aren't made on stage; they're only recognized there. Search within yourself to discover where they're made.

Law of Culture
(people, ideas, alignment, and communication)

The Law of Culture is one of the 7 Laws of Innovation, presented by Phil McKinney, the former Chief Technology Officer of Hewlett-Packard. The law states that the establishment of an innovation culture sets the foundation for organizational success.

Slightly adapted, this means: People drive ownership. Ideas fuel action. Alignment connects agendas. And communication creates trust.

Everything of value involves people. The debate is ongoing whether innovation is more about people or process. We're working with a chicken-or-the-egg question. Without people, a process wouldn't be followed. Without a process, people would, in theory, wonder what to do.

IDEO, one of the world's leading industrial-design firms, is a leader in innovation and design thinking to solve complex problems. Tom Kelley, a general manager at IDEO, co-authored a book entitled, *The Art of Innovation: Lessons in Creativity from IDEO, America's Leading Design Firm.*[65] The book captures how IDEO is dedicated to making innovation the defining value of its business.[66]

Many companies attempt to copy IDEO's processes, straining to achieve even a 20 percent improvement on innovation initiatives. Yet, somehow, despite hiring similar people and establishing similar processes, they fail. These imitating companies fail because they miss the spirit of the book. The book is about cultural transformation. Sure, the people and processes help, but, if you ask IDEO co-founder David Kelley for the company's secret, he'd likely say, "It's the innovative processes that our company IDEO formed." This difficult-to-emulate spirit is the essence that differentiates IDEO from every other design and innovation firm in the world.

Many of us aren't running IDEOs. We've been burdened with legacy people, process, and technology and are required to make the best of what we've got. A serious cultural transformation is likely not in our organization's future.

We do have options. You can transform a team. That's within your power. This brings us back to the Law of Culture. Culture can be organic. If you put 20 people in a room for a common goal, eventually, patterns will surface. We, as innovators, aren't looking to organically allow just any culture to form. Some cultures could negatively impact performance. We, as innovators, design culture. We're culture designers. When developing a team, whether you're building it from scratch or making small adjustments to a team you inherited, consider how you, as an innovator, are designing a culture for success. What type of culture will benefit your objectives? Are those objectives short-term or long-term? Is the spirit of the culture visible?

The cultural success will be apparent when people are producing, ideas are flowing, alignment is a norm, and the team is communicating effectively.

Law of Diffusion of Innovation

The Law of Diffusion of Innovation was first introduced by Everett Rogers, a professor of communication studies in the Department of Communication and Journalism at the University of New Mexico, in his 1962 first edition of *Diffusions of Innovations*. The book, now in its fifth edition, explains how consumers adopt new technology.

THE ORIGIN

The original work studying diffusion goes back to the 19th century with French sociologist Gabriel Tarde and German and Austrian anthropologists and geographers such as Friedrich Ratzel and Leo Frobenius.[67] This concept first took off in the 1920s and 1930s when the technology of agriculture was accelerating and scientists started to explore the diffusion or spread of farmers' adoption of hybrid seeds, equipment, and techniques. Growing from corn studies, the diffusion of technology has since enveloped medical sociology, communications, marketing, development studies, health promotion, organizational studies, and knowledge management as well as complexity studies to understand how organizations adapt.

ADOPTION CATEGORIES

Overlaying a bell curve (representing technology adoption) on a logistic function (representing market share) provides categories of adopters for emerging technology. Each innovation and technology passes through every category, if ever so briefly. There are five categories of adopters:

1. Innovators: risk takers
2. Early adopters: hedgers
3. Early majority: waiters
4. Late majority: skeptics
5. Laggards: slowpokes[68]

The innovators will be the first to experiment, because they're comfortable taking risks. The early adopters are often more educated, hold a greater social status, and use a degree of discretion when adopting. The early majority also have elevated social status and are rarely responsible for opinion leadership (e.g., domain leadership). The late majority defines the average adopter, who's skeptical of new innovations and has lower than average social status. The laggards adopt last and are averse to technological and organizational changes.

Intentionally classifying stakeholders into different buckets enables leaders to focus on the group most likely to adopt. Spending time trying to move a group when their probability of adoption is low is effort and time wasted that could move another initiative forward. Physically modeling these groups by creating heat maps or ven diagrams provides a better understanding of where these groups are today in their adoption cycle and the distance you must cover to reach critical mass.

KEY ELEMENTS
Diffusion research and the study of technological spread draws from five key elements:

1. Innovation
2. Adopters
3. Communication channels
4. Time
5. Social system

Innovation is the idea, practice, or thing that's understood to be emerging. The adopters are individuals or organizations that accept and use the technology. Communication channels enable the transfer of information from one entity to another. Time is the duration that must expire for the innovation to be adopted. Lastly, the social system encompasses the external influences (social, political, legal, environmental etc.) that represent the total vantage position of an adopter.

STAGE OF THE ADOPTION PROCESS
With new technology comes new challenges. The largest challenge isn't the creation of the product or service; the biggest challenge is building adoption. When you're preparing to launch an idea, internally or externally, first consider where you are in the adoption lifecycle. The specific stage doesn't matter as much as the thinking around why you aren't at the

next, more progressive stage. Who's inhibiting the idea? Why has adoption not occurred faster?

To design a strategy for adoption, we first must start with a view of the adoption process. There are five stages of the adoption process:

1. Knowledge
2. Persuasion
3. Decision
4. Implementation
5. Confirmation

The knowledge stage is exploratory; the adopter isn't yet interested in what, why, or for whom the innovation provides value. At the persuasion stage, the adopter is interested to learn more about the innovation. During the decision stage, the adopter weighs the advantages and disadvantages of adopting or rejecting the innovation. The implementation stage delivers the innovation to the adopter for consumption, also allowing for increased education and awareness of the innovation. Lastly, during the confirmation stage, the adopter decides whether the innovation provided the outcome desired.

Consider the stage of each adopter as the project matures. Are adopters moving through the adoption process? Is there a bottleneck in the process? Are you exploring approaches to increase the innovation-pipeline velocity to move adopters through the lifecycle faster?

REACHING A DECISION
Every decision is driven by two primary factors: (1) who's making the decision, and (2) whether the decision is made freely and implemented voluntarily.

We identified the adoption categories, assessed the key adoption elements, and reviewed the stages of adoption. Now we must determine how the decisions will be made. This is relevant to how we, as innovators, influence decisions affecting the innovation's diffusion.

There are four main types of decisions:

1. Optional innovation-decision
2. Authority innovation-decision
3. Collective innovation-decision
4. Contingent innovation-decision

Optional innovation-decisions are made by an individual and are independent of decisions made by other members.

Authority innovation-decisions are made by two entities: the adoption unit and the decision unit. These can be the same individual. However, often the adoption unit (AU) is a single individual or small group of two or three members that can accept or reject the innovation. The decision unit (DU) is a group that has a higher level of authority; e.g., a steering committee or governance board. The DU makes the final adoption or rejection decision.

The collective innovation-decision is a decision made by a group through agreement or consensus. Collective decisions require five steps before consensus is achieved:

1. Stimulation: interest
2. Initiation: new idea
3. Legitimation: social system
4. Decision: to act
5. Action: idea execution

The contingent innovation-decision is a conditional choice to either adopt or reject the innovation only after a certain event, action, or point in time.

How people adopt can change over time. The spread of innovation is a process. Thus, innovators can and should model and monitor the adoption process and take corrective action when the results don't align with their desired outcomes.

The Law of Diffusion of Innovation is a process that requires active supervision.

Theory of Innovation Alignment

The theory of innovation alignment presents the alternative that innovators shouldn't own innovation but support and collaborate to enable it.

Every company has an innovation strategy these days. Even if that strategy isn't formally articulated, ownership typically leads us to a single individual. This could be the Chief Information Officer, the Chief Financial Officer, the Chief Innovation Officer, the Chief Marketing Officer, the Chief Digital Officer, or the Chief Medical Information Officer. If no one volunteers to own it, ownership falls naturally on the Chief Executive Officer.

Innovators often are leaders that help other leaders. That leader could be the Chief Executive Officer, or it could be another leader much lower down the chain. Regardless, even if you're fortunate enough to own innovation within your organization, I'd challenge that you shouldn't. Here's why.

Innovation isn't an individual sport like running or skiing or competing in triathlons. There's something refreshing about these sports, as success or failure solely depends on your individual performance. That's not the case when leading an innovation team or organization. Success depends much more on the people in the organization and the speed at which they adopt change. It's not about your individual performance as an innovator; it's about our performance as a team to evolve. It's important to make this mental shift before you build the vision for the team.

You lead. You create. You perform. If you didn't, you wouldn't be reading this book. Now I'm telling you that doesn't matter. What matters is how you grow those characteristics within your team. What matters is how your team continues to evolve.

Evolution requires growth—both internally and externally. It sounds straightforward. It's not. This is the difference between a "smart person" and an "innovator" who transforms teams to produce exceptional results—results that, frankly, without the leader, would have never occurred.

This is where the innovation mindset comes into play. It's a totally new way of engaging with your peers and your team. You're an enabler. You're a collaborator. No one cares how fast you run or ski or bike. What they care about is how you develop teams and how you build a renewed purpose for a team that may have fallen.

You can strengthen your team by building it and, therefore, making it stronger. If you lead at the spear, it's hard to see where adjustments are needed. You have a choice to make at this point. If you lead the innovation team, you must acknowledge that it's possible it won't be as successful as it would be if you supported the work. Alternatively, if you support (which also could be in a senior role, just not with direct accountability), you'll be better positioned to guide the team over, around, and through obstacles as they pop up. Do you want to be in charge, or do you want the team or innovation to win? This is the quintessential decision every innovation leader must make. It's the decision of innovation alignment. Are you aligned with where you'd like to be today?

Consequences of Adopting Innovation

The art of managing innovation is the art of managing risk. Operational, commercial, and financial are the primary innovation risks every innovator must tackle. As you protect your innovation initiatives, so must you protect your business initiatives. Both require active oversight.

Your objective as an innovator is to build value-driving partnerships. Balancing the processes that you introduce, with allowing your team flexibility to perform, will accelerate the pace of your team's innovation mindset. Additionally, be proactive and filter innovation initiatives before the innovation pipeline is jammed up. This is accomplished by managing the innovation pipeline through innovation portfolios.

GOVERNANCE AND SPACE

An accepted form for managing risks is to establish innovation-program governance. This includes accountabilities, roles, people, processes, resources, and desired outcomes. This process provides a forum for discussion and debate. By keeping discussions centralized, even when heated, they're easier to control.

The challenge with governance is that it can stifle innovation. The solution is to actively provide a venue where individuals can go when they want to think and be creative. This space could be a game room, a nap room, or even a quiet space for meditation. Some teams block off rooms or even have "no meeting zone" times. For example, a company could establish that on Mondays from 10 am to 12 pm, no meetings can be conducted, or individuals can opt out without negative impact if they're using that time to be creative.

PIPELINES AND PORTFOLIOS

It's a rare company that only has one idea for its innovation program. All too often, the volume of ideas far exceeds the team's ability to deliver on them. As a result, these ideas need to be prioritized. The flow of ideas that moves downstream within an organization is called the innovation pipeline. Use management tools to evaluate risk and measure uncertainty as ideas are flowing through the pipeline. These processes shouldn't stop progress, but they should create additional questions to keep folks thinking about risk.

The innovation initiative will have different variables and scenarios that could help predict their future value. Grouping like or similar ideas allows the team to assess risks against initiatives that have close risk profiles. By establishing innovation portfolios measuring pipeline activity, forward progress is simplified. Building innovation portfolios is about prioritizing the most impactful or valuable work first. This process decreases the redundancy of discussing the same risks when each innovation initiative is raised. The process also ensures that risks are visible across the portfolio.

The Halo Effect

Are you persuasive? Can you influence others effectively? Do you accurately judge positive intent and abilities?

The "halo effect" or the "physical attractiveness stereotype" or the "what is beautiful is good" principle is a phenomenon in which it's assumed that people doing good will continue to do good and, inversely, people doing bad will continue to do bad.

The term "halo effect" was first coined by Edward Lee Thorndike, a psychologist and professor at Columbia University. Thorndike was also president of the American Psychological Association in 1912. Thorndike was a respected psychologist and is the ninth most cited of the 20th century. His paper entitled, "A constant error in psychological ratings," was published in the *Journal of Applied Psychology* in 1920 and was based on his study of 137 aviation cadets' flying abilities and the method by which army officers rated their soldiers. Soldiers were rated in five areas:[69]

1. **Physical** qualities: voice, energy, and endurance
2. **Intelligence**: accuracy, ease in learning, and ability to assess a new situation
3. **Leadership**: decisiveness, tact, ability to inspire loyalty, and cooperation
4. **Personal qualities**: dependability, readiness for responsibility, and freedom from selfishness
5. **General value to the Service**: professional knowledge, skill and experience, and ability to get results

The soldiers were evaluated and the observations were documented along with the findings. It was determined that instructors experienced the halo-effect error when evaluating their students, and this error manifested itself in the job-performance appraisals of their subordinates. Thorndike noticed that the correlations among the officers' evaluations of cadets were too high and too even; there was a recurring error appearing in the results—the halo effect. A cognitive bias was injected into the process without the knowledge of the officers.

As innovators, you and I must study and learn from the halo effect. How does this increase influence? Why does influence spread? How do we prime the halo pump?

We study and take note of this 1915 military study analyzing the officers' ranking of subordinates to ensure we judge new talent correctly. Loyalty must mean intelligence. Values must mean leadership. Dedication to the purpose must mean results. None, some, or many of these correlations could be true. Be conscientious about how you engage rising innovation talent and how you evaluate existing teams you adopt.

The halo effect isn't only applicable in the teaching environment of classrooms and innovation labs. This phenomenon can be applied when examining executive leadership and support for an initiative, how quickly adoption will occur within a group, and why it's hard to spot shifts in support for an innovation. Acknowledging this bias will help ensure you're fairly and accurately evaluating yourself, your team, and your supporters—each of which is critical for success.

An offshoot of the halo effect is how niche expertise of an individual can be leveraged to create a broader assumption of greater knowledge. For example, an individual might be an expert in mathematics. One might assume this person is also knowledgeable in statistics. However, that person might have a very weak understanding of statistics.

, draw the assumption that the knowledge of an individual or team is, in fact, more widespread. Not all food at Subway is low-calorie. Not every person that runs eats healthily. We assume that if someone is running, they likely are eating a balanced diet and have better fitness than someone who isn't running. However, the reality might be they're running to reduce the mental drain caused by their smoking habit.

The halo effect can be flipped from a detractor to an accelerator of adoption. Your first team excels at engineering, and they suggest a new testing methodology for the company. The new product that the second team develops is a SaaS service, and they introduce a new interface for client analytics and data interactions. The first team isn't an expert in testing. The second team isn't an expert in analytics. The halo effect is at work. Studies of the halo effect have demonstrated that judgment in one area of competency affects judgment in other areas.[70] If you, as an innovator, are aware of how the halo effect and cognitive bias impact decisions, you place you and your team on the winning side.[71]

Influence

No discussion on influence would be complete without the mention of Robert Cialdini and his 1984 book entitled, *Influence: The Psychology of Persuasion,* which has sold over three million copies. Cialdini, a professor of psychology and marketing at Arizona State University, identified what he described as the theory of influence based on six key principles: reciprocity, commitment and consistency, social proof, authority, liking, scarcity, and unity (which he added later).[72]

Guiding initiatives that require people to believe in them place the burden of influence on the leader. If a leader is unable to influence, a team comprising even the most brilliant minds may have ideas and products that will never reach consumers. We, as innovators, must influence. To do this, we'll lean on Cialdini's wisdom.

Principle of Reciprocity

Have you ever supported a colleague only to find, to your surprise, they supported your next idea? This principle dials into the give-and-take rule. The feeling and need to repay is powerful—very powerful. The rule of reciprocation is an excellent tool for every innovative leader. This rule instills an unsaid obligation for future repayment. Be mindful of how you're building the obligation to pay in actions that are outside your direct innovation initiative but that that could come in handy later.

Principle of Commitment and Consistency

Your confidence level changes once you're committed. In a study from the University of British Columbia, a pair of Canadian psychologists found something curious just after bettors placed a bet on a horse at the racetrack—their confidence in the horse's ability to win rose dramatically. Nothing had changed within the environment.[73] The odds were the same, the conditions of the track were unchanged, and the horses competing on the field were the same. Yet, somehow, the bettor felt better about these collective factors. If you're able to win interest in an innovation, that interest will soon become a positive bias in your favor that will spread.

The principle of consistency states that it's difficult to be positive one minute and negative the next or happy one minute and then sad the next. This technique, as Cialdini suggested, has been used by telemarketers for years to encourage donations. When the caller asks, "How are you feeling today?" or "How are things going today?" they don't care how the person on the other end of the phone feels but are leveraging the principle of consistency to prompt a consistently positive contribution to their charity. It's difficult to not answer these questions with, "I'm doing great today, thanks for asking" and, instead, reply with a curt response of, "I'm not interested" or "No, I can't give you anything." The solicitor has established your baseline and hopes to draw future positive responses from that positive exchange.

When requesting adoption for an innovation initiative, factor in how your question, prior to the ask, will establish the foundation for future answers.

Principle of Social Proof

People like to imitate. Ever been to a store and seen a long line at a counter, only to find yourself stepping in line to find out what's going on? This fascination with what others are doing is a natural instinct.

Humorous examples of this principle are plentiful. Someone aimlessly stares into the sky, only to create a crowd of on-lookers peering up into the clouds and seeing nothing. Folks get into an elevator and stand with their backs to the door, which causes others to do the same for no apparent reason.

As you design meetings to move people toward an objective, reflect on all the indirect ways to influence. Could you have four or five peers attend who support the idea? What if they asked hard questions but were seemingly persuaded during the meeting? Who does the stakeholder look to for influence? Consider building the social-proof foundation before you present the idea or before your team launches the demo.

Principle of Authority

Stanley Milgram, a Yale University psychologist, Milgram conducted experiments later referred to as the Miligram experiments that began in 1963.[74] The experiment involved three roles: the Experimenter (an authoritative role), the Teacher (intended to obey orders), and the Learner (the recipient of stimulus from the Teacher). The Learner appeared to be strapped into an electric-enabled chair (not real), and the Teacher would administer a shock to the Learner if the answer to the question was incorrect. If, at any time, the Teacher

98

didn't want to proceed in consideration of the Learner, the Experimenter would recite a series of commands to encourage the Teacher to continue.

While you might think such an experiment wouldn't last long, the power of authority was significant, and 65 percent of all participants proceeded to the final shock (pretending to increase the shock strength as questioning progressed).

This level of influence can be leveraged in a much lighter sense to persuade middle management and other stakeholders who might be undecided. Agreement can be reached more quickly by using the principle of authority and engaging support from an authority figure two or three levels above the individual in question. The person in authority doesn't have to be on the same team or even in the same department: what's relevant is that they buy in and are significantly more senior.

Principle of Liking

People are more persuaded by people they like. Being likable is the goal of every innovator. Not many fat people sell diet pills. There aren't a lot of shy people at Costco selling smoked sausage. The probability of locking down a customer increases when the individual doing the selling is positive and overall likeable. This isn't to say that only the physical attractiveness stereotype is applicable here. Being likeable is about more than looks. It's your attitude and how you carry yourself. Attractiveness is how others view you.

However, some of these biases do originate from physical appearance. Your height and weight might be fixed, but what about your clothes and your grooming? Think about how you'd respond if you presented an idea to yourself. Answer the question, "Am I likeable?"

Principle of Scarcity

The concept that fewer of something creates an increased demand stems from economics and how the availability of a commodity can impact buyers' desire for it—which, in turn, affects the commodity's price (or value).

Toy stores regulate demand for toys during the holidays to create post-holiday buying interest. Nintendo regulates access to games to grow market share. This concept has affected each of us personally. Have you ever taken a shower knowing there was limited hot water? Even though you normally don't take a long shower, for some reason, you wanted to take a slightly longer shower that day.

These same concepts can apply to building innovation capabilities. Initially limit access to a product demo—for example, have it be invite-only. Select an alpha group that will provide first-hand information before the product, service, or interaction goes public. Increase the level of exclusivity to increase demand and, ultimately, interest in the innovation event. Create an environment where colleagues, peers, and executives desire to be included. This also applies to the customer side. Slow rollout access to allow the excitement to build as awareness of the innovation initiative ripples through the organization.

Principle of Unity

Unity builds a shared identity. People that are more "like" us have a greater influence over the actions we take and the decisions we make.[75] This concept is the basis for Cialdini's recent book, *Pre-Suasion*. Family, ethnicity, nationality, politics, and religion are categories Cialdini classifies as contributing to unity. The categories aren't only about common things like reading a newspaper or owning a dog. The principle of unity is how an individual defines themselves.

Harley Davidson motorcycles, a love of the arts, or a passion for CrossFit can connect people to build extremely strong bonds. Many bonds likely already exist among people in your organization; you just have to want to discover them. You'd be well advised to identify them before you begin on your innovation journey.

If the unity categories don't come to you quickly, there are ways of building a category or community of your own. By creating a language only known to your team, organization, or leadership, you bring the group together in ways that otherwise aren't possible.

Have you ever watched or participated in a CrossFit workout? There's a lot of jargon. They've created an entirely new language:

- WOD: workout of the day
- AMRAP: as many reps as possible
- T2B: toes to bar
- ATG: ass to ground
- K2E: knees to elbows
- Unbroken: perform all workouts in a row or start over at the beginning

These words heard around "the box" (CrossFit gym) build unity among the participants.

Building unity isn't only about Harleys and CrossFit. Building unity is necessary for every successful team. How has the organizational design you've established united your team?

Conclusion

You don't have to solve problems that have already been solved. Think about the biggest problem you're facing today in business—not the problems that surface and, 24 or 48 hours later, submerge but the organizational challenges that threaten jobs and change the future of organizations; e.g., the monumental and pivotal decisions that launch new revenue opportunities and close others. Do you think you're alone? Are you the only innovator, executive, or pioneer to confront such an obstacle? Doubtful.

Has another industry faced the same challenges recently or even decades earlier? Designing the architecture of a successful idea or innovation is a balancing act. Leveraging the laws governing innovation creates a path toward success. It's not only up to us to take it. By collaborating, we create a shared sense of ownership. This ownership leads to a curiosity to discover new opportunities. By releasing control, we receive the gift of creativity. As a new strategy begins to take shape, welcome innovative ideas—both the good and the less good.

It's not possible to quickly accelerate to scale with this model. We must add co-opetition to obtain exponential growth. We grow stronger together. Ultimately, sharing ideas empowers and creates a shared inspiration for innovation. Start you day by asking these key questions:

- Who am I collaborating with?
- Do I allow my team to intentionally wonder?
- How am I building curiosity in my organization?
- Are the innovation initiatives aligned with corporate strategy?
- Have we built an open environment to foster innovation?
- Which organizations have I contacted to create a shared purpose?
- How has my team shared publicly their inspiration and passion with the organization?

CHAPTER 6

THE ART OF PREDICTION

"Everyone wants to live on top of the mountain,
but all the happiness and growth occurs
while you're climbing it."

— ANDY ROONEY

Chapter Objectives

After reading this chapter, readers will be able to:

- Define the art of innovation
- Explain the future of forecasting
- Discuss the business value of cooperation and co-creation
- Explain events in terms of uncertainty and how this impacts new ideas
- Describe black-swan and micro black-swan events
- Internalize why crowds affect markets and ultimately perception

The Art and Science of Predictions

Wheels on a horse-drawn carriage was a horrible idea until it wasn't. Hoverboards were a fantastic idea until they weren't. There's a nondescript quality held by leaders who can predict the adoption of visionary and futuristic technologies.

New technology is spawned every day. CIOs are under constant pressure to evaluate capabilities, explore new products, redesign existing processes, and formulate useful applications that are cost-effective and add value safely. Technology is forever evolving, and keeping pace with the sprint of ultra-efficient solar, nanopore-DNA sequencing, crowdfunding, 3D transistors, augmented reality, and quantified self is extremely time consuming.

Technology executives are curious. CIOs know that while even a mainstream concept such as artificial intelligence (AI) is appealingly straightforward, it could impact business today with recommendation engines and tomorrow by creating new products that are unimaginable today.

Value is a fascinating concept. The same principles used to evaluate value in technology can be found in the principles of assessing the value of art. In May 1837, a painting by John Constable, "Salisbury Cathedral from the Meadows," sold for only $6.87 in today's dollars. The fine-art industry estimated the value of the work in 2013 at $760 to $1,200, yet a passionate art enthusiast paid $5,212. Insane, right? On Jan 29, 2015, this same painting sold for $5.2 million, almost 1,000 times the initial professionally estimated value. During the week of May 11, 2015, Constable's "Dschungel" (1967) sold for $27.13 million, three times the previous price for one of his works, according to Sotheby's. "Riot," by Chris Wool, sold for $29.93 million, even though the art industry estimated this piece would sell for a mere $12 million to $18 million.

DEFINING THE ART

In art, there are three steps to estimating the value of a piece: 1. validation (size of artwork, date of artwork, condition, auction venue), 2. appraisal (purpose, market analysis, statement of professional qualifications of the appraisers, provenance), and 3. authentication (performed by an expert). In technology, we can also apply three steps for estimating value: 1. culture (global, local, beliefs, values, and opinions), 2. shared economy (quantified self, consumptive collaboration, ownership models), and 3. network effect (network externality, social networks, product or service, wealth creation, the opportunity for demand-side economies of scale).

Microsoft Vista was supposed to be the flagship release of 2007. CIOs that adopted the platform likely experienced compatibility issues with older PCs, slower processing than on XP, and a host of other problems. iTunes Ping was a weak attempt to merge the Apple music store and social networks, and it didn't last; security challenges quickly inspired Apple to kill off Ping. Netbooks also ultimately failed. Who's at fault? Manufacturers were only trying to provide a low-cost alternative to the laptop. Who could have predicted that Steve Jobs would launch the iPad in 2010?

Predicting trends in and adoption of technology is an art. Evaluating technology can't be done on a spreadsheet. Sure, the benefits and risks can be written down, but that won't help. Predicting technology trends requires executive leaders with "social sight." Social sight is the unique ability to see trends before they become mainstream. Some leaders have this capability and others don't. You know who they are. They think differently.

Will sensors change your consumers' daily routine by 2030? Will artificial intelligence change the modern office? Will blockchain change tomorrow's healthcare? Inside your organization are technology artists. They can predict trends before they go mainstream. They have the unique ability to see value where others find little. This value could originate from technologies, individuals, or even predictions of behavior.

Technology artists see the value of blockchain. Microsoft's Azure blockchain-as-a-service (BaaS) solution partnered with BitShares, BitPay, Eris Industries, and Factom. Digital Asset (blockchain technology developer) partnered with Accenture, Broadridge, and PwC. BitGo partnered with HYPR to integrate the HYPR-Secure biometric login with BitGo's multi-signature platform. Technology artists can discover hidden value.

Do you remember when a CIO suggesting cloud-hosted services was considered reckless? It was reckless until the point when, if your organization didn't have a cloud strategy, even your board wondered about the organization's ability to keep pace with technology and contain costs. Remember when bring-your-own-device (BYOD) was considered ridiculous? Many held that viewpoint until Blackberry was removed from just about every enterprise and replaced by Android and iPhones.

Data-driven decisions make sense—most of the time. What happens when there isn't the data upon which to base decisions? When data doesn't exist, technology artists must forecast predictive trends. We trust technology leaders to help provide the social sight. Lean on technology artists who have the uncanny ability to predict trends. These trends could be the future revenue backbone of your company's business.

The process of evaluating predictive technologies and the impact on society is an art, not science.

Prediction Markets

What if decentralized prediction markets could improve health? Patients will soon be managing their chronic diseases as in-person support goes global and as collective wisdom produces clinical insights surpassing the knowledge of any single physician. Market predictions will be part of the future of health.

The wisdom of the crowd opens conversations around treatment options, symptoms, and options for improved patient care. Thinking and information processing (cognition), coordination (optimization of the utilization), and cooperation (how groups form networks of trust) can be applied to artificial intelligence, analytics, co-creation, and principles of the sharing economy. Social networks are creating new sources of health information with disease-associated support groups (think crowd analytics). The collision of social media and healthcare creates global crowds. These groups no longer need to be led by the smartest people. How clinical experience and insights are collected is changing.

WISDOM OF THE CROWD

Are irrational mobs capable of wisdom that can be used to predict markets? In the age of socially and globally connected economies, can crowds make you healthier?

These principles are harnessed in the wisdom of crowds. The psychology of crowds is explained in James Surowiecki's book, *The Wisdom of Crowds*. His primary thesis on the wisdom of the crowd is captured in this statement: the collective opinion of a group is superior to that of a single expert. Surowiecki expanded on the 1841 work, *Memoirs of Extraordinary Popular Delusions and the Madness of Crowds*, by Charles Mackay. Mackay is famous for saying, "Men, it has been well said, think in herds; it will be seen that they go mad in herds, while they only recover their senses slowly, and one by one." Mackay didn't see a lot of intelligence in crowds. Surowiecki took a different perspective in response to Mackay's work, saying that, given the right circumstances, crowds or groups may have better information and make better decisions than even the best-informed individual.

BETTER HEALTH FUELED BY CROWDS

PatientsLikeMe is a great example of where connecting to people like you and learning from others can improve your personal health. PatientsLikeMe provides a more efficient method for patients to share real-world health experiences to improve patient health and connects other patients like you with organizations that focus on your condition. Nurses-RecommendDoctors is changing the way patients find quality doctors. The premise is that nurses know which doctors have the best reputations, the best technical skills, and the best outcomes. Why? They see it every day. Sermos is the number-one social network for doctors globally. This "crowd" of doctors has ballooned to over 600,000 verified and credentialed physicians to create a big meeting of the minds. Sermos operates across 80 countries including US, UK, Mexico, Germany, Sweden, Canada, and many others. Patients, nurses, and doctors are creating crowds for wisdom.

However, as it turns out, not all crowds are wise. Surowiecki breaks down four criteria that separate the wise crowds from the irrational ones:

1. Diversity of opinion—each person should hold their opinion independent of those around him or her.
2. Independence—individual opinions aren't determined by the opinions of those around them.
3. Decentralization—individuals specialize and can offer local knowledge.
4. Aggregation—the mechanism exists to turn private judgments into collective decisions.

Today, we rush to schedule doctors' appointments, only to wait to be seen. If we apply Surowiecki's thesis about the wisdom of the crowd to healthcare, we can posit the following: there's no need to chase the expert.

THE FUTURE OF FORECASTING
Social-media platforms have helped to increase the collective knowledge of the crowd. These media platforms include wikis, blogs, social networks, video sharing, online forums,

and video blogs like blab.im. From WebMD to WEGO Heath, social networks are integrating into the healthcare-delivery system.

Augur is the future of forecasting. Augur is a prediction-market platform that rewards users for correctly predicting future events (it's a decision market to capture collective wisdom). Augur prediction markets allow users to purchase and sell shares in the outcome of an event. The current market share of an event is an estimate of the probability of an event occurring. On Augur, the price of each share adds up to $1.00 USD, so, if you buy a share at even odds, it will cost $0.50 USD, and if you predict correctly, you'll earn $1.00 USD for that share. Augur combines the magic of prediction markets with the power of decentralized networks to create a stunningly accurate forecasting tool.

This all happens on the blockchain. In a centralized prediction market, one person has to report back on the outcome of the event. This encourages mistakes or even corruption. Augur is decentralized and uses blockchain, with thousands of users reporting on outcomes using reputation. With Augur, anyone anywhere in the world can create a market by asking about anything. Augur was one of the first applications built on Ethereum, a decentralized computing platform featuring digital contracts and a turing-complete programming language.

What if there was a healthcare market-prediction platform that used the wisdom of the crowd, social media, and analytics to make everyone healthier by becoming an expert on their health?

TOMORROW'S PREDICTIONS

The global healthcare-analytics market is expected to reach $84.3 billion by 2027 from $11.7 billion in 2019, according to Valuates Reports. While descriptive and retrospective analytics offer historical information, it's predictive and prescriptive analytics that will move the economics of global health forward. The predictive-analytics market will impact everyone in the healthcare value chain including payers, private insurance companies, government agencies, employers and private exchanges, providers, hospitals, physician practices and integrated delivery networks (IDNs), ambulatory settings, accountable care organizations (ACOs), health information exchanges (HIEs), managed care organizations (MCOs), and third-party administrators (TPAs).

Growth will occur across five core prediction-analytics markets:

1. **Clinical analytics**
2. **Population health management** (precision medicine and health)
3. **Quality improvements** (clinical benchmarking, operational and administrative analytics)
4. **Comparative** (effectiveness analytics, clinical decision support)
5. **Payment integrity** (fraud, waste, and abuse)

Big data evolutions, mHealth, and customer centricity all disrupt health insurance and the business of health. Likewise, market predictions will be part of the future of health.

Is it possible to predict factors that have greater insight and influence over patients' behaviors? Can we use prediction markets to forecast infectious-disease activity? Will prediction markets help align incentives to create long-term behavioral change that supports healthcare payment reform? As the frequency of chronic diseases rise and we move toward outcomes and value-based care, can we use prediction markets to forecast the demand for hospital services? It's going to be an exciting road ahead. Prediction markets will be part of the future of healthcare.

Surowiecki believed that groups are remarkably intelligent and are often smarter than the smartest people in them. Let's use the collective wisdom of the crowd to produce clinical insights and make the world healthier. Monumental change starts with believers.

Uncertainty of Events

Until 1696, it was believed by Europeans that all swans were white. Willem de Vlamingh, a native of Holland, was a skipper for the Dutch East India Co. and ventured out to a shipwreck on the western coast of Australia. In late December 1696, de Vlamingh's ship anchored off Rottnest Island, and the crew went ashore to the mainland. It was there—after rowing 10-miles up the river called Swaanerivier—that de Vlamingh discovered black swans.

Until there were black swans, they didn't exist, and there wasn't a known method to forecast that they might exist (or could occur in Nature).

Later, the statistician, former trader, scholar, and risk analyst Nassim Nicholas Taleb developed the theory of black swans and uncertainty, which is described at length in his book, *The Black Swan.*[76]

"Black swans" are highly improbable events that have enormous effects—what isn't known is more important than what is known. This concept is one manifestation of the "known knowns" (white swans), "known unknowns" (gray swans), and the "unknown unknowns" (black swans). Rephrased, we don't know what we don't know.

It's important while innovating to clearly classify (to the best level we can) which type of swan we're hunting on a given day. What type of risk are we discussing? Where do we have options for egress should an outcome from an event not be favorable? It's important to understand that swans can represent positive and negative events—both disasters and triumphs. For simplicity, I'll be focused on negative events. The parallel is to consider, throughout the explanation, how this could impact your ability to innovate, create, and design value.

1. **White swan**: an event less likely to happen but easy to anticipate (medium probability, low impact)
2. **Gray (near-black) swan**: an event that's rare but somewhat predictable (low probability, high impact); events that are unlikely but can be modeled; impact usually cascades
3. **Black swan**: an event unexpected to happen (unknown, extreme impact)

Black-swan events have three similar characteristics:

1. **Rarity**: these events are rare and outside our past experiences.
2. **Extreme impact**: massive impact, where a single event will dominate all others.
3. **Retrospective predictability**: an illusion that these rare, black-swan events are predictable, leading to "black-swan blindness" or "black-swan denial."

Combined, these three factors result in a phenomenon wherein these random-chance events have very large impacts. Often, the severity is measured on a historic level.

BLACK SWANS

Taleb's black-swan theory shouldn't be confused with the "black-swan problem" in philosophy (i.e. the problem of induction or the "Hume" problem).

Black swans are hard to predict, and rare events can't be factored into models based on science, history, or technology. In fact, these black-swan events are considered non-computational due to the extremely minimal chance of their occurrence. Our challenge in identifying these potential events revolves around psychological biases that, collectively, blind us.

What do we think of when we see traffic backed up on the highway? How do we handle delays in program delivery? We ask why, and then we search for patterns. This approach can be fruitful. However, in the case of black swans, there's no pattern; those events or conditions are unpredictable. If it just hailed outside or a project leader was in an accident, those events are extremistan—but they aren't black swans.

Examples of black swans:

- Personal computer
- World War I
- Emergence of the Internet
- Dissolution of the Soviet Union
- September 2001 attacks

Taleb defines a black swan as "the outlier, the important event that is not expected to happen."[77]

GRAY SWANS

Gray swans are rare but predictable. We could model and therefore largely predict these events. The problem is that we don't. Gray swans are all but ignored until they happen in practice.

Benoit Mandlebrot, a Yale University professor of mathematical sciences and a Fellow Emeritus at IBM's Thomas J. Watson Laboratory, is the inventor of fractal geometry. A student of natural patterns for 40 years, Mandlebrot offers brilliant perspectives on gray swans and their effect on markets. Mandlebrot defines gray swans as events that can't be rationalized with fractal geometry.

Gray swans are events that are rare but not improbable, and they materialize so infrequently that they're often overlooked until they're inevitable.

Disasters are a good way to characterize these unlikely occurrences. At the time they happen, these events were difficult but not impossible to predict and, retrospectively, models can be generated to anticipate future events of a similar nature.

Examples of gray swans:

- Earthquake
- Best-seller book
- Tsunami
- Flood
- Climate change
- Epic stock-market crash

Gray swans—known unknowns—can occur in theory, but, due to their unlikely appearance, in practice they're mostly ignored until their presence makes it vital that we pay attention to them.

WHITE SWANS

The color of the swan represents our level of uncertainty. White swans represent uncertainty; however, the probability is only absolute after a given point of time.

White swans are high-probability but random events. When they do occur, their impact is relatively low. Our challenge is that, while these white swans are theoretically knowable, it may cost more than is reasonable to find them (i.e. in the 9th standard deviation). These white swans—unlike black swans—aren't magical. They don't just appear unannounced, but the time it takes to find them may be more than we have available.

Examples of white swans:

- Tire recall
- Oil spill
- Food-contamination event
- Network outage
- Business-service interruption

Whether we're speaking of white swans, gray swans, or back swans, the presence of uncertainty shouldn't encourage the absence of planning or project management. Some swans will say hidden forever—or until they decide to present themselves (e.g., an accident in a nuclear-power plant or a death in a NASA mission to space). But not every activity we participate in is one of life or death. Most have success or failure associated with the event, but the outcomes are less dramatic.

For these events, planning isn't only suggested but required. Leading teams involves an anticipation of risk and an acknowledgment of the type of swans you're hunting for. Some will spend a lifetime searching for black swans (the paranoid) and never find them, while others will ignore white swans (known risks) and trip over them at an almost daily cadence. Choose your path.

Take a minute to think about the type of swans you and your team see as you travel on your innovation safari. It's good information to have, but it's also not an excuse for success to be deemed unattainable. Ask yourself if the consequences can be tolerated and to what degree. What level of planning is reasonable for the risks you could potentially face?

MICRO BLACK SWANS

Not every swan event involves a disaster or a travesty. Many are positive. These events also take different forms—small (micro black swans), larger (black swans), fat (short duration but extreme), and narrow (longer duration but less extreme). Events that occur as a lead-up to a larger swan event we call micro swans or micro black swans.

Taleb suggests that every scientific discovery is an attempt to produce a micro black swan. We strain to qualify and quantify the highly improbable. In our weak attempt to become forecasters of the future, we lose perspective on the present reality of our situation. Practically, just as a rogue wave could surface, the likelihood is low. It's also more probable that a micro event (a single rogue wave as opposed to a tsunami) will occur. Yet, all our time is spent on events that, while catastrophic, rarely occur.

Maybe we'd be better served working through the daily grind of challenges and using our present environment to establish a climate for success. Of course, coupled with the knowledge that it's possible for that rogue wave to surface, we'll have a plan B, but we just won't spend 90 percent of our time away from plan A to address it.

Micro black-swan events occur on a smaller scale and, therefore, are generally less interesting to study. Micro events occur in business as well. These events don't present themselves loudly but nonetheless can impact business operations. This could be a price move by a competitor that was totally unexpected or a dramatic change to a known business model that was unanticipated by competitors. The oscillations in the normal pattern of business disrupt the flow or pattern of a network. This network could be a group of vendors or a communication hub for distribution. Regardless, micro black-swan events inject a random variability into your business. Your ability to innovate is also impacted. You, as a leader, must adjust the innovation engine to quickly react when you're made aware of these events.

A great first step is to ensure you have a governance model to address and prioritize risk. By establishing a formal model and communication structure, you ensure there's at least a plan A for these types of micro black-swan events. You also validate that there's a clear communication approach that your team is aware of should one of these micro but rare events occur.

There's nothing better than having a great contingency plan and never having to use it. While black swans can't be anticipated, you should take a proactive approach and have a well-thought-out plan for general categories of events.

Examples of micro black swans:

- Twenty-minute stock market drop
- Single-bomb event
- Unexpected death

- Winning the daily lottery

Freak drone crash (i.e. versus a black-swan event like the Space Shuttle Challenger disaster)

Conclusion

Have you been able to predict an event when no one else could forecast it? Did you have a gut feeling about a product launch that you felt would be great? Predicting events, outcomes, or results involves uncertainty. We can do a lot of things to mitigate that uncertainty, but it will never go down to zero percent.

This means innovation is just as much about art as it is about science. If you're launching a new product, you can do a lot to ensure the product is working to specification. Testing, quality control, and inspections can all improve the likelihood the product will work. However, who would have accurately predicted that starting a new restaurant business in the first quarter of 2020 would occur in the middle of the COVID-19 pandemic? Essentially, no one.

Whether you're building a product, offering services, or providing interactions, innovation has risk. The more ideas you generate, the more likely that one or more will be sticky.

CHAPTER 7

INSPIRATION FROM NATURE

"Look deep into nature, and then you will understand everything better."

— ALBERT EINSTEIN

Chapter Objectives

After reading this chapter, readers will be able to:

- Explain the difference between problem-focused and solution-focused solvers.
- Understand the powerful effect of Nature on innovation.
- Define mimicry and apply it to create new behaviors.
- Take a lesson from Nature on where we find innovation.
- Explain how the order of Nature mirrors modern innovation.
- Define the principles of swarm intelligence.
- Explain why swarm intelligence depends on innovation.

Innovation Inspired by Nature

Innovation inspired by observing Nature captures the power of design. Today's business architects must construct new business models for innovation. Visionary leaders begin with Nature.

Solved first by Nature, efficient business designs may drive the next technological innovations. Mimicry can advance innovation through design thinking. When balancing the power of physical design with design thinking about living things can teach new innovation principles.

The Architect and The Scientist: A Balancing Act

According to the Biomimicry Institute, "Biomimicry is an approach to innovation that seeks sustainable solutions to human challenges by emulating Nature's time-tested patterns and strategies." Why try to resolve problems that Nature has already solved over thousands of years?

Steve Jobs was quoted as saying, "I think the biggest innovations of the 21st century will be at the intersection of biology and technology. A new era is beginning." Maybe he wasn't talking only about the advances of biotechnologies; he was talking about what we can learn from Nature. We missed concepts and lessons that were in front of us, because we were too busy recreating them.

Janine Benyus is a biologist focusing on innovation inspired by Nature and has written two great books on the subject: *Biomimicry: Innovation Inspired by Nature* and *Secret Language & Remarkable Behavior of Animals*. Benyus believes that designers can discover new powers of design by looking at Nature. Michael Pawlyn, a TED speaker and the author of *Biomimicry in Architecture*, summed it up well: "You could look at Nature as being like a catalog of products, and all of those have benefited from a 3.8-billion-year research and development period. And given that level of investment, it makes sense to use it."

Problem-Focused vs. Solution-Focused Solvers

Design thinking promotes the idea of visual thinking to form practical and creative solution-focused thinking. It jumps ahead in the scientific method. Instead of defining all the parameters of a problem to construct a logical solution, design thinking starts with a better future in mind—not with a specific problem to solve. This approach unlocks the mind and removes the mental obstructions for new growth. The conflict in design thinking challenges the [business] architect and the scientist.

In 1972, Bryan Lawson conducted investigations into the variance between problem-focused solvers and solution-focused solvers. Nigel Cross, a British academic and Emeritus Professor of Design Studies at The Open University in the United Kingdom, deduced that scientists problem solve by analysis, using Nature's genius, while designers solve problems using synthesis. Design thinking uses both design analysis and synthesis.

Mimicry

Mimicry is the art of acting as or imitating someone or something. This is best described as WWND—What Would Nature Do?

This imitation could be represented by an animal's deceptive behavior such as Batesian mimicry (involving a palatable, vulnerable species—the mimic—resembling an unpalatable species; e.g., an edible bumble bee protected by its resemblance to a noxious flower); Mullerian mimicry (the display of particular patterns of colors warning that both the model and the mimic are toxic; e.g., a Monarch butterfly resembling the Viceroy butterfly); Masmannian mimicry (resembling the host entity; e.g., a jumping spider representing an ant); and Peckhamian mimicry (aggressive mimicry where the predator mimics its prey to capture it; e.g., the same approach of the bird dropping spider hunting moths by mimics the sex

121

smells released by female moths by producing the moth pheromones). Deceptive behavior or camouflage is often foremost on the mind when the topic of mimicry surfaces.

There is, however, another form that applies to business. Mimicry can be applied to advance innovation through design thinking by leveraging mimicry's foundational constructs. One example is how biomimicry can improve supply-chain models by creating sustainable solutions for business. We can use our observations of Nature to discover potential solutions for eco-efficient improvements, use Nature's genius in business architecture, gain new social perspectives in business interactions, and expand gamification theory for applications.

The Power of Nature's Innovation

The Sanyo Shinkansen 500-series electric train was placed into production in 1997 and, because of a maximum operating speed of 320 km/h or 200 mph, the travel time between Shin-Osaka and Hakata was shorted by 10 percent. What made this innovation successful were the design-thinking principles applied to achieve the world-record speed at the time and meet strict noise standards of 70-75 dB(A) as measured 25 meters from the center of the tracks.

Eiji Nakatsu, the general manager for the Technical Development Department of Japan Railway West and Japan Railway Kyushu, was charged with solving three train-related problems:

1. Ground vibration during high speeds
2. Aerodynamic noise generated by the train's body and the pantographs (connecting the train to overhead wires)
3. The sonic boom created during the train's exit from the departure tunnel

An article in the *Zygote Quarterly*—abbreviated zq9—titled, "Auspicious Forms: Designing the Sanyo Shinkansen 500-Series Bullet Train," is the most comprehensive article on this subject and well worth the read.

One of the problems, pantograph vibrations, was solved by applying the principles of flight from owls. Specifically, how an owl's natural concave face and down absorb the vibrations of movement as a result of tiny serrations on its primary feathers.

Problem two, wind resistance creating aerodynamic noise, was solved by reshaping the pantograph's supporting shaft to look more like the body of the Adélie penguin. The result was a shape like a spindle, which lowered wind resistance.

Problem three, the sonic boom, was solved by understanding the bill of the Kingfisher—a revolving, paraboloid shape. Trains in service before the 500 series had wedge-shaped nosecones; this shifted to a modern, rotational, parabolic body (squashed diamond shape) that is a mathematical constant.

A Lesson from Nature

Many of the most efficient designs tested were derived from Nature and taught efficient forms. New models developed from living things and the trend to apply mimicry to advance design thinking are growing globally. Germany's Bionics Competence Network (BIOKON) focuses on deciphering "inventions of Nature" and transferring them into technological innovations. France's Centre Européen d'Excellence en Biomimétisme de Senlis (CEEBIOS) focuses on the development of biomimicry as a tool for scientific and societal transition at the international level. At the Centre, they actively disseminate biomimicry information to innovators.

Eco-mimicry, the practice of mimicking the natural world in the technological world, is merging with products, platforms, processes, and services to create new interactions and behaviors. As design thinking searches for new innovations, maybe the answer is hidden in Nature. Will the most amazing technological advancement be traced back to mimicry?

Business can learn much from Nature, and, as Janine Benyus put it, "When we look at what is truly sustainable, the only real model that has worked for long periods of time is the natural world."

The Order of Nature

Can intelligence be amplified by thinking together? Ants do it. Birds do it. What about humans? Collective intelligence is the next wave of intelligence. Swarm intelligence connects systems with real-time feedback loops. Individual efforts combine to form a greater value.

Fish school. Birds flock. Bees swarm. A combination of real-time, biological systems blends knowledge, wisdom, opinions, and intuition to unify intelligence. There's no central control unit. These simple agents interact locally, within their environment, and new behaviors emerge.

Swarm intelligence is the self-organization of systems for collective, decentralized behavior. Swarm intelligence enables groups to converge and create an independent organism that can do things that individuals can't do on their own.

Why can't humans swarm? Fish detect ripples in the water. Birds use motion detected through the flock. Ants leverage chemical traces. Until recently, there's been little research conducted on "human swarming." If other groups in Nature can work together, why can't humans use similar decision spaces to arrive at a preferred solution? Will the next generation of breakthrough innovation stem from the wisdom of the crowd—swarm intelligence?

Whether we're talking about Nature, humans, or robots, swarm intelligence creates a virtual platform to enable distributed engagement from system users. Through this engagement, feedback can be provided in a closed-loop, swarming process.

INDIVIDUAL FORCE FOR UNIFIED OBJECTIVES

Swarm intelligence draws from biologically inspired algorithms to enhance robotics and mechatronics. Evolutionary optimization is more than ant-colony optimization algorithms (ACO), bee-colony optimization algorithms (BCO), or particle-swarm optimization (PSO). Swarm intelligence can be applied to immune systems, computer vision, navigation, mapping, image processing, artificial neural networks, and robotic motion planning.

Bio-inspired systems bring new intelligence to the design of robotics and are used in aerial flying robots, robotic manipulators, and underwater vehicles.

The physical, biological, and digital worlds benefit immensely by learning from Nature. These bio-inspired applications are creating swarm algorithms empowering a newly discovered digital autonomy.

ANTS AND DISTRIBUTED SYSTEMS

Technology-based distributed systems are collections of independent computers that appear to work as a unified, coherent system. This same effect is found in swarms. The common element is that control is distributed across individuals or entities, and communication isn't localized.

Why is Bitcoin so fascinating to us? Could it be that the Bitcoin network is a self-organizing, collective intelligence similar to that mesmerizing school of fish?

The collective intelligence, or COIN, framework was first introduced in a paper published in 2000 by John Lawson and David Wolpert of NASA's Ames Research Center.

This framework helped identify—using similar system attributes—where collective intelligence might exist. The framework comprises:

1. A multi-agent system
2. No central operator
3. No centralized communication

4. Unified utility function.
5. Agents running reinforcement-learning algorithms for validation

Bitcoin is a large version of a multi-agent, reinforcement-learning system. The same challenge injected into swarms is inherent in Bitcoin: How are rewards to individuals, agents, or entities assigned? The social aspects of swarms are both simple and complex. Group behavior emerges as more significant than individual actions—complexity out of simplicity.

Swarms can solve more than just static problems. Units interact in localized ways and can solve online, offline, stationary, time-varying, centralized, distributed, and dynamic problems.

How does a swarm live? How does a swarm communicate? A unique "life" takes shape when a swarm forms, and it has everything to do with spatial intelligence. When observing swarms, we start to notice certain principles:

1. Work division
2. Collective behaviors
3. Navigation
4. Communication
5. Self-organization
6. Social survival

Dinosaurs weren't social. Ants are social, and they have outlasted dinosaurs and are able to survive in a range of environments and climates. How do ants build their nests? How do ants navigate? Why can ants locate food fast? There's a one-word explanation: sociality.

The key to human survival isn't having sophisticated intelligent robots that will floss your teeth while you're in the shower. The secret is sociality. We must build social systems when we design intelligent systems. There are many examples of Nature's social systems we can draw from:

- An implausibility of wildebeest: They move through rivers in sheer numbers to avoid crocodiles.
- A rabble of butterflies: Monarch butterflies migrate to escape the cold North American winters.
- A rookery of penguins: Emperor penguins converge in a huddle to stay protected from the Antarctic winters.
- A business of mayflies: These insects form swarms of 8,000 to attack predators in volume.
- A plague of locusts: Synchronize their wing beats to make travel more efficient.
- A shoal of fish: Silver carp leap into the air as a unit to avoid predators.
- A pod of dolphins: Superpods of dolphins, which can exceed 1,000 individuals, form a pod for protection and hunting.
- A flight of birds: Budgerigars, a type of parakeet, assemble to act as a unit to make decisions, fend off predator attacks, and find food.
- A cloud of bats: a social vortex of bats forms for communication and to make decisions on foraging.

Nature's progression and technology's evolution are amplified with social systems. The end of social abnormalities may be the introduction of swarm intelligence.

IS THERE A BETTER WAY TO BUILD SUPER-INTELLIGENCE?

Let's collect lessons from Nature, insights from humans, and the unified benefits of intelligent systems and create something smarter than ourselves. These intelligent systems—things smarter than ourselves—appear to think and act. The algorithms, robotics, and systems are only a piece of the system we'll create. Instead of creating and designing complete intelligence systems, maybe we should apply simple rules to form collections of behaviors or swarms.

These swarms could respond by connecting real-time human insights into more intelligent systems with morals, values, emotions, and empathy. Swarm intelligence won't be something you watch on a Ted Talk. Swarm intelligence will be a feeling that transcends Nature through a collision of the digital and physical worlds.

Tomorrow's systems will be designed with swarm intelligence and spatial judgment.

The Coordination of the Natural World

We find universal coordination throughout the natural world. Dynamic environments enable indirect interactions for the production of unified objectives. Let's explore the four principles of stigmergic collaboration and their application in the design of intelligent systems. Stigmergy derives from the Greek words στίγμα, "stigma," meaning "mark or sign;" and ἔργον, "ergon" meaning "work or action." Stigmergy is the universal coordination mechanism: a consensus mechanism of indirect coordination within an environment among agents or actions. While we don't fully understand all the interactions of self-organizing organisms, the concept of self-organization is found in both robotics and social insects.

DO NATURE'S PRINCIPLES APPLY TO INNOVATION?
Have you ever examined the path on which you find yourself standing today along with all the antecedent steps that brought you to the current moment? The modern path of artificial intelligence is a mix of cognitive science, psychology, and dreams.

Is there a secret to how organisms collaborate? Methods to coordinate aren't only found in science labs and the basements of research buildings. Universal coordination mechanisms can be found in many places, if we look. Environmental traces, mass collaboration, and group interactions have much in common.

Remy Chauvin (1956) conducted the earliest work on stigmergy-based coordination in the biological sciences. However, the foundation of stigmergy was envisioned by Pierre-Paul Grasse in 1967, making use of his 1950s research on termites. The idea is that an agent's actions leave signs in the environment—signs that it and other agents sense and which determine and incite subsequent actions. Stigmergy is also used within artificial intelligence in the study of swarming patterns of independent actors that use signals to communicate.

A better understanding of stigmergy, sociometry (a quantitative method for measuring social relationships), and group dynamics offers new insights into the world of multi-agent coordination, which is the essence of swarm intelligence.

The essence of stigmergy is that traces left within an environment—the result of an action—stimulate the performance of a future action. This combined positive- and negative-feedback loop enhances a mutual awareness, fostering the coordination of activity without the need for planning, control, and communication.

Ants use pheromones. People use wikis. Wasps use secretions. These multi-agent coordination mechanisms function because agents exchange information within a dynamic environment. The agents modify their environment, which triggers a future response.

When open-source systems blossom from five users to 50,000 users, we might find our answers buried in the evolution of group work. Stigmergic collaboration has four distinct principles:

1. Collaboration depends upon communication, and communication is a network phenomenon.
2. Collaboration is inherently composed of two primary components—social negotiation and creative output—without either of which collaboration cannot take place.
3. Collaboration in small groups (roughly two to 25 members) relies upon social negotiation to evolve and guide its process and creative output.

4. Collaboration in large groups (roughly 26 to n) is enabled by stigmergy.

STIMERGIC COLLABORATIONS

Stigmergic collaboration is when agents or individuals work without explicit knowledge of others. Adding a block to a blockchain isn't controlled by a central function; it's organic. Editing or changing a wiki page relies on a shared pool of content for mass collaboration and consumption.

Stigmergic interactions are coordinations of activities that, over time, use decentralized control. Primitive rules guide the orchestration of activity. There are no instructions, and there's a self-awareness of actions and the sharing of information.

How can stigmergic principles be used in your mobile designs? How does the communication and messaging of self-organizing systems improve your IT landscape? How do unstable systems evolve into stable states in which order and organization are the norms? You can apply these theories to your technological environment.

Innovators are using these theories to design interactions that don't presently exist within conventional artificial-intelligence environments. Future artificial-intelligence systems will be designed with an awareness of stigmergic collaborations.

The Future: Self-organizing Software

The future of artificial intelligence is self-organizing software. Multi-agent coordination and stigmergy will be useful in our quest to discover dynamic environments with decentralized intelligence.

In every field, there's a pioneer, a prototype, an individual, or a group that blazed the path forward to uncover previously hidden value. Observing the giants in artificial intelligence allows us to revisit the early instrumental concepts in the development and maturation of the field. Biological principles are the roots of swarm intelligence, and self-organizing, collective behavior is its organizing principle. A better understanding of these foundational principles results in the ability to accelerate the development of your business applications.

PIONEERS OF ARTIFICIAL INTELLIGENCE

Four pioneers shaped artificial intelligence as we know it today.

Allen Newell was a researcher in computer science and cognitive psychology at the RAND Corporation and Carnegie Mellon University's School of Computer Science. His primary contributions to information processing, in collaboration with Herbert A. Simon, were the development of two, early A.I. programs: the Logic Theory Machine (1956) and the General Problem Solver (1957).

Herb Simon was an economist, sociologist, psychologist, and computer scientist with specialties in cognitive psychology and cognitive science, among many other fields. He coined the terms "bounded rationality" and "satisficing." Bounded rationality is the idea that when individuals make decisions, their rationality is limited by the tractability of the decision problem, the cognitive limitations of their minds, and the time available to make the decision. Satisficing (as opposed to maximizing or optimizing) is a decision-making strategy or cognitive heuristic that entails searching through the available alternatives until an acceptability threshold is met. Simon also proposed the concept of the preferential-attachment process, in which, typically, some form of wealth or credit is distributed among individuals or objects according to how much they already have, so that those who are already wealthy receive more than those who are not.

John McCarthy was a computer science and cognitive scientist who coined the term "artificial intelligence." His development of the LISP programming language family—which heavily influenced ALGOL, an early set of a programming language developed in the mid-1950s—emphasized the value of timesharing. Timesharing today is more commonly known as multiprogramming or multitasking, where multiple users share computing resources. McCarthy envisioned this interaction in the 1950s, which is nothing short of unbelievable.

Marvin Minsky, a cognitive scientist, was the co-founder of MIT's artificial intelligence laboratory. In 1963, Minsky invented the head-mounted graphical display that's widely used today by aviators, gamers, engineers, and doctors. He also invented the confocal microscope, an early version of the modern laser scanning microscope.

Together, these framers laid the foundation for artificial intelligence as we know it today.

COLLABORATION FOR SCALE

Do we understand collaboration? Thanks to Kurt Lewin and his research on group dynamics, we understand how groups interact much better than we did. I ask again, do we understand group interactions? Is there an ideal group size? What's the best balance of independence? Is the group interaction better or worse when we design in patterns for group activities?

We have defined paradigms of productive and unproductive group interactions. Our challenge comes from the fact that these models don't scale. It's also the same reason that the suggested agile team size is seven people plus or minus two team members. As group size increases, so does the complexity in the lines of communication. A team of six people has 15 lines of communication, a team of seven people has 21, and a team of nine people has 36 lines of communication [n members in a group produces n(n-1)/2 lines of communication]. Yet, in spite of the problem of the complexity in lines of communication, colonies of ants reaching 306 million workers interact just fine as does a mayfly swarm of 8,000 flies. Both groups are organized around common goals.

How is this possible if the lines-of-communication principle is absolute? To state it simply, it's not absolute. We can change the lines of communication by adjusting how the group interacts. This same concept can be applied to swarms of drones and self-organizing software. The limit that prevents us logically from adding agents due to communication complexity—a system we, as innovators, can simply redesign—is defined by our communications systems.

Psychologist Norman Triplett concluded that bicyclists performed better when riding with others. He found a similar result in the study of children: pairs performed better than solo actors.

Lewin, Lippitt, and White later studied what happened to the behavior of young boys (10-11 years old) when an adult male joined the group. The group adopted one of three behavior styles, which the authors named autocratic, democratic, and laissez-faire. The results were surprising. The autocratic style worked when the leader merely observed the boys' behavior. The democratic style worked when the leader wasn't present with the team. The laissez-faire style was found to be least effective. Does democratic mass collaboration result when the leader is absent?

AI PRINCIPLES APPLY TO INNOVATIONS

Sociometry is the quantitative study and measurement of relationships within a group of people. Does sociometry apply to swarm interactions?

A swarm is simply a group, right? What if we could design intelligence systems to optimize learning? These systems wouldn't only exemplify stigmergic environmental properties. They would also build on properties of traditional group dynamics. If you're in the gym and notice people are staring at you, you're able to bike a little harder, run a little faster, or lift a little more. What if we could design artificial-intelligence systems that would be intelligent enough to embrace these same feelings? Sure, we're talking less about feeling and more about procedures or rules that we apply in context—but the term "feelings" sounds better to me.

Collective behaviors contribute to solving various complex tasks. These four principles are found in insects that collectively organize. They should also be found in the artificial intelligence systems we create:

1. **Coordination**: organizing using time and space to solve a specific problem.
2. **Cooperation**: agents or individuals achieve a task that couldn't be done individually.
3. **Deliberation**: multiple mechanisms are employed when a colony or team faces multiple opportunities.
4. **Collaboration**: different activities are performed simultaneously by individuals or groups.

Whether we're adding blocks to a blockchain or changing the rights that individuals have to shared content, the study of interactions might hold the key to unlock the next generation of artificial intelligence. Before exploring the benefits of dynamic systems and chaos theory, we must apply the principles of artificial intelligence, mass collaboration, and group dynamics to expand our knowledge of how systems self-organize.

Conclusion

You've been trying to solve a problem. You went online for answers. You asked a friend for help. You sat alone trying to think. In all those years of mentally exploring spaces, how many times did you go outside and observe Nature? I'm not talking about taking a walk or going for a run. I mean you left your house with the pure intent to be inspired by Nature. Probably none.

Nature's concepts, such as mimicry, go deep into the heart of innovation. When you're trying to step outside your existing knowledge, begin with Nature. From multi-agent systems to the swarm intelligence of bees, as inventors, we find that often we aren't creating something new and original but rather mimicking Nature. One day, it's as obvious as a stop sign and, another day, the pattern is as subtle as an ant's behavior.

Creators of inventions and innovative ideas need to be consumers of inventions, even the natural ones.

CHAPTER 8

INNOVATION PLATFORMS AND ECONOMIC SHIFTS

"There exist limitless opportunities in every industry. Where there is an open mind, there will always be a frontier."

— CHARLES KETTERING

Chapter Objectives

After reading this chapter, readers will be able to:

- Explain the impact of the sharing economy on innovation.
- Highlight the primary impact on revenue of the sharing economy.
- Explain how to gain entrance into the billion-dollar club.
- Explain how platforms lift value.
- Understand the phenomenon of network effects.
- Define the four types of innovation platforms.
- Describe the difference between direct network effects, indirect network effects, local network effects, and two-sided network effects.
- Appreciate the history of artificial intelligence.

The Sharing and Collaborative Economy

How we work, how we earn, and the skills required are taking on a shared purpose.

Shifting from hyper-consumption to collaboration consumption has given a renewed belief in the value of reputation, community, and shared access.

Technology is present in virtually every part of an individual's life. The iPhone alarm wakes you up. The Waze app gets you where you're going. LinkedIn, Facebook, and Twitter are the new playgrounds where you nurture your social networks. Technology is ever-present.

Survival Means Adaptation to Changing Environmental Conditions

How will organizations learn? Organizations—both big and small—will need to adapt to new challenges to survive. Applying a learning curve can be a great approach to position companies for change. Some aspects of this learning curve include:

1. Redefinition of social capital: personal, not corporate, brands are determining business relationships.
2. Redistribution markets: unwanted or underused goods are resold.
3. Collaborative lifestyles: non-product assets such as space, skills, and money are exchanged and traded in new ways.
4. Product-service systems: pay to access a product or service without ownership.

Redistribution markets, collaborative lifestyles, and product-service systems have spurred the rise of consumptive collaboration—new, shared reinvesting through technology. Traditional sharing—bartering, lending, trading, renting, gifting, and swapping—is redefined through technology, and peer communities are blooming into a sharing economy.

This collaborative economy places value on a combination of reputation, community, and shared access. Underutilized assets and resources are offering alternatives, making space for on-demand platforms that reach critical mass based on the efficiency of crowds and the trust of communities. Products and services that align groups of users in a two-sided network is called a platform. These platforms provide the foundational infrastructure to link groups of users.

Competing forces and evolving priorities have created a new world born on the back of business fragmentation feeding off the influence of social environments. Here, technology breakthroughs are the norm, and resource scarcity is a driver in the global shift of power.

THE BILLION-DOLLAR CLUB

Today, every industry is getting involved in the sharing economy. Companies that make up hospitality (Feastly, Leftover-Swap), transportation (Lyft, Zipcar), consumer goods (Etsy, Poshmark), entertainment (SoundCloud, Pandora), healthcare (MedZed, Heal), logistics (Instacart, Uber Rush), and odd jobs (Fiverr, Upwork) all contribute to form the sharing economy. Given the surge of sharing companies, it might not be surprising that Uber's valuation of USD $60.3 billion is 2.12 times Southwest Airlines at USD $28.4 billion as of October 2020, and T. Rowe's latest valuation lifts Airbnb's assessment to USD $25.5 billion, 1.48 times that of Marriott International at USD $17.2 billion.

The collaborative economy is here to stay. *HBR* published a great piece titled, "What Customer Want from the Collaborative Economy," that stated, "We now have research to show that companies need to embrace the core innovations of the collaborative economy if they want to thrive in the era of Kickstarter, Uber and TaskRabbit." Maybe we'll all be relegated into three simple worlds: Orange (small is beautiful), Green (companies care), or Blue (corporate is king) as suggested by PwC's "The Future of Work: A Journey to 2022" report. The future of work will include companies that innovate around their core values.

PLUNGING INTO THE SHARING ECONOMY

The future of work involves learning (Udacity, Chegg), municipal (Musketeer, MuniRent), money (Bitcoin, CircleUp), goods (yerdle, shapeways), health and fitness (VINT, Medicast), space (HomeAway, ShareDesk), food (VixEat, Blue Apron), utilities (vandebron, fon), transportation (Ola Share, DriveNow), services (CloudPeeps, Fiverr), logistics (nimber, deliv), and corporate (warpit, TwoGo). The makers, co-creators, crowd funders, peers, and companies that are successful all empower people. The sharing economies are creating partnerships between traditional incumbents and bleeding-edge tech companies.

Healthcare companies are launching a flurry of interaction applications to capture the attention of patients and their loved ones.

- Ease delivers medical marijuana delivered in minutes or less. Think of a slick decision-support tool for medical marijuana. Ease offers a high-quality, lab-tested menu with fast and convenient delivery and a technology that provides an experience for patients that's safer than the alternatives.

- Helparound addresses the daily drain on caregivers of chronically ill patients. Part of Helparound is Diabetes Helpers, a help network available on mobile and desktop in which people help each other navigate life with diabetes. People with type 1 or type 2 diabetes, gestational diabetes, and their caregivers respond to each other about the symptoms of diabetes, how to lower patients' a1c, and how to learn more about diabetes diet and management.

- Stat provides on-demand doctors, medical care, medical transport, and companionship. Stat is healthcare-on-demand and, with a simple push of a button, patients can reach a doctor, CNA, HHA, or a medical transport in minutes for themselves or loved ones.
- Popexpert gives users an opportunity to learn life and work skills directly from top experts to be happier, healthier, and more productive. From getting fit to staying healthy, Popexperts offers the latest in life, work, and play.
- Medicast is helping hospitals and health systems bring back the house call. This new platform offers care delivery for the on-demand age. Medicast helps hospitals and health systems modernize their care-delivery networks with sophisticated, easy-to-use technology designed in collaboration with patients and physicians.

The sharing economy is bringing people together. In our small and beautifully connected world, reputation, community, and shared access matter.

PLATFORM ECOSYSTEMS LIFT VALUE

Platforms shift value from products and services to interactions. Ecosystems promote scale through interactions, not volume. Platform ecosystems build better businesses. Historical growth drivers focused on consumer goods will transition to business models where platform-enabled, connected interactions are at the center of the ecosystem. The orchestration of interactions enhances an ecosystem's value as organizationally siloed processes transform into a shared ecosystem—a community of trust.

A NEW STRATEGY FOR GENERATING PROFIT

Emerging business models are moving from pipelines to platforms—toward communities of value and away from the traditional pipeline value models originating from manufacturing supply chains. Shifts in markets, shifts in competitive advantage, and shifts in value creation have highlighted that value can no longer be created solely by company processes rearranging labor and resources. Value creation stems from scale grown out of interactions.

Platform-based companies employ 1.3 million people with a total market capitalization of $4.3 trillion, making platform ecosystems a critical component of corporate strategy. Today, success demands that business leaders understand how platform-based ecosystems are reshaping traditional organizational hierarchies and building new value. Not surprisingly platform-based business account for 20% of the S&P 500 returns.

A sure way for companies to become obsolete is to maintain a narrow focus on internal products and services. Managerial incentives and new organizational cultures are stimulating business curiosity about ecosystem profits and asset-light platforms. The issue of profits raises questions about what competitors are working on next. Yesterday, a firm's competitors were known. Today, competitor identification isn't so simple. How are competitors defined? Should we focus on incumbents or emerging markets? Do we weigh risk by market capitalization and value or agility? Nielsen, Forrester, Gartner, Millward Brown, Ipsos, and Capital IQ are all discovering the challenges of defining industry outlooks.

THE PROFIT CONSIDERATIONS OF MULTIHOMING

The speed and explosion of platforms have created platform competition for horizontally differentiated platforms that offer complementary interactions. When two-sided markets contain more than one competing platform, the configuration of users affiliating with more than one platform is called multihoming. Carrying credit cards from more than one bank is an example of multihoming. This concept isn't the same as switching costs, as these users don't terminate one service when switching to a second platform. They use both platforms.

Have you used LinkedIn and Twitter? You didn't cancel your LinkedIn account when you joined Twitter, right? This is an example of multihoming. The "homing" costs are what's important. These costs comprise all the expenses incurred by a user's affiliation with different platforms. When multihoming costs are high, users are less willing to be affiliated with multiple platforms that provide similar services. As industry regulations mushroom, multihoming costs rise, increasing the likelihood of industry consolidation.

Outside-in, technology-driven business models define the platform economy. These models don't create value from inside the organization; value is created by the community outside the organization. These technological changes disrupt business models and alter the global macroeconomic environment. The economy is undergoing a rebirth with platform ecosystems that bring the enterprise to scale in months rather than years. Every company across every industry has the potential to unlock the power of platform-based business models. Unparalleled growth has arrived: Dogs of the Dow estimated that the top 15 public platform companies represent $10.8 trillion in market capitalization worldwide. "Unicorns" (companies with valuations of $1 billion or more) and "decacorns" (companies valued at over $10 billion) are realizing profitability by leveraging profitability with platform ecosystem strategies. Platform strategies have fueled the growth of over 168 unicorns, with private unicorn companies reaching a cumulative valuation of $500 billion. Platforms that utilize network effects place producers and consumers together to create new value—co-creation of value through communities.

Traditional brick-and-mortar companies are embracing platform ecosystems and developing new emergent strategies. In fact, Accenture identified traditional companies that are embracing dynamic platform strategies including Fiat (connected car), Kaiser Permanente (digital health), Disney (MagicBands), Caterpillar (connected machines), Schneider Electric (smart cities, buildings, and homes), Walgreens (retail pharmacy), Goldman Sachs (customer analytics), Bank of New York Mellon (financial services), McCormick/Vivanda (FlavorPrint), Houghton Mifflin Harcourt (education)—and the list goes on.

The platform world has arrived. Business profitability depends on platform-based business models leveraging communities to build value.

The Value of Co-Creation

The digital transformation isn't about moving to digital; it's about moving your business to platform ecosystems. Generating value starts with understanding the four types of platform ecosystems.

Industry competition is constantly redefined through transformation. Fragmented industries are using open-platform ecosystems, reputation systems, and ubiquitous connectivity to connect communities to create value. Unlocking the hidden value starts with an understanding of the capabilities of the four main platform ecosystems and the communities they connect.

Seductive Platforms for Profitability

Platforms magnify profitability by offering non-linear ecosystem growth. Network effects are the primary driver for scale, and community management is replacing human-resource management. As more users participate in ecosystem interactions, the value of the ecosystem increases. More people equals more value. The network effect or network externality is the value as it relates to the number of users participating in an ecosystem.

The concept of network effects was developed over 100 years ago. Theodore Vail, president of American Telephone & Telegraph between 1885 and 1889, leveraged the power of network effects to build a monopoly on US telephone services.

By 1908, he'd signed up over 4,000 local and regional carriers. The concept of network effects matured through 1995. Robert Metcalfe, co-inventor of the Internet, popularized the term "network effect." Today, platforms are the greatest benefactor of network effects and embody the largest potential for value and profitability.

The Center for Global Enterprise does a great job of segmenting platform ecosystems, and it classifies platforms that leverage network effects into four categories:

1. Innovation: co-creation of value
2. Investment: portfolio of value
3. Transactional: exchange of value
4. Integration: production of value

INNOVATION PLATFORMS

The major innovation-platform companies include Microsoft, Intel, Oracle, Salesforce, and SAP. Innovation platforms co-create value with producers and consumers. New decision-makers are improving the ability of platforms to orchestrate interactions by exploring user journeys rather than stretching conventional sales funnels. Co-creation unifies multiple parties to jointly produce a mutually valued outcome. In the search for the wisdom-of-the-crowd, these products, services, and interactions are co-created or built based on shared value. This new co-creative enterprise model aims to satisfy the needs of all the stakeholders, not just a select group. Co-creation differs from the classic process-design approach, which might ask, "How do we redesign this experience to decrease consumer touchpoints?" Alternatively, co-creation begins with a different starting point. The focus isn't on a single stakeholder; e.g., the consumer or customer. Co-creation focuses on all the stakeholders. The renewed focus asks, "How do we together create new value?"

Innovation platforms co-create value for a redesigned interaction experience.

INVESTMENT PLATFORMS

Investment platforms provide a different value by offering back-end infrastructure to enhance the front-end user experience. Typically, these experiences span multiple brand categories. This platform approach is appealing to multinational companies challenged to provide global consistency for consumers. Significant investment platforms include Priceline Group (U.S.), Rocket Internet (Germany), Naspers (South Africa), Softbank (Japan), and IAC Interactive (U.S.). Academics could argue that these companies are not, at their core, investment-platform companies. However, I'd disagree. It's hard to argue that their strategy isn't tightly coupled with the success of platforms and is an integral part of emerging company portfolios. A prime example is Priceline Group, a diverse portfolio that now includes Booking.com, Kayak.com, agoda.com, Priceline.com, rentalcars.com, and OpenTable. Naspers made a bet big with the Chinese platform, Tencent, and now has a broad mix of investments in over 30 platforms. As mentioned earlier, the digital transformation isn't about moving to digital; it's about moving from business models to platform models.

Investment platforms improve the consumers' interactions by connecting platforms for a better consumer experience.

TRANSACTIONAL PLATFORMS

Transactional platforms have a total market capitalization of $1.1 trillion, and most transactional platform companies are private—although that may soon be changing with the emergence and industry adoption of blockchain technology. In 2008, in response to the global financial crisis of 2007-08, Satoshi Nakamoto wrote a paper titled "Bitcoin: A Peer-to-Peer Electronic Cash System." The paper suggested that "trusted third parties" could be eliminated from financial transactions using blockchain technologies. Blockchain makes it possible, for the first time in history, to remove—or disintermediate—the middleman from business transactions and, by doing so, improve the value of existing products, services, and interactions. Transactional systems are preparing for disruption. IBM, Microsoft, Intel, and J.P. Morgan have already invested heavily in blockchain technology. Through 2015, $1.2 billion was invested in blockchain technology. By the end of 2018, that cumulative number reached $4.2 billion. Not to mention, the first half of 2019 had $783 million in investment funding. Blockchain technology is a foundational element of many trust-based platforms. Companies aren't just talking about blockchain; they're investing their company's future in it. Firms remember what happened in 1995 with the Internet. Profitability is lost when you're an industry laggard.

Most economic and social platforms fall into the category of transactional platforms. These include social media, marketplaces, media, music, money, financial technology (fintech), and gaming platforms. Daimler AG was a first mover in this space, with two purchases extending its platform capabilities. Daimler AG's first acquisition was US-based moovel (formerly RideScout), a technology platform that aggregates public, private, and social ridesharing. The second acquisition was the German-based MyTaxi, one of the world's first taxi applications. Today, MyTaxi boasts over 10 million international users across 45,000 taxies. MyTaxi is a transaction-based platform for ridesharing similar to Lyft. Daimler AG challenged Uber Technologies Inc. in the ride-hailing space when it merged with a well-known cab-calling service, Hailo. The result was the creation of Europe's biggest transactional platform for hailing a taxi.

Transactional platforms reduce transaction costs through disintermediation-enhancing interactions using connected technology.

INTEGRATED PLATFORMS

Integrated-platform companies contain aspects of transactional platforms and largely depend on third-party developer networks and multi-sided markets to build value. Multi-sided markets connect multiple distinct groups that value each other's participation. A simple example of a two-sided market is Airbnb. There are consumers on one side (renters) and, on the other side, there are producers (hosts). In multi-sided markets, the participation is more complex due to the many varieties of consumers and producers. Health insurance is a good example of a multi-sided market.

With over $2 trillion in market capitalization, there are six, well-known, integrated-platform companies: Apple, Google, Alibaba, Facebook, Amazon, and XiaoMi. Integrated-platform companies are considered platform conglomerates, because they utilize multiple platforms. These companies have fewer traditional platform characteristics, as they may have large, physical fulfillment facilities and manufacturing supply chains.

Integrated platforms combine platforms to produce new value, leveraging seamless consumer interactions with new behavior designs.

These new platform strategies are reinventing how we do business and opening new economic markets. By working together, we create new value.

TWO-SIDED MARKETS

An integrated social platform is at the epicenter of Groupon. Despite the more than 600 sites offering daily coupons for a limited-time. Groupon did narrow its coverage from 27 countries to 15 in November 2016.[78]

Groupon's use of social platforms encourages mobile adoption through incentives and built communities that benefit from network effects, increasing discounts as others join.[79] Low switching costs coupled with open information platform systems exposes opportunities that only technology can unlock. Low entry barriers promote value extensions by creating relationships between merchants and consumers.

Technology and business-process integration are critical elements of Groupon's success and operational vision for continual growth. Although a rip-and-replace approach sounds logical, this model would prove ineffective when absorbing new lines of business because of the uniqueness of each business acquisition. Allowing new Groupon entities to continue operating as primarily independent is a strategic decision that preserves the start-up mentality and harnesses the energy that rigid corporate structures would erode. Groupon's Lego approach to building customer interest and monetizing network effects revolves around acquisitions. Between 2010 and 2014, acquisitions drove a competitive advantage for Groupon via its purchase of technical capabilities in order to innovate and compete with industry competitors. From the start, in Q2 2010, when Groupon took shape at $38.7MM, to current revenues in 2019 of $2.2 billion, Groupon has established itself as an industry-wide, low-cost leader through acquisitions and has assembled an integrated social platform (Statista, 2015). Groupon made 41 acquisitions between January 2010 and October 2020, building strategic strength.[80] [81]

SOCIAL NETWORKS

Extending existing social networks is a primary objective of the Groupon operational vision in reaching beyond the United States. Groupon's acquisitions are global. From its beginning in 2010, Groupon was looking for opportunities outside the United States. To this end, it teamed up with Digital Sky Technologies of Russia and raised $135MM in new venture capital. Groupon's purchase, Swarm Mobile, based in San Francisco, provides shopper analytics and omni-channel marketing, but its global acquisitions abound. These include CityDeal in Germany, Needish and ClanDescuento in Chile, Disdus.com in Indonesia, Crowdmass in Australia, Beeconomic in Singapore, Darberry in Moscow, OpenCal in British Columbia, TMON in Korea, and Blink in Spain.

NEW METHODS TO MONETIZE INNOVATION

Making money by giving things away isn't new. Monetizing FREE is the spirit of platform competition in two-sided markets, where the value of a product shifts with the number of users. Facebook and Twitter are both good examples of this type of platform competition. A classic example of a two-sided market is the credit card linking consumers and merchants. To build value, the two groups of users—in this case, consumers and merchants—need to be brought together. The platforms don't always need to be digital or online to demonstrate value. One example is Shopping Mall, which connects shoppers and stores and illustrates a "shopping" platform. Another example of platforms are gas stations, first introduced in 1905, that later aligned owners of the Model-T with the needed gas required for fueling their transportation.

"In traditional value chains, value moves from left to right: To the left of the company is cost; to the right is revenue. In two-sided networks, cost and revenue are both to the left and the right,"[82] Groupon knows that, in order to realize this revenue on both or, typically, one side of the network, a platform is required. This desire to monetize the network effect is driving its acquisition strategy. Is this a sustainable competitive advantage? Yes.

Although we may normally categorize network businesses in this way, we see these models in use every day, and they're booming. LinkedIn has a two-sided network of giving away resumé listings but charging for power searches. Amazon Associates gives away free content while earning referral fees. Travelocity gives away some travel services but gets a share if you rent a hotel and car on the same trip. Van Alstyne suggests that, despite the ubiquity of network businesses, strategic value has largely gone unexplored. (Eisenmann, Parker, Van Alstyne, 2006). If we see value in LinkedIn and Travelocity, there might be room yet for Groupon.

Conclusion

New situations create new markets. Similarly, new environments will create new platforms. The sharing economy, gig economy, second-hand economy, and on-demand economy all shift how consumers buy, sell, and trade products.

Understanding the digital landscape is useful for innovators. How people learn, absorb information, and consume data is changing. This shift, in turn, changes usage patterns. From transactional platforms to integrated platforms, how we, as innovators, leverage information is becoming a game changer. Be mindful of the platform you build on, in, or around and how that will impact the consumer side of your experience.

CHAPTER 9

DISCOVERING INNOVATION

"Without change there is no innovation, creativity, or incentive for improvement. Those who initiate change will have a better opportunity to manage the change that is inevitable."

— WILLIAM POLLARD

Chapter Objectives

After reading this chapter, readers will be able to:

- Recite the three major models of discovery.
- Understand the 5A's method for ideation.
- Explain the four models for managing digital at your organization.
- Explain to a friend the four backbones of innovation.
- Create a mental image of the what "discover" means and how you leverage your internal ideas.
- Understand what defining a problem really means.
- Create a go-to-market strategy.
- Describe steps required to create "business as unusual" practices.
- Identify when shifts occur.
- Prevent yourself from getting trapped in the innovation vortex.
- Look outside your norm for innovative inspiration.

Organizational Innovation

Innovation is a process, not an event. Innovation can be described as the process of idea management. Sure, you can have your team randomly come up with ideas; however, without a process and path for the ideas to follow, they soon fade and disappear.

Good ideas need a place to grow. These ideas need an environment to mature, and they need funding. Investment and execution require a process—a repeatable process.

Three Discovery Models

There isn't a single best-case example of how to be innovative. Are Apple, Google, and Amazon innovative in your mind? Like most companies, some areas of these organizations are innovative, and others are much less inspirational.

After an extensive and thorough examination of innovation models, a discovery was made—there aren't many good ones. There was one observation that was significant: the process of innovation or innovating is very similar to the process for conducting research—the research process model.

We'll first look at three major models of discovery.

1. THE BIG6

This model was developed by Michael Eisenberg and Robert Berkowitz in 1987. The model is straightforward and has six key steps for how people solve big problems.

1. **Task definition**: define the problem, and identify the need.
2. **Information-seeking strategies**: explore all sources, and select the best.
3. **Location and access**: locate sources, and find information within them.
4. **Use of information**: engage and extract the relevant information from the source.

5. **Synthesis**: organize from multiple sources, and present the information.
6. **Evaluation**: judge the product (effectiveness) and the process (efficiency), and tune where required.

2. FLIPIT!

First introduced to a 7th grade class in 1988, this model was designed by Alice Yucht to help students move through the library faster and get what they needed out of their "library time." Not surprising, this methodology has a similar flow to The Big6 and is anchored by four steps.

1. **Focus**: on the topic or subject.
2. **Locations**: determine where to find the resources you desire.
3. **Information implementation**: investigate the information you found.
4. **Product**: present the results of the findings.

The process is similar to the BIG6 and has been used for over 20 years in academic settings to help students conduct research more productively.[83]

3. I-SEARCH

This process, designed by the late Ken Macrorie, focuses on the writer's (or innovator's, in our case) passions. It's not so much about being objective but more about focusing on topics that interest the researcher. Simple, really: Focus on your passion.

There are three areas of focus in this technique.

1. **Purpose**: synthesize information you care about.
2. **21st-century skills**: identify the topic and correlate events and ideas to develop a deeper meaning or context.

3. **Change in focus**: most academic efforts center on the outcome—the final research paper. Here, the focus is on the process—the assumption being, if the process is done correctly, powerful outcomes will follow.
4. **Higher-order skills**: group by ideas, not sources, and build groups around practical ideas.

The elegance of this research approach is that, although it's structured, it allows the researcher to wonder without stepping outside the lines. Wondering is encouraged and is similar to allowing employees to take 20 percent of their time on a Friday to explore an area of interest to them that might benefit the company—only this approach came about 20 years earlier than the 20-percent day at Google.

Many other research approaches exist. The DIALOGUE process model evolved in 1988 and is an acronym for define, initiate, access, locate, organize, guide, use, and evaluate. The 5A's method was pioneered by Ian Jukes and comprises five key steps: asking, assessing, analyzing, applying, and assessing. Of course, there's the scientific method, also with five steps: observe, question, hypothesize, predict, and communicate. Annette Lamb's 8W's model surfaced in the latter 1990s. This was a light-hearted attempt to make the research process more fun with an eight-step approach: watching, wondering, webbing, wiggling, weaving, wrapping, waving, and wishing.

It really doesn't matter that Big6 was used for middle school students and I-Search was used for high school students. Each process provides insight into how to look at a problem, do something, and eventually come up with new solutions. Isn't this exactly what innovation is all about—finding solutions to old problems or even redefining the problem altogether?

There's no perfect solution. All solutions were found to work, if they were applied correct. The lesson is, you need an innovation process. That's obvious. However, that innovation process can vary and still be effective. You, as an innovator, need to think differently and design an innovation process that best suits your environment—your organization, team, environment, or desired outcome.

Four Models for Managing Innovation: Your License to Explore

There are seven well-known innovation models in the evolution of innovation, beginning with five identified by Rothwell in 1994.

1. **Technology Push Model**: research-and-development science
2. **Market Pull Model**: market-driven innovation
3. Coupling Model: integrating marketing and research and development
4. **Interactive Model**: bridging push and pull models
5. **Network Model**: integration through sophisticated technology linkages
6. **Open Innovation Model**: shared ideas for market advancement in standards
7. **Distributed Model**: peer-to-peer architectures tailored for scale[84]

The first generation of innovation model, the "Technology Push Model," was seen from the 1950s to the mid-1960s during the rapid industrial expansion. This was characterized by an emphasis on research and development with a linear process. The second-generation "Market Pull Model" began in the mid-1960s and continued through the early 1970s and focused on the market. New products were extensions of existing product lines in the battle for market share. The third-generation "Coupling Model" was persuasive from the early-1970s to the mid-1980s, during the demand saturation, or stagflation, that occurred and had a renewed focus on scale, consolidation, and benefits. The fourth-generation "Interactive Model" was visible in the 1980s through the early-1990s and combined push and pull models centering on a firm's integration capabilities. The fifth-generation "Network Model" emerged in the mid-1990s and was prevalent until 1997. The networking generation drove development in system integrations and extensive networking between systems, with an emphasis on pervasive innovation.[85] The sixth-generation "Open Innovation Model" was popular from 1997 to 2008, when firms were encouraged to use external ideas as well as internal ideas along with internal and external paths to market as they advanced their business and technological capabilities.[86] The seventh-generation "Distributed Model" began to take hold in 2008 after the global financial crisis. Disintermediation was considered a reasonable path to limit risk within ecosystems by using distributed technologies to connect products and consumers.

While these seven models are unquestionably the backbone of the evolution of innovation, we'll be focusing on four flavors of these models:

1. **We Discover**: identify multi-sided markets
2. **We Choose**: select the strategy
3. **We Extend**: define the innovation boundary
4. **We Evolve**: adapt to the environment

Model 1: We Discover

Discovery is a model of differentiation. It introduces new services, new products, and new interactions to form a new value, either perceived or realized.

We're all familiar with Porter's Five Forces model of competition: determinants of supplier power, threat of new entrants, determinants of buyer power, threat of substitute products, and rivalry among existing firms. We're not talking about building sustainable competitive advantages. If fact, it's debated if there is such a thing as a sustainable advantage in this new world of platform economics.

This is a shift to discovery is a shift toward differentiation through platform selection. Discovery is a four-step process.

1. Select the platform
2. Identify the multi-sided market
3. Engage for network effect
4. Determine the monetization method

There could be 50 steps, but there are only four. There only need to be four.

1. SELECT THE PLATFORM

First, select your platform:

1. **Innovation**: co-creation of value
2. **Investment**: portfolio of value
3. **Transactional**: exchange of value
4. **Integration**: production of value

Innovation platforms orchestrate interactions. Investment platforms offer back-end infrastructure to enhance the front-end user experience. Transactional platforms reduce transaction costs. Integration platforms combine platform types to produce new value.

I haven't seen a better framework for exploring the types of innovation than Doblin's, a framework that Larry Keeley has matured since its emergence into the corporate world in 1988.[87] We briefly mentioned this in Chapter 4; however, this framework, summarized for brevity below, is worthy of a more detailed elaboration to briefly explain the 10 models.

1. **Profit model**: the way in which you make money
2. **Network model**: connections with others to create value
3. **Structure model**: alignment of your talent assets

4. **Process model**: signature of superior methods for doing your work
5. **Product performance**: distinguishing features and functionality
6. **Product-system model**: complementary products and services
7. **Service model**: support and enhancements that surround your offerings
8. **Channel model**: how your offering are delivered to customers and users
9. **Brand model**: representation of your offerings and business
10. **Customer-engagement model**: distinctive interactions you foster

2. IDENTIFY THE MULTI-SIDED MARKET

Second, identify the multi-sided market. Airbnb has renters and hosts. Uber has riders and drivers. Aricanduva has retail stores and shoppers. Facebook has friends and advertisers. eHarmony has men and women. Apple iOS has users and application developers. Epoca has readers and advertisers. American Express has cardholders and merchants. These examples are two-sided markets. Of course, some markets are multi-sided.

Make an active decision, and craft the sides of your market ecosystem before you build.

3. ENGAGE FOR NETWORK EFFECT

Third, engage for network effect. This is a reference to Metcalfe's law, which states that the utility of a network is proportional to the square of the number (n) of its users. Networks are more valuable to their users if more people use that same service. Not many of us still use a land-line phone, so that example may not be relevant. However, how impactful would LinkedIn be with two users on it? Not very. To grow the value of our network, we need to build this network equally for both producers and consumers.

Amazon uses network effects for its recommendations engine. eBay uses network effects for competitive auctions. For Google Adsense, more publishers means more advertisers. Are you hoping consumers will come to you, or are you actively building and thinking about network effects? Social networks aren't only about chatting with friends; network effects are essential to growing a business or idea to scale.

4. DETERMINE THE MONETIZATION METHOD

Fourth, we need to determine how to make money from this idea. How do smart companies design the product around the price? They think beyond the price point and understand that how you change trumps what you charge.

Below are five primary monetization models. I'm sure you can be creative and generate another 10, but these are the core models utilized by most platforms that reach scale:

1. Subscription model
2. Dynamic pricing model
3. Market-based pricing
4. Alternative-metric pricing model
5. Freemium pricing model

HOW IS DISCOVERY APPLIED?

Now you know the platform, market, and effect.

The subscription model requires payment for access to extended features. LinkedIn is a good example of this. Basic access is free; however, extended functionality through Sales Navigator, which is used for prospecting new sales leads, requires a fee to access.

The dynamic pricing model is variable pricing contingent on factors not controlled by consumers such as weather, seasonality, or demand and supply. In the case of Uber providing ride services, their rate is largely flat. However, they have

161

what's called "surge pricing," which can create variation in the fixed rate by a multiplier—2x or 3x normal fares depending on the demand on drivers.

The market-based pricing model uses the price for similar or competitive goods. Google Adsense delivers Google AdWords ads to websites, and Google pays web publishers for ads displayed on their websites based on clicks or impressions. The price of these ads is based on market competition.

The alternative-metric pricing model or the pay-as-you-go model is largely based on transactions. This per-unit transactional fee is typical of PayPal, Stripe, Google Wallet, Shopify, Payoneer, and Payline Data. Each of these services has payment models centered around transactional volume.

The freemium pricing model or "land and expand model" presents customers with two or more pricing models, one of which is free. The theory is that, when a service is free, more consumers will experiment with it. Once they're convinced of the value, they're more likely to purchase additional features.

Determine which model is best for your innovation depending on who the innovation impacts and your competition's approach. You may choose to deviate from that or support a similar monetization model.

Model 2: We Choose

Selecting the right innovation isn't about the right technology or processes. It's all about selecting the right partners.

If you have a strong team, you probably already have mock-ups, MVP, prototypes, or other ideations in flight.

DEFINE THE PROBLEM

The Innovator's Method presents an alternative strategy for thinking about innovation and where to start an end-to-end innovation process. The backbone of this model is that innovations are only valuable if they solve problems. To begin this process, we'll apply four steps of the Innovator's Method:

1. **Insight**: savor surprises
2. **Problem**: discover the job to be done
3. **Solution**: prototype the minimum awesome product
4. **Business Model**: validate the go-to-market strategy[88]

The Insight, or "where do we look?" begins with a curiosity about where to explore, why to look, or how to discover something that only yesterday didn't exist. The Problem, or "Why does this help?" asks the right questions—questions that may have seemed obvious but didn't address the raw, underlying root cause. The Solution, or "What gets us there?" addresses the shortest path to a minimal viable product (MVP) or minimal awesome product (MAP). The Business Model, or "How do we get there?" addresses the go-to-market strategy. Using these simple steps in combination can provide a useful guide when starting down the innovation path. They also act as a methodology to help field question from stakeholders. All questions should nicely fit into one of the four steps or phases.

DEFINE THE GO-TO-MARKET STRATEGY

After you ideate and build stuff, quickly determine the business model you'll be using. Then, evolve the product, service, or interaction around that model using the following:

1. Value proposition
2. Pricing strategy
3. Consumer acquisition
4. Customer acquisition
5. Cost structure by activity
6. Cost structures by resources[89]

One concept we don't often hear about is how go-to-market strategies are developed. These strategies can and should be developed while innovations are embryonic and still taking shape. The benefit of conducting leadership and team discussion before the product is finalized is the added benefit of ex-

163

ploring new approaches to achieving scale, which might not be overt once we're looking at a real product or service.

Model 3: We Extend

Where do the boundaries of innovation end? Is the answer to this an edict that comes down from above or a gut feeling that your team is wandering outside the boundaries of acceptable exploration?

We could extend our channel intermediaries to expand our distribution reach. We could push corporate goals through new innovation policy, but we're not going to. Every meeting and every discussion inside the corporate office at some point becomes a discussion of time. How fast can it be done? When will I receive it? Why can't it be done faster? In this cyclone of perceived progress, everything done yesterday is always better.

We Extend takes a different perspective by extending or slowing down the process. By observing the behavioral sciences, the analysis of quantitative and nonquantitative data, economics theories, and process analysis, we know the evolution of Total Quality Management is a long-term approach to customer satisfaction. Everyone participates, strengthening processes, services, and the culture in which members live and work.

W. Edwards Deming, an American electrical engineer, was a master of continual quality improvement. *The New Economics for Industry, Government, Education* was published after his death in 1993 and was the culmination of a life's work presenting The Deming System of Profound Knowledge:

1. **Appreciation of a System**: understanding the overall processes involving suppliers, producers, and customers (or recipients) of goods and services (explained below)

2. **Knowledge of Variation**: the range and causes of variation in quality and use of statistical sampling in measurements
3. **Theory of Knowledge**: the concepts explaining knowledge and the limits of what can be known
4. **Knowledge of Psychology**: concepts of human nature[90]

TQM and the Deming System of Profound Knowledge both center on the organization—not individual components or units—working as a system for optimal productivity.

When we innovate, we need to work as a system, not a cluster of individual units supporting similar objectives. We can learn from Deming and accelerate our ability to innovate as a team to improve organization cohesion.

Deming also published 14 points for Total Quality Management.:

1. Create constancy of purpose for improving products and services.
2. Adopt the new philosophy.
3. Cease dependence on inspection to achieve quality.
4. End the practice of awarding business on price alone; instead, minimize total cost by working with a single supplier.
5. Improve—constantly and forever—every process for planning, production, and service.
6. Institute training on the job.
7. Adopt and institute leadership.
8. Drive out fear.
9. Break down barriers between staff areas.
10. Eliminate slogans, exhortations, and targets for the workforce.
11. Eliminate numerical quotas for the workforce and numerical goals for management.
12. Remove barriers that rob people of pride of workmanship, and eliminate the annual rating or merit system.

13. Institute a vigorous program of education and self-improvement for everyone.
14. Put everybody in the company to work accomplishing the transformation.

As you consider new approaches for growth, discovery, and delivery, apply Deming's 14 Points of Total Quality Management as your team moves through the innovation process.

Model 4: We Evolve

Variation, selection and competition are the challenges of navigating today's digital ecosystem of value. Identify the struggle between individuals and competitors to discover tomorrow's game changers. Innovation is the modern struggle for existence. Will your organization survive?

Consumers buy your products, services, and interactions for reliability. Partners seek your alignment for greater stability. Employees join your company for predictable results. Disruptive innovation can be identified when best practices no longer produce predictable results. Our modern, knowledge-intensive economy depends on organizational capabilities. Is your organization having trouble identifying why the margin is eroding? Disruption in disguise may be the answer.

Struggle for Existence

Charles Darwin's *The Origin of Species* is unquestionably one of the greatest works in human intellectual history. In this seminal book, Darwin develops the argument of why the theory of special selection is incorrect and why the theory of natural selection is more favorable. Eventually, reputable scientists arrived to acknowledge that evolution—the transformation of species over time—had, in fact, occurred. Darwin elaborated that variance isn't an anomaly but rather an inevitable result of orchestrated processes.

Causes of variability and the difficulty in distinguishing among varieties and species weren't only challenges for Darwin. Today, a complex ecosystem of offerings makes the identification of value-based innovations difficult to delineate in markets with multiple offerings.

Buried under the struggle for existence, many innovators incorrectly assume that natural selection requires competition among individuals. Darwin defines this struggle as not between individuals as competitors but in a metaphorical sense where predation, parasitism, or environmental conditions dictate a new struggle. Natural selection eliminates competition. All modern innovation organizations should pay attention to lessons of selection in the struggle for existence—a modern struggle for variability through innovation and predictable results. Industries are looking less to their neighbors and more toward unrelated industries for innovation insights. You're not competing with your business neighbor.

Natural Selection Redefines the Rules

Industry leaders are searching to discover tomorrow's game changers. Will a new technology improve efficiency? Is the current business model changing? How do we compete tomorrow in this explosive sharing economy? There are multiple methods to ensure corporate survival. The accepted method favors players that evolve and adapt. The winners define new rules and establish new games.

This year will unlock opportunities—ones that weren't afforded last year. Start with these questions before you set your organizational agenda:

1. Is your organization creating and capturing value?
2. Does your organization not only find the right strategies but make good decisions when selecting future strategies?

3. Is your organization in competition or cooperation? For example, is your organization building walls against the competition or establishing relationships with unlikely allies?
4. Are you playing an old game, or are you redefining a new game?
5. Has your organization clearly identified complementors (the situation in which customers and suppliers play symmetric roles)?

Natural selection may preserve favorable variations and reject injurious variations. As with natural selection in animals, all inferior businesses aren't immediately destroyed; they evolve out of existence. Darwin suggested that natural selection is "the daily and hourly scrutinizing, throughout the world, [of] every variation, even the slightest, rejecting that which is bad, preserving and adding up all that is good." Isn't this happening in business—every hour of every day? The change we experience in business is natural selection. Consider the value your organization adds as environmental conditions change. Is your organization evolving out of existence?

Several mistletoe plants growing on the same branch of a host tree may struggle for existence. It might be truer that the struggle for existence isn't against the thousands of seeds of the same kind or against other fruit-bearing plants but against any attempt to devour the seeds and thus prevent dissemination. Disruption isn't an event; it's evolution, a transformation of convenience. Aspects of your business are transforming as did cloud computing, consumerism, and mobile—focus beyond the seeds of your company and observe the broader struggle for existence.

Business as "Unusual"

How do you prepare your leaders for what's coming?[91] We encourage our teams to welcome change. It's comforting to know that your teams and core leaders are comfortable handling—always in motion—dynamic environments. But how we do we handle the change that accepting change creates.

Price Pritchett, PhD, a specialist in merger integration strategies, captures this concept well. Organizational change creates new risk factors. There's a certain irony here. Your change initiative is intended to solve problems, but, any time the organization makes major changes, you must deal with the problems of your solutions.

Everyone wants to avoid business disruption. Few would argue that business performance doesn't matter. Fewer still would challenge that the right business behaviors are essential to survival. But how do we dodge the big industry disruptions? What's the best mix of academic and practitioner-based strategies for optimal business performance? How do we define those behaviors we all know are critical? These are the questions that don't get answered. Each innovator must discover the truth alone—or at least that's what's we each hear.

THE SIGMOID CURVE

The Law of Diffusion of Innovation, covered earlier, helps to explain how ideas and innovative technologies spread. Five categories of adoption anchor this theory: (1) innovators, (2) early adopters, (3) early majority, (4) late majority, and (5) laggards.

Reflect for a minute on where you'd place your company on the diffusion of innovation bell curve. Consider your industry, the products you create, the services you offer, and the interactions orchestrated by your organizational platform. Not surprisingly, most place their organization on the near side of the diffusion of innovation bell curve. This would indicate an early adopter (ahead of industry) or an early majority (with the industry but leading). Shockingly, very few innovators place their organization on the back side of the curve—in the categories of late majority (tail end of the opportunity) or laggards (missed the window).

How do we discover the truth about our product, service, or interaction maturity? We must look back to look forward. Our first step starts with the inspiration of Charles Handy's *The Future of Work* (1984)[92] and later sequels *The Age of Unreason* (1991)[93] and *The Empty Raincoat* (1995).[94] Nature, organization, and the future of work were amplified thanks to Charles Handy. Handy noticed that change was occurring when he penned *The Future of Work*.

It was during the 1970s that the familiar scenery of our working lives began to show visible changes. The large employment organizations that had been daytime houses for so many people all their lives began to decline. Jobs began to become a scarce commodity, and work started to mean other things besides the conventional full-time job. Second and third careers, moonlighting, and the (informal) economy became part of our language as did the chip and the video—new words to herald new ways. The old patterns were breaking down; new patterns were forming. Handy's concepts of radical thinking were re-examined in *The Age of Reason*.

We're fixated, both as a nation and as individuals, on the employment organization. Work is defined as employment. Money is distributed through employment. Status and identity stem from employment. Therefore, we hang on to employment as long as we can. We measure our success in terms of it, we expect great things from it for the country and for ourselves, and we cannot conceive of a future without it.

Corporate enterprises were fixtures of industry, but something was changing. Jobs were no longer guaranteed. Handy asked readers—in 1989—to stop pretending. He demanded acknowledgment that industry, employment, and entities that bound us were shifting in front of our eyes without our awareness.[95] Fast forward almost 30 years, and I ask: Are we still pretending? Are we pretending change isn't already here?

THE INNOVATION VORTEX

Are you in an innovation vortex? Vortices are disruptions. The phenomenon of a smoke ring. The spin of a whirlpool. The wake of a boat. Vortices don't only occur in tornados or inside nature's dust bowl. They also occur with innovation.

In *The Empty Raincoat*, Handy re-introduced the sigmoid curve, a special case of the Logistic function. The sigmoid curve is a mathematical function with a notable "S"-shaped curve. Typically, this curve represents time (on the horizontal axis) and activity (on the vertical axis). Handy's representation is two, interlocking S-curves. Initially, the A-curve is ascending, and the B-curve is declining. However, as time passes, what occurs is the A-curve ascends and then declines, while the B-curve declines and then ascends. If we took a picture earlier in time, it would appear that the A-curve (representing the incumbent) is leading and the B-curve (representing the startup) is declining. Quickly, the gap between the incumbent and the startup narrows, and soon the A-curve is rapidly declining and the B-curve is ascending. The startup just surpassed the incumbent, against all reasonable odds. The lesson is that nothing is permanent; all that rises must decline. Our role as innovators is to determine when we diverge from A-curve thinking (business models) and adopt B-curve thinking. The challenge is convincing people while they're successful that, in fact, they're unknowingly in a slow decline.

The sigmoid curve can be used to chart empires, nations, and even political movements.[96] The path to sustained success—whether conquering a country or a new product—is knowing how to ride the sigmoid curve. You must use your success as a security parachute while you experiment.

You shouldn't be afraid to fail. Just like with pilots, captains, or expedition scuba divers, once you lose your ability to acknowledge fear, you become complacent—which is the first real step toward failure—and therefore more—not less—likely to make mistakes.

The innovation vortex is the enclosed space in which the two S-curves connect. This vortex represents doubt and uncertainty. The business-model shift happens inside the innovation vortex.

IDENTIFY THE SHIFT

Even when we're really paying attention, it's hard to identify the business-model shift. The reason is that success depends on your ability to convince your team and your organization—while they're successful—that their strategy no longer works. It's like walking up to a blackjack player that just won a $5,000 hand after a series of smaller wins and convincing them that their strategy isn't sustainable and is, in fact, failing. It's damn near impossible. Thus, even if you do successful identify the shift, you might not be able to rally enough organizational support to act on your instincts.

Individuals believe that once they've been successful, they'll continue to be successful. It's hard to swallow the raw truth—the pattern of success is constantly changing. The pattern of success today won't be the pattern of success tomorrow. Success doesn't last. Those that continually find it always discover success in a new place, not a familiar one.

Dispassionately evaluate everything. Taking bold risks isn't only for innovators. It's for anyone who wants to maintain sustainable success in business.

We must honestly assess where we are on the diffusion of innovation bell curve, focusing on the first three categories: innovators (startup), early adopters (scale), and early majority (performance). Then, overlay the S-curve. There are a lot of great examples online of this innovation curve. Acknowledge where your organization is today, and estimate the time before you're into the innovation vortex.

172

Looking Outside for Innovation

When you're looking for innovation, where do you start? Do you start with the big brands? What about looking under rocks searching for innovation incubators? How about non-governmental organizations (NGOs)? NGOs might have been you very last stop. They should be your first.

Limited resources. Non-existent budgets. Dreams of changing the world. NGOs provide a model for all innovators, and NGOs are everywhere. Globally, there are over 10 million NGOs. In 2019, 31 percent of the world donated to an NGO charity and on average 25 percent volunteered at one. In fact, collectively, NGOs do have capital and, if they were all combined, they'd form a country with the fifth largest GDP.

Observing innovations at NGOs can reframe our thinking about what's required for resources and capital within standard enterprise-innovation programs.

It might appear that a not-for-profit and a for-profit company would have radically different approaches to innovation. Surprisingly, that's not the case. A lot of insight can be gained by exploring NGOs and how they stay creative.

NGO: GIVE DIRECTLY

There have been many NGOs that have successfully created new innovative business models while starting from some of poorest places on earth. Innovation isn't optional for NGOs; it's part of their survival. With limited budgets and restricted resources, not having the cash flow to support short-term and long-term initiatives is part of daily life.

Give Directly is based around the concept of "a radically new way to give: directly." Give Directly doesn't use donations itself but rather directly routes money to individuals and families in need, thereby removing the middleman or go-between that often results in financial leakage. The concept behind Give Directly is beautifully simple and has four pillars:

1. Supporters donate through its webpage.
2. Give Directly locates poor households in Kenya and Uganda.
3. The NGO transfers the donation to the recipient electronically via their phone.
4. The beneficiary uses the contribution to pursue his or her goals however they wish.

NGO: APOPO

APOPO started small in 1997 but has recently received a lot of attention in 2020. APOPO is the acronym in Dutch for Anti-Persoonsmijnen Ontmijnende Product Ontwikkeling, which translates as Anti-Personnel Landmines Detection Product Development in English. This is a Dutch social enterprise that researches, develops, and implements rat-based detection technology for humanitarian purposes. Wait, what was that? Did you say rat? Yes, rats!

This company has a "fleet" of rats—HeroRATS—that are specially trained to face—head on—the most challenging development issues in Africa including landmines and tuberculosis. These are giant African pouched rats. (I was going to include a picture, but I think it's best if we just use our imagination. The visual might be too disturbing.)

Bart Weetjens, the founder, was a pioneer in the use of indigenous African rodents to detect unexploded mines and weaponry in the earth and TB in sputum samples. NGOs are creating innovation to solve the hardest of the world's social and healthcare problems.

NGO: ZANAAFRICA

Migrating 1,400 kilometers north to Kenya, another innovative and interesting NGO has surfaced. ZanalAfrica is a hybrid healthcare and girl's education NGO that's working to help young women stay in school and reach their potential. Its mission is to tackle two main humanitarian issues at the same time: (1) a lack of access to appropriate healthcare information and products, and (2) the rate at which young girls in Africa drop out of school.

Here's how it works. The ZanaAfrica supports the promotion of affordable sanitary pads combined with health education presented in a fun and interactive comic-based pamphlet. The objective is to help girls make informed decisions about their reproductive life and keep them in school. ZanaAfrica has generated some amazing results, with research demonstrating that these pads help girls win back 75% of their learning days by staying in school. The adoption growth rate was frankly amazing. This idea is taking off so well that the NGO plans to reach five million girls by 2025, supplying over 10 million comics across East Africa.

NGO: TOMIKE HEALTH

Another interesting NGO out of Africa is the less well-known Tomike Health. The inspiration for this came from a friend of the founder during childbirth. The mission of Tomike Health is to ensure women across Africa have access to maternity care. Most NGOs depend on begging for grant funding or donations by claiming (usually inaccurately) that the NGO "eventually" will be self-funded. However, that wasn't the objective of Tomike Health; its vision was to be self-funded from day one!

To meet this aggressive target, Tomike Health combined business, job training, and clinical innovations to create a self-sustaining and scalable solution to reproductive health. In a continuous fashion, this NGO introduced new and innovative ideas and products into its ecosystem including mobile health and electronic medical records as well as financial and marketing innovations in an attempt to reach the one million-plus women who give birth each year in urban West Africa. Sometimes, it takes believers to make a difference. The best creative ideas aren't sold on the first attempt.

Tomike Health is a great example that shows how thinking beyond borders can grow new value for those in need.

NGO: COLALIFE

Shifting focus to the United Kingdom, charity is the focus of the NGO called ColaLife. The mission of ColaLife seeks to embrace the ideas of social networks to reach one of the world's biggest brands and provide health resources to people living in rural and remote locations that are underserved.

The ColaLife mission is based on three principles:

1. **Access**: You can buy a Coca-Cola almost anywhere you go in the world, even in the most remote parts of developing countries.
2. **Prevention**: In these same places, one in nine children dies before their fifth birthday from preventable causes. Most die from dehydration caused by diarrhea.
3. **Change**: Child mortality figures haven't changed significantly for at least three decades, which would indicate that current initiatives aren't working.

The distribution network of Coca-Cola is one of the most diversified and expansive of any product sold around the world. If the Coca-Cola bottles in the world were laid end-to-end, they'd reach to the moon and back more than 1,677 times. There are nearly 10,450 different soft drinks produced by Coca-Cola, as every country and region has its own specific flavors. Coca-Cola has been in the cola business since 1931.

The basic premise of ColaLife is there's no need to recreate the distribution channel that it took Coca-Cola almost 100 years to build. Instead, ColaLife is leveraging the success and reach of Coca-Cola to tap into some of the most remote locations in the world.

ColaLife also developed the AidPod, a small, wedge-shaped container that fits in the space between the neck of Coca-Cola crate. The model piggybacks on Coca-Cola's distribution system. ColaLife is doing well for an NGO with limited resources and limited funding. Fortunately, it's rich in unique ideas.

Conclusion

As soon as we select a technology or envision an idea, we first look inside our team, department, or company for insights. We search for unique perspectives in an environment that we largely already know and understand.

What if, instead of looking inside, we look outside our physical and digital spaces? Innovation is happening all around us. We tend to associate innovation with Bell Labs or IBM Watson types of technologies. It's true that innovation does live inside those companies. Innovation also lives and flourishes outside as well.

If I mention the word innovation and ask you to quickly associate a company with that word, you'll likely come up with Amazon, Apple, Sony, Tesla, and others. What you won't come up with is APOPO, Give Directly, or ZanaAfrica, which are all non-profit organization driving original ideas.

The next time you're looking for market insights, a new market segment, or attempting to design a new platform, look for ideas in places that others aren't looking.

PART III

ENABLING ORGANIZATIONAL INNOVATION

We've discussed innovative ideas and how to create them, and we understand where original ideas come from and how to envision them. Now, how do we enable innovation within our companies?

Creating ideas is one thing; making them come to life is another. It's widely known that companies are where great ideas go to die. In a plot twist, we're going to make our ideas transformative and sustainable, so they endure.

We'll begin with discovering innovation models and how our outside thinking helps us now. Then I'll introduce a well-known framework to evaluate what type of idea you're dealing with. Does this new idea have huge potential, or has the product already matured? From there, we'll get into some of the huge potential of robotic process automation and blockchain. This section will help you understand how small and large ideas can be disruptive. We'll cover the architecture of innovation, introduce the power of data science, and wrap up with the humor of innovation. Let's go!

CHAPTER 10

THE IDEA REVOLUTION

"Any institution faces two basic choices if they hope to spark new ideas. One is to leverage the brains trust within their organization by creating a special event dedicated to new thinking. The other is to look outside themselves to stimulate solutions."

— SIMON MAINWARING

Chapter Objectives

After reading this chapter, readers will be able to:

- Identify the steps in the industrial revolution.
- Know the history of the Hype Cycle and why it's used.
- Understand the Hype Cycle for emerging technology.
- Provide examples of innovations in each stage of the Hype Cycle.
- Delineate between hype and legitimate good ideas that have low adoption.
- Identify when you're in the Hype Cycle.

Fourth Industrial Revolution

The fourth Industrial Revolution merges the physical, digital, and biological worlds. The need for human connections has never been greater.

Companies can find talent. They just can't attract it. Fifteen years ago, corporate was king, and bigger was better. Companies such as Bank of America, Qualcomm, Cisco Systems, Intel, Sun Microsystems, and Merck were the most desirable companies for employment. That mindset has evaporated. Today Hilton, Ultimate Software, Wegmans Food Markets, Cisco, Workday, and Stryker are among the 100 best companies to work for, according to *Fortune Magazine*.

CHANGE IS COMING

Worker preferences are changing. It's no longer good enough to tout social responsibility and entice talent with the sparkle of high earnings. Employees want flexibility and inclusion in decisions affecting their future. Companies are fracturing, and disintermediation isn't only an outside force pressing upon companies. It's a force creating disruption from the inside out. Today's workers are looking for a corporate family, a group of like-minded individuals that share beliefs and hold similar values. Business is getting personal. Large enterprises aren't able to complete.

According to the MIT Sloan School of Management, the roles of startups and big business are shifting. According to Vladimir Bulović, associate dean for innovation and a professor at MIT, 15 to 20 percent of MIT graduates join startups. Interestingly, 5 years ago, only about 1.5 percent joined startups. The primary reason for the swing is that innovation has shifted to smaller companies. These little companies house tight groups of individuals who are committed—the seduction of the modern startup—even with low pay, horrible hours, and only a slight chance of changing the world. Interested?

THREE DECADES OF PROGRESS

The influx of freelance and contract workers into corporate America has changing the landscape of work. Job polarization, although a relatively new economic term, started with an investment in robotics, removing middle-skills jobs and relocating many jobs overseas. The effect of job polarization has resulted in a sharp reduction of middle-class jobs. These jobs are classified as of moderate-skill level when compared to low-skill and high-skill jobs. When observing the index of computing over the last 30 years, there have been tremendous advances in computer power, cost per unit, labor cost per unit, cycles per second, and rapid memory.

COMPLETE POWER

Significant growth in computing power, performance, and productivity began in the mid-1940s. Moore's Law—observed in 1965 by Gordon Moore, co-founder of Intel—started a trend that would last for decades. This surge in productivity accelerated from 1969 to 2004, when the price index for computers fell by 23 percent. The GDP price index measures inflation in the prices of goods and services produced in the United States as presented by the Bureau of Economic Analysis (BEA). *The Future of Work in the Age of the Machine*, by The Hamilton Project, illustrates the exponential gains in computer buying power between 1980 to 2010.

American Economic Review published a paper titled, "The Growth of Low-Skill Service Jobs and the Polarization of the US Labor Market," written by David H. Autor and David Dorn. Their hypothesis posited "a critical role for changes in labor specialization, spurred by automation of routine task activities, as a driver of rising employment and wage polarization in the United States and potentially in other countries." The structure of jobs is changing. Jobs are moving away from middle-skill roles and branching toward low-skill and high-skill roles.

THE REVOLUTION

The future of work is also broader than collaboration technologies. We're on the brink of a new industrial revolution. In 1784, the first Industrial Revolution was driven by steam and mechanical production equipment. The second Industrial Revolution, starting in 1870, was characterized by the mass production of electricity and divisions of labor. The third Industrial Revolution was driven by automated production and electronics and information technology beginning in 1969.

What will be the fourth Industrial Revolution? The Internet of Everything (IoE), robotics, sharing economy, cyber-physical systems, nanotechnology, biotechnology, materials science, energy storage, and quantum computing all compete for the new title.

Professor Klaus Schwab was born in Ravensburg, Germany in 1938. He's the Founder and Executive Chairman of the World Economic Forum of the International Organization for Public-Private Cooperation. In January 2016, he published *The Fourth Industrial Revolution*, which steps through the impact of this revolution:

1. Economy: growth, employment, and the nature of work
2. Business transformations: consumer expectations, data-enhanced products, collaborative innovation, new operating models
3. National and global changes: governments, countries-regions-and-cities, international security
4. Individual disruption: identity, morality, and ethics

The need for human connection and the necessity to manage public and private information have increased in signal strength as this revolution changes society.

With virtually unlimited possibilities, business-model shifts are occurring across every industry. How we work and communicate is undergoing a profound paradigm shift—and asking every member of society to rethink their values and goals.

Hype Cycle

How do you make the decision to adopt a technology into your organization? The Gartner Hype Cycle can help leaders make informed decisions on innovative new technologies.

A Clear Definition of Hype

To absorb the massive virality and impact of innovation, we must first address the hype. Hype, please square up!

What is hype? The Oxford Dictionary defines hype as, "promoting or publicizing (a product or idea) intensively, often exaggerating its importance or benefits." Simply put, hype is an exaggerated advantage, a benefit that doesn't align with the future reality of the product or service. As with many new technologies, there's excitement. However, the buzz and excitement around blockchain, virtual reality, and cogitative computing are more than hype; it's the realization of the potential to transform industries.

A Framework for Emerging Technology and Innovations

The "Hype Cycle," introduced in 1995, is a graphical representation of the stages of emerging technology from its introduction to widespread model adoption, focusing on model relevance in solving real business problems. The Hype Cycle helps to identity how to exploit new technological opportunities and is a tool created to illustrate the risk associated with a technology and the present stage in a technology's lifespan. The five phases of the Hype Cycle are: (1) innovation trigger, (2) peak of inflated expectations, (3) trough of disillusionment, (4) slope of enlightenment, and, lastly, (5) the plateau of productivity.

The Hype Cycle can be used to evaluate a technology across five major categories:

1. **Inception**—When did the technology start to create a following?
2. **Evaluation of claims**—Does the technology deliver the benefits initially claimed?
3. **Validate commercial viability**—Will this product, service, or new interaction create profit for a business?
4. **Maturation**—Has this technology reached end-of-life—or, more specifically, has enough time been spent exploring the technology—to determine the useful life remaining if we invest today?
5. **Risk profile**—Each level of the Hype Cycle is associated with a degree of risk. Understanding a technology's Hype Cycle stage is a useful measure of risk.

Remember the hype over the telegraph in the 19th century? The telephone has matured, but was that invention all hype? We all know how overstated the possibilities of the telephone were by the end of the 19th century and start of the 20th century. How about the buzz and over-promising related to canals and railroads in the 1700s and 1800s? Hype probably isn't the best word to describe the development of railroads, which was one of the most important phenomena of the Industrial Revolution. The list doesn't seem to end. It continues with the likes of automobiles, radios, and then the jet engine, rockets, and atomic energy and proceeds into the 1950s and 1960s with biotechnology, nanotechnology, and genomics. Do we consider the canals, railroads, telegraphs, automobiles, and cell phones hype? If these hyped technologies landed us here, how can emerging technologies change the future of society?

The Hype Cycle Explained

Each time the concept of the Hype Cycle is raised, I'm reminded of how much I already know of it. You probably have a similar reaction. There is one reaction I need to constantly remind myself to do.

When you're in your next meeting, instead of yawning at the fact you just thought of the Hype Cycle—stop and think. Ask yourself, where in the lifecycle does the technology we're discussing fit. Is this technology barely tested or is it at the end of it's maturity? What new technologies could be replacing it today? This is where the innovation mindset kicks in.

The five phases of the Hype Cycle can be summarized as follows:

1. **Innovation Trigger**—Embryonic technology

2. **Peak of Inflated Expectations**—Inflated expectations
3. **Trough of Disillusionment**—Technology misses expectations
4. **Slope of Enlightenment** - Realization of practical benefits
5. **Plateau of Productivity** - Benefits widely accepted and understood

There are no constants with innovation. In general, the lifecycle from Innovation Trigger to Plateau of Productivity takes 10 or more years. Let's explore the five phases of the Hype Cycle in detail.

Phase 1: Innovation Trigger

The Innovation Trigger is the early phase of a new and rapidly developing technology. Typically, technologies at this stage have just been officially released—beyond alpha and beta releases—with their first stable build available for industry consumption. During this phase, research and development has started, and several startup companies have already secured their first round of venture-capital funding.

DRONES

Triggers solve problems. This may be a new compliance regulation—for example, from the U.S. Federal Aviation Authority (FAA) for routine commercial use of small unmanned aircraft systems (UAS or "drones"), which opens pathways toward fully integrating UAS into the nation's airspace. This new regulation affects multiple industries including precision agriculture (higher productivity while utilizing the same land), insurance (survey of physical facilities), and real estate (appraisals and 360-degree views for buyers). Innovation-trigger technologies impact existing supply chains, commercial platform manufacturers, parachutes and recovery, components and systems, and the software that runs drones. If you're a supplier or retailer for incumbent products, this new technology could impact your entire supply chain: sell, buy, make, move, and plan.

Here are 10 questions to assess whether a technology is in the Innovation Trigger phase:

1. Has research and development just started to explore the innovation potential?
2. Are founders receiving first rounds of venture-capital funding for the innovation?
3. Has the media started to show interest in the innovation?
4. Is the product only available to a select number of suppliers?
5. Does the innovation require heavy customization for the majority of corporate consumers?
6. Are suppliers having trouble identifying references due to early adoption?
7. Is the innovation being talked about at conferences but not picked up by social media?

8. Have science or engineering journals recently published information on how the technology works?
9. Was the innovation, product, service, or interaction launched within the last year?
10. Are functional market studies limited to prototypes with primarily proofs-of-concept?

If some or many of these questions result in an affirmative response, the innovation is going through the Innovation Trigger. Pay close attention. This phase is often quick and lasts typically only one to two years.

Phase 2: Peak of Inflated Expectations

The Peak of Inflated Expectations occurs when everyone is talking about the innovation, and the innovation is covered in a variety of industry magazines. The innovations are technically stable but require heavy customization, driving up commercial prices for access to the first-generation technology. This is the stage at which the early adopters take action. Suppliers work hard to monopolize distribution channels, and mass-media hype begins. Industry thought leaders claim the innovation can work across industries and solve an extremely wide range of business problems. While significant improvements were made over the first-generation, price and performance don't match the inflated expectations.

DNA SEQUENCING

New regulations may have transpired that create a challenging environment for the innovation to thrive into greater adoption. Several innovations require an extremely long incubation period, as in the case of precision medicine. The first DNA sequencing started in the early 1970s, but this was slow and extremely costly, which prevented scaling to benefit population health. By the 1990s, many new methods of DNA sequencing were developed and, by 2000, these processes were implemented commercially by DNA sequencers (a scientific instrument used to automate the DNA sequencing process).

Next-generation sequencing is high-throughput DNA sequencing, which sequences millions or billions of DNA strands in parallel, decreasing the need for the fragment-cloning methods used in Sanger genome sequencing and improving the speed critical for patient usability. The cost to sequence your DNA is decreasing. According to the National Human Genome Research Institute, the cost per genome in 2001 was $100 million. By 2007 that was down to $10 million, and, in 2020, the cost was between $100 and $1,000. In the case of mapping the human genome, it took almost 50 years.

Here are 10 questions to assess whether a technology is in the Peak of Inflated Expectations phase.

1. Have companies gone public to announce that the innovation or technology was unusable?
2. Are companies considering the technology for early-adopter advantages?
3. Are trade shows and conferences focused specifically around the innovation or technology potential?
4. Have the number of suppliers that carry the innovation started to rapidly expand?
5. Are suppliers able to show specific client examples in which customer benefits were realized?
6. Have marketing campaigns for technology and consulting companies focused on their "expertise" in this area with a fog of non-specific marketing slogans?
7. Does there appear to be a bubble in which expectations don't align with the current stage of the innovation's potential?
8. Has the press covered the innovation from top to bottom?
9. Are companies aligning their campaigns around the innovation?

10. Have a number of innovation success stories emerged that are recycled throughout the media?

Phase 3: The Trough of Disillusionment

The Trough of Disillusionment phase indicates waning curiosity. The technology failed to meet expectations. At this point, the press has zero interest in covering the topic or technology. The technology is locked in a closet and not being talked about, because it's out of fashion. Early adopters that were initially excited about the technology's potential have lost patience waiting for results that never materialized.

Innovators desperately look for new success stories—but there are none. A reexamination of those early stories discovers cracks and potentially inappropriate uses of the technology. The technology has lost creditability due to overinflated expectations.

SLIDING INTO THE TROUGH

Although the technology slides into the trough, early corporate adopters can squeeze out benefits if applied with precision to impact business outcomes. The slower pace of adoption drives supply-chain consolidation. This consolidation is visible across the four primary levels that must be effectively coordinated and integrated to improve organizational operational performance: buy (purchasing), make (operations), move (logistics), and sell (marketing). R&D teams decrease in size. New innovations are slow to be incorporated into the product, and addressing specific customer challenges is the norm. Creating distribution channels to potential corporate consumers is the focus. The voice of marketing becomes quieter.

It's popular to repeat the Drucker mantra of, "Do what you do best and outsource the rest." However, not all companies have this option or can afford to leverage it. The result is they are stuck fixing the problems. Let's assume Microsoft

Dynamics isn't practical, and a SAP end-to-end solution is out of the budget. As an organization, how do we achieve operational performance? The answer is, we get creative and look to innovation.

A review of technology as it slides into the Trough of Disillusionment, tell us that it will take years before real productivity gains are realized.

Companies run out of steam selling the idea of "uncovering hidden insights." The Trough of Disillusionment can mean the technology doesn't work. However, more commonly, the stage is a sign that the technology will take longer to mature to become commercial grade. 3D printing is a good example.

3D-PRINTING

The potential applications for 3D printing are almost limitless. Hushang Tengda in Bejing, China printed a 400-meter-square villa on site in 45 days. The Institute of Advance Architecture of Catalonia in Barcelona, Spain used an army of robots that build as a unit, removing limitations associated with a single large printer, with the ability to create skyscrapers. INNOprint, in Nantes, France, has mastered emergency accommodations, leveraging printers to create shelters ready to go in 30 minutes. MX3D, in Amsterdam, Netherlands, created a 3D-printed steel bridge across a canal. 3D printing is solving simple challenges such as producing a piping hot pizza and starting to tackle more challenging problems. NASA isn't interested in creating Space Age food. It's interested in the ability to create a tool on demand in space. That concept is a bit distant, so let's make this more personal.

America's population, on average, is getting older. The population of Americans age 65 and older is forecast to more than double from 46 million in 2016 to over 98 million by 2060 (Mather, 2016). Education levels are increasing, life expectancy is on the rise, and older adults are working longer. Inevitably, at some point, we all need healthcare. Surgery is about to dramatically change. Soon doctors will have the ability to scan a patient and print a life-size model of a patient's organ—for example, a heart—to allow a surgeon to identify where they must operate and anticipate future complications. 3D printing will give doctors the ability to review medical problems much like an architect views building plans in 3D (Conner-Simons, 2015). Is 3D printing an indicator of the reversal of the Industrial Revolution—a shift from mass production to individualized manufacturing on demand? China may have to cede its title as the world's manufacturing powerhouse (Morrissey, 2015).

3D printing will introduce new business models and design freedoms to create a flexible manufacturing system with personalized products (PA Consulting Group, 2016). 3D printing is disrupting traditional business paradigms, and digital technology is an anchor for the fourth Industrial Revolution, altering the way we live, work, and relate to one another (Accenture, 2016; Schwab, 2015). The fourth Industrial Revolution—a digital revolution—will blur the physical, digital, and biological spheres.

Before 3D printing climbs out of the trough, three obstacles must be solved that prevent its broad adoption: (1) organizational readiness, (2) software automation, and (3) labor-force experience (Heller, 2014).

This is the phase where, if you believe in the technology, you should double down on initial investments. Experience pays, so be very selective. Opportunity does exist for the informed early adopter.

Here are 10 questions to assess whether a technology is in the Trough of Disillusionment phase:

1. Have the media and press lost interest in the technology?
2. Are early adopters disappointed with early trials?
3. Have startups that initially launched the technology into the market started to thin out?

4. Has investor capital all but evaporated in the space for new companies touting the same wares?
5. Are user interfaces improving access to the underlying technology benefits?
6. Do weak monetization models exist around the technology?
7. Technology must slide in and out of the Trough of Disillusionment to reach the Plateau of Productivity. Does the technology look like it may find its way out of the trough?
8. Is the market questioning the validity of the technology for industry transformation?
9. New technology generates new questions. Are suppliers refocusing on what's truly important about the technology?
10. Have expensive attempts to make the technology work become expensive public failures?

Technologies that reach the Plateau of Productivity each painfully walked through the Trough of Disillusionment. How deep the technology falls into the trough will depend on the skepticism of the pundits.

Phase 4: The Slope of Enlightenment

The Slope of Enlightenment is the phase before the technology becomes useful. When the technology is more mature, and initial expectations find traction, it's started to ascend the Slope of Enlightenment.

Often at this phase, the initially weak value propositions become solidified, in part as a result of the now second- and third-generation products appearing with shortened delivery cycles to provide higher-quality products with improved features. This increase in the volume and quality of newly released features help to fuel education about the technology. While the press has stopped covering the technology innovations, the cadence of new features keeps the technology in the mind of decision makers.

How do companies endure through the Slope of Enlightenment? Integration. Gathering insights into broader markets. Stepping back and looking at the four components of growth segmentation:

1. Total Available Market (TAM)
2. Serviced Available Market (SAM)
3. Service Obtainable Market (SOM)
4. Target Available Market (TAM).

Sustainable penetration into a Target Available Market requires analysis of the broader picture. The alignment of business impact, financial impact, and social impact reinforces the value proposition. In context, the ability to demonstrate business value demands collaboration and, ultimately, vendor integration—e.g.; open-source compatibility.

When experiences are improving, and both startup leaders and incumbents have announced their offering in this technological space, that means the technology is climbing the Slope of Enlightenment.

VIRTUAL REALITY

One practical example of the Slope of Enlightenment is virtual reality. The divergence from TV networks and the convergence toward live streaming is a symbol of the 2020 sports fan. The development of new state-of-the-art stadiums will radically shift how fans experience sports games. Sony and Oculus revolutionized game day with virtual reality (VR) in 2016, and the game experience of today will be unrecognizable to the 2020 sports fan. The fans, players, and coaches are beginning to grasp how disruptive this will be to sports and smile at the enormous potential for growth for new distribution experiences. Are fans getting the content they can't get at home? Is the consumer delivery mechanism reflective of a COVID-19 enabled global environment? If fans receive new content, that's real value, and draws more fans into each game.

A report (Future of Sports) mentioned that cord-cutting is popular with millennials and that 25 percent of late millennials went completely cable-free within the last 12 months. Is this the death of broadcasting? Meanwhile, fans are being priced out of live sporting events. With the introduction of Bitcoin and other cryptocurrencies, augmented reality (AR) will unleash a new world of virtual, real-time sports betting. Fans won't need to have cable TV to experience this new, virtual, game day. Fans will want to share these new experiences. Forget about the wooden seats of yesteryear; soon, new state-of-the-art seat sensory upgrades will be offering (4DX) including motion, smell, wind, heat/cold, and other sensations, enriching the experience of watching the game at the stadium.

Disruption starts slowly. If you're paying attention, small cracks in the foundation of normal will be visible. Observance of these slow-forming cracks is contingent on awareness. Most of us are too busy chasing rabbits to notice slow transformational change occurring in the sports experience or your customers' experiences. If you pay attention, you'll spot it.

Here are 10 questions to assess whether a technology is in the Slope of Enlightenment phase:

1. Has early feedback of the product resulted in significant improvements in its adaptability; e.g., scale, switching cost, or functionality?
2. Have providers started to be more inclusive with the range of tools they offer within the core suites; e.g., early products that were feed-based are now inside the core feature set?
3. When evaluating cost, is there more benchmark data from companies to illustrate hypothetical, ongoing cost savings?

4. Have vendor-to-vendor integrations started to occur?
5. Are vendors able to demonstrate business value based on hard metrics from previous experimentations or proof-of-concept engagements?
6. Is company data tied to outcomes the technology solves?
7. Have the majority of incumbents publicly launched their market offerings for the technology?
8. Are open-source frameworks a hot topic when discussions of vendor-capability comparisons are raised?
9. Are newly released features exceeding initial expectations?
10. Is the possibility of huge potential for other industries beginning to create interest?

Phase 5: The Plateau of Productivity

The Plateau of Productivity is achieved when mainstream adoption of the technology is attained. The most obvious evidence of a technology clearly venturing into the Plateau of Productivity phase is scale. At this point, companies are supporting thousands or millions of users leveraging the technology.

Questions quickly shift from scale to timing. Respected publications have been consistently publishing about new scientific and technological advancements regarding the technology. Vendors quickly move solution discussions from custom and tailored to "out-of-the-box" and "commercial-off-the-shelf." The technology has matured. Customers are confident the technology works; there have been enough success stories to validate previous claims of successful outcomes.

PREDICTIVE ANALYTICS

While some technologies are entering the exciting Innovation Trigger phase of the Hype Cycle, predictive analytics is already resting comfortably in the Plateau of Productivity phase.

Predictive analytics is getting noticed by aerospace for maintenance, repair, and overhaul (MRO). Canned and ad hoc reports are legacy terms at Airbus. Airbus's Aircraft Maintenance Analysis (Airman) is a real-time, aircraft health-monitoring system that transmits warnings to ground control and is already used by hundreds of customers. In comparison, Boeing's Airplane Health Management (AHM) is leveraged across 2,000 aircraft supporting 53 customers, providing insights on aircraft availability. Experts believe that predictive analytics for aircraft maintenance will reduce maintenance budgets by 20-40%. In an aircraft, lack of data is never a problem. Today, this data is used for flight-monitoring, and tomorrow it could be used for predictive maintenance.

Here are 10 questions to assess whether a technology is in the Plateau of Productivity phase:

1. Is the technology trusted?
2. Have COTS solutions started to emerge or become the norm?
3. Are larger companies acquiring smaller innovation startups to "buy innovation" capabilities for their shops?
4. Have initially niche markets that began as industry-specific expanded into multiple-industry sectors?
5. Is research more available that highlights not only success stories but success stories across industries?
6. Is scale of existing user bases at thousands or millions instead of tens or hundreds of customers?
7. Are clear leaders rising from the market that command large or majority share of markets?
8. Have specialized products started to mature around the core technology; e.g., as in the case of cloud SaaS, BPaaS, and aPaaS?
9. Has the technology reached mainstream adoption?
10. Is terminology commonplace; e.g., texting, blogging, and googling?

If we consider that blockchain's Innovation Trigger Phase started in 2014—based on when serious investors began to weigh in—the phases of the blockchain Hype Cycle would be the following: Innovation Trigger (2014-2015), Peak of Inflated Expectations (2016 to 2020), Trough of Disillusionment (2021 to 2030), Slope of Enlightenment (beginning 2030), and, lastly, the Plateau of Productivity (if applicable, after 2030).

If you're looking for additional sources on the Hype Cycle, Jackie Fenn and Mark Raskino have an excellent book titled, *Mastering the Hype Cycle: how to Choose the Right Innovation at the Right Time.*

The Hype Cycle Research Methodology highlighted the phases of the Hype Cycle on emerging and collaborative tech. It could be argued that the Hype Cycle isn't a cycle, and that outcomes don't depend on the nature of the technology itself or that it's less than scientific in nature without accounting for changes over time of the speed at which technology develops. However, it does effectively show how society feels about new technology and when historically inflated expectations and disenchantments should likely occur.

Conclusion

Why do we care about a Hype Cycle? It's been discussed more than almost any other innovation concept in everything from articles to research papers to books. Why are we still talking about it? Because the concept offers a framework for innovation.

Is the market or product being adopted on the rise in its lifecycle, or is that same offering reaching maturation and at the end of its lifecycle? In your company, you have products, services, and interactions. Nothing new. Have you taken the time to model or chart those entities to determine which are due to be replaced? Likely no.

Do you want to know what will have the greatest effect on your company or organization? Begin with the products, services, and interactions that will be required. A great way to do this is by analyzing which products are due to be replaced.

CHAPTER 11

EMBRACING THE THREAT OF INNOVATION

"Entrepreneurs always pitch their idea as 'the X of Y,' so this is going to be 'the Microsoft of food.' And yet disruptive innovations usually don't have that character. Most of the time, if something seems like a good idea, it probably isn't."

— ERIC RIES

Chapter Objectives

After reading this chapter, readers will be able to:

- Explain the relationship of RPA to process re-engineering, intelligence automation, artificial intelligence, cognitive intelligence, autonomics, and machine learning.
- Identify the importance of the shift from transactional to analytical.
- Explain the top benefits of RPA.
- Identify tools that are leveraged in RPA engineering and innovation initiatives.
- Explain the advantages of robotics and autonomous systems.
- Explain why blockchain has the potential to influence innovations of the future.

Robotic Process Automation

Autonomics and multi-agent systems will be applied in healthcare to definable, repeatable, and rule-based processes. Robotic process automation (RPA) will be a competitive advantage, not replacing humans but enabling them.

Autonomics, which ultimately aims to develop computer systems capable of self-management, was started by IBM in 2001. These self-regulating autonomic components are driving the research of multi-agent systems (MAS). MAS are computerized systems composed of multiple, interacting, intelligent agents within an environment. Robotic process automation is capable of automating activities (by creating software agents) that once required human judgment. This is the evolution of automation—the automation of automation.

Transactional to Analytics

In 1990, traditional onshore labor was the norm. By 2000, offshore labor was ripping through every industry. Huge cost savings were realized in shifting from the traditional onshore model to an offshore model. The subsequent revolution of digital labor is called "no shore." This robotic process automation is an autonomic, self-learning, and self-healing system.

The Institute for Robotic Process Automation (IRPA) published an excellent report highlighting the top 10 benefits of robotic process automation that cross industries.

1. **Decreased operational costs** – no-shore models (digital software agents)
2. **Improved data analytics** – tasks executed by robots allow for analysis
3. **Increased regulatory compliance** – steps are tracked, traceable, and documented
4. **Increased efficiency** – software robots never need time off

5. **Higher employee productivity** – software agents address repetitive functions, freeing workers to participate in more value-added activities
6. **Improved accuracy** – employees are human, and all humans make mistakes
7. **Increased customer satisfaction** – decreased errors build deeper customer relationships, improving retention and customer happiness
8. **IT support and management** – it's easier to scale software than it is people
9. **Logistical upside** – minimize or eliminate complications with offshore labor
10. **RPA and business processors** – presentation-layer automation software, mimicking the steps of rules-based non-subjective processes

Automation Process Cycle

When do labor efficiencies become labor elimination? To better understand how RPA can enable your organization, we first need to identify the five phases of the automation process cycle:

1. **Manual execution** – one-off, non-repeatable processes
2. **Scripting** – linear tasks, standard and repeatable
3. **Orchestration** – activities that are complex, standard, and multi-scripted
4. **Autonomics** – dynamic processes that are non-standard, contextual, and inference-based
5. **Cognitive** – self-aware systems that are predictive, self-learning, and self-healing

If we want our employees engaged in activities that involve personal interactions, problem-solving, and decision making, we first need to get them out of tedious and repetitive activities.

What if you were told a new team member would be joining your team? You're not sure where they're geographically located, but you manage to get some intel from your colleague. You're told this new person never complains, doesn't want a desk, never needs coaching, and loves daily performance reviews. This is the resume of the modern robot, a leader in process automation. The competition just got stiffer.

Multi-Agent Systems

Robotic process automation begins with an understanding of agents. Typically, multi-agent systems refer to software agents, but these systems could equally be robots or hybrid robot-and-human teams.

There are three primary types of agents: passive agents (simple—agents without goals), active agents (advanced—agents with simple goals), and cognitive agents (complex—with complex calculations and activities). The environments in which these types of agents reside can be divided into three categories: virtual, discrete, and continuous. Also, each agent environment has one or more associative properties:

1. **Accessibility** – when possible, to gather complete information about the environment
2. **Determinism** – whether an action performed in the environment causes a definite effect
3. **Dynamics** – the number of entities that influence the environment at the moment
4. **Discreteness** – whether the number of possible actions in the environment is finite
5. **Episodicity** – whether agent actions in certain time periods influence other periods
6. **Dimensionality** – whether spatial characteristics are important factors of the environment and the agent considers space in its decision-making

Transparency Market Research predicted that the global IT robotic automation market would be worth USD $4.98 billion by 2020. Robotic automation is a powerful alternative to offshore outsourcing. It's curious how these processes managed to escape automation. Regardless, there are many areas where RPA can be applied to healthcare including account management, claims processing, underwriter support, customer support, billing, collections, reconciliation, and reporting and analytics consolidation.

RPA Applied

The HfS Blueprint Report helps us identify precisely where RPA can be applied within the healthcare ecosystem:

1. **Claims administration** – claims adjudication and processing, payment integrity complaints, and appeals
2. **Member management** – account setup, eligibility, enrollment, billing, benefit management, and customer service
3. **Provider management** – provider credentialing, provider data management, contracting audits, and network management
4. **Health and care management** – population health and wellness, utilization management, care coordination and case management, and remote monitoring
5. **Administration** – finance, accounting, and training

Intelligent automation is entering the business world, and CFOs are happy, because RPA is delivering the promised cost savings. However, cost-only value propositions are no longer attractive to top executives. They're looking for cost-plus value propositions (transactional plus judgment-intensive plus analytics). Global labor arbitrage, the disintegration of barriers to international trade, or moving to where costs of doing business are low is no longer sufficient. In this quest for greater cost-plus value propositions, technology plays a critical role.

Start by understanding where repetitive tasks hurt your organization. First, identify the opportunity; second, validate the opportunity; third, design the mode; and fourth, deploy a pilot. Health plans and providers are discovering software agents as a cost-effective alternative to enhancing or replacing platforms.

The conversation has expanded beyond cost reduction to quality, engagement, and innovation. This new phase of sourcing will engage and manage resources to shift workers from mundane tasks to activities with deeper customer interactions.

Innovators are using robotics process automation to drive the next stage of transformation—at affordable costs. Robotic process automation isn't coming soon; it's here.

Medical Robotics

Star dusted predictions get everyone talking, separating the mythical from the magical in robotics healthcare.

Robotics health threatens to challenge how patient care and treatment are performed, redefining the word "preventive." All too often, we hear about the benefits of mobile or 3D printing, but how often do you hear about medical nanobots or nanomites? The average life expectancy of Americans is increasing. In 1960, the average life expectancy in the U.S. was 69.8 years. That rose to 75.2 years in 1990, and today it's around 78.8 years, according to the Centers for Disease Control and Prevention (CDC). New approaches to medicine and treatment are no longer optional, they're essential. Robotic health offers some answers.

From telemedicine (clinical healthcare at a distance) to bioelectronics (stimulation and monitoring of the nervous system), the health ecosystem is evolving quickly. The greatest medical achievement in the last 100 years is the advancement of personal genome sequencing mapped to repositories of population diseases—introducing the migration from population health to personal genome diagnosis, i.e. the N-of-1: one patient, one trial. Combine this with nanobots, and we have a world in which nanoids, nanites, nanomachines, and nanomites all reference nanomachines and nanomotors. This means biological machines could be used to identify and destroy cancer cells. In this future world, disease isn't a setback but merely a distraction, like a low-oil light. The car isn't sick. It just needs a repair or tune-up, and it's back on the road.

Medical nanotechnology is expected to employ nanorobots that will be injected into the patient to perform work at a cellular level. Ingestibles and internables bring forward the introduction of broadband-enabled digital tools that are consumed by the patient and "smart" pills that use wireless technology to help monitor internal reactions to medications.

Medical nanotechnology is just the edge of the cliff. Let's jump off.

Dermables—digital stickers for the skin—open up a vast range of possibilities. Netatmo's JUNE bracelet adds some class to UV monitoring, and UVSunSense makes monitoring sun exposure fun.

"The day before something is a breakthrough, it's a crazy idea."

— PETER DIAMANDIS

Why don't we hear about these advancements in robotics every day? How come the population isn't demanding small pilots that will undoubtedly extend life? I honestly don't know.

We can start by understanding the stakeholders in robotic health. Hint: They're not only the mad scientists in labs looking for new breakthroughs. They're your wife, husband, daughter, son, grandmother, or grandfather. These are the stakeholders, and they all have a similar goal—to stay healthy.

A draft journal article by Simshaw, Terry, Hauser, and Cummings titled, "Regulating Healthcare Robots in the Hospital and the Home," suggests that family members and their caregivers, healthcare providers, technology providers, and aging or physically challenged individuals have similar goals. Their collective goal is to provide independence, preserve dignity, empower those with special needs, and provide peace of mind to all the stakeholders. These stakeholders' goals are aligned, despite how rare aligned stakeholder goals might be.

The "Healthcare Robotics 2015-2020: Trends, Opportunities & Challenges" report was released by the *Robotics Business Review*. This report provided strategic information on the global robotics industry. The findings were intriguing and helped segment the robotic health market.

In the search for the value of medical robotics, there are three main areas of robotic health:

1. **Direct patient care robots**: surgical robots (used for performing clinical procedures), exoskeletons (for bionic extensions of the self, like the Ekso suit), and prosthetics (replacing lost limbs). Over 500 people a day lose a limb in America, with two million Americans living with limb loss, according to the CDC.

2. **Indirect patient care robots**: pharmacy robots (autonomous robots that perform inventory control, reducing labor costs), delivery robots (providing medical goods throughout a hospital autonomously), and disinfection robots (interacting with people with known infectious diseases such as healthcare-associated infections or HAIs).

3. **Home healthcare robots**: robotic telepresence solutions (addressing the aging population with robotic assistance).

In January 2016, the Population Reference Bureau report, "Aging in the United States," showed that Americans 65 and older will more than double moving from 46 million in 2016 to 98 million by 2060. The 65-and-older population is projected to grow from 15 percent of Americans to nearly 24 percent. Who will take care of the influx of aging individuals when timely healthcare today is already questionable?

Medical robots will change healthcare. They have to.

Benefits of RPA

Cognitive automation technologies are changing our business. RPA is the first step in that evolution. Be part of the business-value realization with RPA.

Robotic process automation is the game changer your organization doesn't know about. There are only a few leaders in your organization who fully appreciate the potential of RPA. The hype about RPA reminds me of the hype about the Internet in the mid-1990s. We knew it was going to take off, but we didn't know where or how this idea of knowledge-sharing would be adopted.

RPA applies AI and machine-learning capabilities to perform a repeatable task that previously required humans to perform.

Similar to the concept of a blockchain, a large part of the slow adoption of this technology is related to education. Once you've internalized the power of RPA, you'll quickly apply RPA-type concepts throughout your organization.

RPA isn't a physical robot. It won't deliver your FedEx package with a smile. It's also not going to delivery your Amazon package in an air taxi on Sunday. The beauty of RPA is that it can automate activities based on rules and relieve your team of the burden of performing manual processes. Processes that are manual, repetitive, and have high error rates are where RPA excels.

RPA does three things well:

1. It reduces cost.
2. It improves quality.
3. It improves operational controls.

It doesn't matter whether you're using Blue Prism, Work-Fusion, Kryon Systems, UiPath, Automation Anywhere, or NICE. Each of these tools can help you realize better business outcomes.

Let me guess. You need to improve business outcomes quantifiably. You're searching for that 10x game changer for next year. You already promised business leaders some magic, and you have no idea where that magic powder will come from. Not to fear.

RPA has some fascinating applications for the next-generation CIO.

RPA FOR ADVANCED ANALYTICS

Building a data lake? RPA can help. Starting a data-enablement initiative? RPA can help. RPA streamlines and automates time-consuming, high-volume, and repetitive activities. Big data requires data aggregation, curation, data cleansing, normalization, data wrangling, and tagging of metadata.

RPA offers amazing benefits to enable advanced analytics:

- Removing the need to rekey data sets manually
- Migration of data
- Data validation
- Producing accurate reports from your data
- Providing the foundation for an action framework: "good to know" (within tolerances), "interesting" (better than expected), or "need to act" (action required)
- Aggregating social-media statistics
- Processing mining technology to visualize the actual process
- Ingesting from acquired sources
- Linking systems to systems (APIs)

- Assessing data rules for accuracy, consistency, validity, timeliness, and accessibility
- Conducting data deduplication
- Scraping data from websites
- Performing vendor master-file updates
- Performing data extraction
- Creating advanced-processing algorithms
- Formatting

RPA can handle even the most complex environments. If you're able to record and play the activities, RPA can be a welcome operational improvement.

RPA FOR BUSINESS-PROCESS REMOVAL

Data integration is the initiative that never gets finished. Somewhere along that last mile to fully automating the integration of those systems, there's either no budget available or no interest. RPA can pick up and connect that last mile, removing waste in the process. RPA will be leading the next wave of increased productivity, and it can help tackle the eight major types of transaction-processing waste:

- Defects; e.g., highlighting missed deadlines or overspend
- Overproduction; e.g., extending reporting based on the severity
- Waiting; e.g., waiting for approvals
- Non-utilized talent; e.g., issuing and tagging training to employees when necessary based on events
- Transportation; e.g., facilitating handoff between functions—like when an approval system isn't talking to the PO and invoicing system
- Inventory; e.g., processing data for entry into a larger system
- Motion; e.g., removing repetitive keystrokes when switching between applications

- Extra processing; e.g., formatting reports, adding details

RPA is disrupting digital transformation and operational excellence. RPA's fast and inexpensive approach to automation saves labor, extends capacity, increases speed, and improves accuracy.

RPA FOR PROJECT, PROGRAM, AND PORTFOLIO MANAGEMENT

Haven't heard of RPA and project management in the same sentence? News flash: RPA isn't going to replace the human need for project managers.

Managing project budgets, monitoring risks, and balancing resource capacity all are functions central to the role of program and project managers. RPA can freshen up the definition of the standard of what's deemed "good" when it comes to IT portfolio management. There are multiple ways in which automation minimizes risks and can streamline portfolio-management activities. Here are the big hitters:

- Create multi-thread, digital approvals for statements of work
- Generate contracts using the company's "gold standard"
- Automate the creation and distribution of portfolio reports
- Generate documents
- Push communication of project variances
- Balance resources; e.g., reporting on utilization and reallocating resources
- Reduce the dependence on spreadsheets to manage information
- Answer the question, "Are we on track?"
- Collect and disseminate project-specific information
- Screen, filter, and track candidates for the recruitment process

212

- Create financial-scenario modeling based on thresholds
- Automate data ingestion for dashboards; e.g., Power-BI or Clarity PPM
- Provide sensors to continuously identify progress wins and capture value delivered
- Forecast based on historical data
- Assure PMO policy adherence; e.g., process documentation and project audits
- Automate project and program SDLC process-step progression

RPA can play an important role in your IT portfolio ecosystem. The short duration (1-2 months) and low investment cost ($50-100k) make an RPA pilot an easy win for your organization. RPA makes quantifying improvements easy. This metric-driven approach simplifies business-partner discussions when outcomes are immediate and visible.

RPA FOR ASSET MANAGEMENT

Do you know when your licenses are due for renewal? RPA and AI will transform IT asset management (ITAM). The nature of IT asset management is repetitive and standard. This taps directly into the sweet spot for RPA. Several applications exist for RPA within IT asset management. Here are the most impactful:

- Automate software audits
- Compare licenses purchased to licenses contracted
- Manage source-code control
- Oversee vendor and resource onboarding and offboarding; e.g., delete domain users or modify distribution lists
- Provide reporting and analysis
- Manage incident resolution; e.g., server restarts, password resets, etc.

- Self-heal; e.g., system health checks, automating back-ups, and event monitoring
- Automate fulfillment processes; e.g., IT asset requests

RPA won't fix your broken workflows, but it can help automate them to ensure human errors are removed and process-cycle time is reduced. You'll still need to spend time fixing the gaps in the process, but intelligent automation can integrate data extremely well from disparate data systems.

RPA FOR FINANCIAL MANAGEMENT (PROCUREMENT-TO-PAYMENT)

Financial processes are riddled with searching, transferring, sweeping, copying, pasting, sorting, and filtering. Financial-process automation will improve relationships with your suppliers and internal partners as well as improve efficiencies within the finance department. RPA can be used to validate contract terms against invoices and validate that standard data such as addresses and billing information hasn't changed in recent invoices.

While the most obvious benefits are around financial risk and controls, cutting down on manual processes often presents even more positive organizational impacts. Freeing up overworked and overcapacity financial leaders can improve morale. By shifting resources from mundane, tactical activities to strategic, high-value-added activities like performing analysis and predictive modeling, RPA can become a force multiplier for financial-management teams. Let's look at a few of the many use cases for RPA for financial management:

- Supporting the quarterly close
- Calculating and anticipating accruals based on real, invoiced (and what's not invoiced) data
- Moving data from Excel to readable reports
- Uploading transaction data from various financial systems
- Generating standard journal entries

- Identifying atypical and exceptional spending
- Calculating and processing annual vendor rebates
- Communicating to vendors missing or late invoices
- Tracking vendor adherence to billing policies and best practices
- Autoloading quarterly forecasts into the financial system of record
- Reconciling forecast to actuals for departmental category spend
- Monitoring CapEx and OpEx forecasts to actuals variance

Operational financial and accounting processes are great examples of where RPA can shine. These processes often are repetitive and typically result in human error of some kind. Financial review prep, interdepartmental reconciliation, and financial planning and analysis all present opportunities for automation.

RPA FOR SECURITY

Protecting an organization from cyberattacks is a 24/7 job. The problem is that humans need sleep. RPA can humanize the role of the CISO and, almost more importantly, the role of cybersecurity managers. By leveraging RPA, we allow the function of the CISO to "get to human" by being visible in projects, developing organizational relationships, and inspiring new leadership. This isn't possible when resources are consumed by cyberthreat prevention and mitigation at all hours of the night. RPA can strengthen and simplify your security operations in multiple ways:

- Deploy security orchestration, automation, and response to improve security management
- Shut down unauthorized privileged access
- Robotic security and password configurations are encrypted and can't be accessed by company personnel

215

- Identify and prevent zero-day attacks
- Cyber antispam (non-threat-driven spam)
- Cyberthreat identification, bot creation, and threat cleansing
- Filter out false-positive threats
- Issue consistent credentials enterprise-wide
- Automate password rotation
- Review 100% of access violations in near real-time
- Improve security and auditing of data
- Implement intelligent automation using artificial intelligence; e.g., creating tickets in ServiceNow based on threat analysis and immediately shutting down that risk
- Identify atypical user and machine actions based on behavioral analysis
- Lower the cost to detect and respond to breaches
- Rapidly detect, analyze, and defend against cyberattacks
- Identify behaviors that are unlikely to represent human actions

AI-enabled cybersecurity is increasingly necessary. The volumes of end-point data are exploding, and our budgets are not. Organizations need to turn to RPA as threats overwhelm security analysts. Detection, prediction, and response can all benefit from applying RPA to transform your organization's cyber defense.

INTELLIGENCE AUTOMATION SHARES THE WORKLOAD

Becoming more strategic starts when you stop spending all your time on tactical activities. That's a difficult process when these tactical activities are required to keep our businesses running day-to-day.

Step beyond simply establishing an RPA center of excellence (COE). First, find the early adopters (the believers). These are the folks that push normal off the table and continually challenge what worked okay yesterday. Second, be collaborative. Seek out cross-functional leaders that you can educate to be champions in the pilot. Third, identify a problem. Focus in on a specific business challenge and articulate a business case where RPA is fit-for-purpose. Quickly move from a proof of concept (POC) that takes 2-3 weeks to a proof of value (POV) that takes 6 weeks.

Blockchain, cognitive analytics, augmented reality, and robotics all present huge and largely untapped opportunities for organizations. Your business model is changing. Be part of the change. Ideate together. Adopt quickly. Embrace the total value of ownership and apply RPA to accelerate business value.

RPA PLANNING AND TOOL SELECTION

RPA leaders know that doing more with less starts with improvements in accuracy, cycle time, and increased productivity of the existing workforce.

To discover trapped value, you need to know where to look. The rapid economic justification that robotic process automation (RPA) holds is alluring. Starting to explore the potential of RPA begins with a grouping of the software and tools that make up the RPA landscape. Let's start at base camp.

There are two main base camps at Mount Everest, each on opposite sides of the mountain. The South Base Camp is in Nepal at an altitude of 17,598 feet. The North Base Camp is in Tibet at an altitude of 16,900 feet. Each base camp is used for climbing different routes. When climbing the southeast ridge, the South Base Camp is used and, when climbing the northeast ridge, the North Base Camp is leveraged. About 800 people successfully reach the 29,029-foot summit of Mount Everest each year.

There are many situations in which we desire to reach the summit—ranging from mountaineering expeditions for exploration, sports, science, or even philanthropic fundraising.

Any of the 18 different climbing routes on Everest can get you to the top, with the South Col and the Northeast Ridge Standard being the most popular.

RPA isn't much different. Begin by getting acclimated to the software landscape. Plan and choose a route. Hire a professional guide. Let's dive into the potential tools you'll need for the trip.

RPA COMPANIES FOR BUSINESS-PROCESS MODELING AND FRONT OFFICE

UI Path, Blue Prism, and Automation Anywhere are software companies that dominate the RPA landscape. That doesn't mean there aren't many other tools that are worthy of bringing on the RPA journey to maximize your business results and RPA footprint.

RPA alone doesn't change how people work, but it does affect the productivity of those workers when applied intelligently. The same core RPA value proposition can be leveraged in the front and back office. This value proposition promises: Increased productivity. Low technical lift. Increased accuracy. Reduce costs.

The front office—with staff that interact with consumers—and the back office—with behind-the-scenes staff—both can benefit from the intelligence that RPA can offer. As CIOs, we're pushed to do more with less, and RPA quickly moves us to the forefront of our viable options.

RPA introduces the concept of uninterrupted resource pools. These RPA bots are configurable to scale limitlessly across time zones to automate respective tasks. By automating these often-tedious tasks, we increase manual productivity and create a happier and more efficient workforce. This is the essence of robotic process automation—automate the non-revenue-generating, repetitive activities to enable a more productive workforce.

There are several software offerings that provide solutions to tackle automation challenges of the front and back office. These include:

- be informed
- Connotate
- Contextor
- Exilant
- LivePerson
- Jacada
- NICE
- Pega
- Verint

be informed specializes in legacy integration to accelerate digital development. Connotate is dedicated to SaaS solutions and handling web data through managed services. Contextor, recently acquired by SAP, targets complex RPA situations by supporting attended and unattended RPA solutions. Exilant, part of QuEST, can bring automation to platform services such as IoT, cloud, security, blockchain, AI, MR, and mobility options. LivePerson, offers AI-powered chatbots, to automate up to 70% of messaging conversations on your website, SMS, Facebook Messenger, Apple Business Chat, and WhatsApp. Jacada narrows in on end-to-end customer-service automation. NICE is a major solution that delivers both desktop (attended) and server-side (unattended) automation, so employees can focus on productivity—not processing. Pega brings attention to interconnected organizational processes and end-to-end automation. Verint focuses on driving processing consistency and regulatory compliance with RPA.

Each of these industry players understands that revolutionary transformation is much bigger than deploying a few RPA bots. Transformation is about changing the values, beliefs, and behaviors of an organization. Front- and back-end RPA solutions start the conversation to increase capacity, drive compliance, and automate faster.

RPA COMPANIES FOR AUTOMATION

We're beginning to see a trend moving toward specialization in RPA software that's concentrated around the functions of a specific industry.

At the core, RPA creates digital factories to automate and integrate human activities that are administrative or repetitive in nature. RPA's appeal is that these digital factories can be created and destroyed in seconds, depending on the workflow and business logic that's been designed into the intelligent agents or bots.

Several companies have offerings that are making a difference and can handle a variety of business challenges regardless of industry. Improving unified testing, decreasing cycle time, and removing people from dull work are all possibilities that these software solutions can address:

- Automation Anywhere
- Blue Prism
- Jidoka
- Kryon Systems
- UiPath
- WorkFusion

Automation Anywhere creates a digital workforce with the same digital skillsets that employees have to interact with any system or application in the same way humans do. Blue Prism recently introduced an AI-powered supervisor in addition to design tools for human-digital collaboration, workforce management, and process automation. Jidoka, recently acquired by Appian (NASDAQ: APPN), is a world-class solution for workflow, AI, and RPA. Kryon Systems is a business-user-friendly platform that combines advanced IMR and OCR capabilities to record and execute processes on any application (including Citrix, web-based, legacy, and desktop)—without the need for integration (no connectors/API required). The UIPath platform simplifies digital transformation by rapidly automating processes end to end for hyper-automation. WorkFusion, a leading vendor of intelligence agent solutions, brings together AI, RPA and ML to generate new capabilities for business process automation.

These companies combine the process (business-process automation), the bot (software-intelligence agent), and the orchestrator (robot controller) to easily create bots to automate rules-driven business processes.

RPA COMPANIES FOR PRODUCTIVITY AND DESCISIONS

Operational excellence. Agile operations. Lean development. There's an RPA embedded in each of these buzzwords. RPA leaders are leveraging bots to increase employee engagement, bolster financial performance, and boost speed to market. CIOs are looking at organizations that consume RPA, which is a good indicator of digital maturity. RPA provides a competitive advantage by driving revenue higher, taking greater market share, and improving customer service.

RPA is destined to become more pervasive across all functions in the organization. The following companies are creating advancements in software to make that organizational climb easier:

- AntWorks
- Ayehu
- EnableSoft
- Epiance
- Ikarus
- Loopai
- OpenConnect
- PERPETUUITI
- Rimilia
- Softomotive
- T-Plan
- VisualCron

221

AntWorks is a platform for integrated artificial intelligence and intelligent automation powered by fractal science. Ayehu has platforms and managed-service-provider solutions to automate business processes to simultaneously retrieve all kinds of information about how those particular processes are carried out. EnableSoft, recently acquired by nintex, leverages trained bots to quickly and cost-effectively automate routine tasks without the use of code in an easy-to-use, drag-and-drop interface. Epiance is an industry-leading solution that taps into EpiGenie for building, assembling, and dashboarding project execution for individual robots. Ikarus is an AI platform for business-process automation. Loop AI introduced a platform incorporating robots that autonomously learn and reason to retrofit systems with one centralized cognitive platform. OpenConnect, recently acquired by AcitveOps Ltd., specializes in simplifying and optimizing the running of operations. PERPETUUITI is a platform for iBaaS (iBoT-as-a-Service) in which cognitive and capable bots automate a wide range of industry-specific operational and functional processes. Rimilia is the first and only AI-powered automation platform built to manage order-to-cash processes in real time. Softomotive emphasizes the smoothest RPA journey by making it easy to start small, learn quickly, and scale seamlessly. T-Plan's RPA Robot is the most flexible and universal black-box automation tool on the market, specializing in testing automation. VisualCron is an automation, integration, and task-scheduling tool for Windows.

These tools center around productivity and decisions to enhance and augment your human workforce. By integrating AI, ML, RPA, and analytics, repetitive business processes can be automated with intelligent and cognitively aware bots.

RPA LEADERS AND THE REST
Protiviti published a report on the average RPA spend based on RPA maturity level. Beginners were spending $1MM or less, intermediates were spending $1MM to $3.9MM, and

RPA leaders were spending $10MM or more. As you chart your path toward the RPA summit, where does your organization fit in to the maturity level? Are you a beginner, intermediate, or RPA leader?

What is Blockchain—in Five Minutes?

Are you struggling to understand how blockchain works, why blockchains are secure, or why blockchain technologies will transform the world? Here's a five-minute answer to all those questions.

As a leader in your organization, you have a duty to your organization to understand why blockchain technology will transform the economy.

WHY BLOCKCHAIN STARTED

The bursting of the U.S. housing bubble underpinned the global financial crisis of 2007-08 and caused the value of securities linked to the U.S. real estate to nosedive. Easy access to subprime loans and the overvaluation of bundled subprime mortgages all leaned on the theory that housing prices would continue to climb.

Ultimately, the Financial Crisis Inquiry Commission determined the entire financial crisis was avoidable and caused by widespread failures in financial regulation and supervision. There were many reasons for the financial crisis including subprime lending, the growth of the housing bubble, and easy credit conditions. The world believed that "trusted third parties" such as banks and financial institutions were dependable. Unfortunately, the global financial crisis proved intermediaries are fallible. The crisis resulted in evictions, foreclosures, and extended unemployment; it was considered the worst financial crisis since the Great Depression.

In response to this horrible global financial upheaval, in 2008, Satoshi Nakamoto wrote a paper titled, "Bitcoin: A Peer-to-Peer Electronic Cash System." The paper suggested that "trusted third parties" could be eliminated from financial transactions.

WHAT IS BITCOIN, AND HOW DOES IT RELATE TO BLOCKCHAIN?

Bitcoin is a peer-to-peer system for sending payments digitally signed to the entire Bitcoin network. When the "b" is capitalized, "Bitcoin" refers to that network, e.g., "I want to understand how the Bitcoin network operates." When the "b" isn't capitalized, the word "bitcoin" is used to describe a unit of account or currency, e.g., "I sent one bitcoin to a friend." The digital signature is made from public keys (given to anyone for sending assets) and private keys (held by the asset owner).

The public ledger of Bitcoin transactions is called a blockchain. Bitcoin also runs on top of a technology called blockchain. Blockchains are permissionless distributed databases or permissionless public records of transactions in chronological order. Blockchain technology creates a decentralized digital public record of transactions that's secure, anonymous, tamper-proof, and unchangeable—a shared single source of truth. Blockchains apply to any industry where information is transferred and roughly fall into the following six classifications:

1. **Currency** (electronic cash systems without intermediaries)
2. **Payment infrastructure** (remittance; sending money in payment)
3. **Digital assets** (exchange of information)
4. **Digital identity** (IDs for digitally signing to reduce fraud)
5. **Verifiable data** (verify the authenticity of information or processes)
6. **Smart contracts** (software programs that execute without "trusted third parties")

224

HOW BLOCKCHAINS WORK

For the first time in history, blockchain removes—or disintermediates—the middleman from business transactions and, by doing so, improves the value of existing products, services, and interactions in the following ways:

Preventing double spending: With blockchain, you can't spend money more than once. Blockchain presents a solution by ensuring the authenticity of any asset and preventing duplicate expenditures (real estate, medical claim, insurance, medical device, voting ballots, music, government records, or payments to program beneficiaries).

Establishing consensus: In this new model, crowds are networks of computers that work together to reach an agreement. Once 51% of the computers in the network agree, "consensus" has been reached, and the transaction is recorded in a digital ledger called the blockchain. The blockchain contains an infinite, ordered list of transactions. Each computer contains a full copy of the entire blockchain ledger. Therefore, if one computer attempts to submit an invalid transaction, the computers in the network wouldn't reach consensus (51% agreement), and the transaction wouldn't be added to the blockchain.

There are four principles of blockchain networks.

1. **Distributed**: Across all the peers participating in the network. Blockchain is decentralized, and every computer (full node) has a copy of the blockchain.
2. **Public**: The actors in a blockchain transaction are hidden, but everyone can see all transactions.
3. **Time-stamped**: The dates and times of all transactions are recorded in plain view.
4. **Persistent**: Because of consensus and the digital record, blockchain transactions can't catch fire, be misplaced, or get damaged by water.

STEPS TO CREATE A BLOCK (TRANSACTION)

Blocks are a record of transactions, and chains are a series of connected transactions (blocks).

1. **Create transaction**: A miner (computer) creates a block.
2. **Solve the puzzle**: A miner (computer) must do mathematical calculations and, if correct, will receive a "proof of work."
3. **Receive "proof of work:"** The proof of work is a piece of data that's difficult (costly, time-consuming) to produce but easy for others to verify and which satisfies certain requirements. In short, it's difficult to solve the puzzle but easy to verify it's solved correctly.
4. **Broadcast proof of work**: The miner broadcasts its successful proof of work to other miners.
5. **Verification**: Other miners verify the proof of work.
6. **Publish block**: If the miners reach consensus (51% agreement) that the proof the miner presented solved the puzzle, that transaction is published to the blockchain.

WHY ARE BLOCKCHAINS SECURE?

With blockchain technologies, truth can also be measured, and consumers and producers can prove data is authentic and uncompromised.

To create a new block—which we'll call block 101—some of the data is used (or a hash is created by an algorithm that turns an arbitrarily large amount of data into a fixed-length random number) from the previous block, block 100. To create the new block, block 102, information from block 101 is used, and so on. Each subsequent transaction is dependent on the prior transaction(s), similar to a light string on a Christmas tree. If a light bulb were pulled from the string (changing a transaction), the miner would have to change every previous transaction ever made in that string. Probabilistically, this is almost impossible, as not everyone would reach consensus on the proposed change.

The result is an immutable digital record for every agreed-upon transaction: a single source of truth.

WHY BLOCKCHAIN TECHNOLOGIES WILL CHANGE THE WORLD

Blockchain technologies will improve trust in industries where information (assets) is transferred, including these:

1. **Accounting** (auditing and fraud prevention)
2. **Aerospace** (location of parts and chain-of-custody)
3. **Energy** (smart metering and decentralized energy grid)
4. **Healthcare** (medical devices and health information interoperability)
5. **Finance** (remittance and currency exchange)
6. **Real estate** (deeds transfer and speed-buying or selling property)
7. **Education** (better managed assessments, credentials, transcripts)

Blockchain technologies will change everything—from the clothes you wear to the food you eat and even the products you buy.

Conclusion

It takes time to fully understand the potential of an innovation. You must read. Research is involved. And you must think. It's the thinking *after* we read that's done less often these days.

Why are we focused on multi-agent systems, robotic process automation, and blockchain? Each of these technologies and concepts has the potential for huge organizational transformation if leveraged to its full potential.

Are you familiar with the UIPath workflow for RPA? Is IPFS a familiar concept to you regarding blockchain? No?

This is the reading and additional depth of knowledge I challenge you to acquire. You don't need to be an expert. You do need to be aware that the technologies exist and how they apply to business.

So often, technologies that are in front of us have the potential to transform our business and the interactions with our customers. Yet, we do nothing. I'm here to tell you to do something. Start reading. Start exploring. Your mind will do the rest to start connecting dots you didn't even know existed.

CHAPTER 12

INNOVATION AS A STRATEGY

"However beautiful the strategy, you should occasionally look at the results."

— WINSTON CHURCHILL

Chapter Objectives

After reading this chapter, readers will be able to:

- Define strategy.
- Identify what is a strategy is what is not.
- Explain the four components of strategic alignment.
- Explain strategic vs. emergent innovation.
- Defend why strategic alignment drives change.

Strategic and Emergent Innovation

It's easy to overestimate your ability to rapidly build value. Building commercialization strategies helps to ensure sustainable competitive advantages with economic benefits. Strategies broadly fall into two categories: Corporate strategy, or, "where to compete," and business strategy, or, "how to compete." Often companies trip and fall awkwardly somewhere between where to compete and how. Today, we'll adjust that trip to more of a fashionable skip. Innovation strategies are emergent, not planned.

Articles that highlight concepts of strategy are plentiful, but there are few that define the boundary between having a strategy and not having one. Donald C. Hambrick and James W. Fredrickson help us identify what a strategy is not. Outsourcing is not a strategy. Being a low-cost provider is not a strategy. Chasing a global footprint is not a strategy. Surprisingly, operational effectiveness is also not a strategy. Then what is a strategy?

Strategy (n): the art of sustainable value creation to create unique competitive advantages to shape the perimeter of an organization.

Business strategy, operational strategy, marketing strategy, and financial strategy all slide into the dirty fishbowl known as strategy. A strategy is about how people throughout an organization should make decisions and allocate resources in order to accomplish key objectives. Hambrick and Fredrickson's five major elements of a strategy, when applied to innovation, make strategy determination straightforward. Ask yourself these questions to determine if you have an innovation strategy:

- How is the innovation adding new value to the core ecosystem interaction?

- Are we building value rapidly? Are we creating a new value chain or tapping an existing one?
- Is the product, service, or interaction unique, or can it be imitated?
- How does our innovation provide a sustainable competitive advantage?
- Have we established a viable economic model for scale?

While peering into the fishbowl of strategy, it's worth the time to assess whether your organization *has* a strategy. Innovation doesn't have to be planned—it can emerge under a strategy umbrella.

Henry Mintzberg was the first to come up with the concept of "emergent strategy." Emergent strategy, also called realized strategy, isn't intentional. In an article published in the *Stanford Social Innovation Review*, John Kania, Mark Kramer, and Patty Russell say that emergent strategy gives rise to constantly evolving solutions that are uniquely suited to the time, place, and participants involved. Emergent strategies can bend. They can break right off, and reconnect. They aren't linear and can reconnect to form unique, value-creating economic benefits.

Leaders track external and internal factors impacting shifts of customer behavior. Monitor these we should—they can impact strategy, business models, and operational approaches. Emergent strategies acknowledge that oversimplification kills innovation. For example, defining a product aligned to a specific market segment or attempting to create scale on a foundation of underskilled, overworked, and unmotivated resources are oversimplified strategies.

Curious if your organization is leveraging emergent innovation strategies? Answer these questions for a quick pulse:

1. Do you have a mechanism in place to "sense" environmental business-model changes?

2. Are there processes in place for interventions in response to exogenous events?
3. Have you established a co-creation approach for the next evolution of the innovation or interaction experience?
4. Is innovation predictable, or is the organization adapting and sensing as circumstances change over time—e.g., watching the competitors?
5. Is the company dependent on decision-making frameworks, or does the decision-system dynamic appreciate the human dynamics that can accelerate change?

Looking over your shoulder at competitors and copying innovation approaches will never result in sustainable competitive advantages. New directions are required.

Moving to an emergent model for innovation may be the answer.

We can pigeonhole every company into one of eight types of strategies: planned, entrepreneurial, ideological, umbrella, process, unconnected, consensus, and imposed. Mintzberg and co-author James Waters did a great job of articulating how strategic choice drives a strategy in a 1985 *Strategic Management Journal* article titled, "Of Strategies, Deliberate and Emergent." Rarely does an organization purely adopt a single type of strategy. More often, strategy development is a combination or hybrid of multiple types that, together in orchestration, establish the organizational direction and intent.

Have you ever tried to follow someone in a car going to an unfamiliar location? It can be difficult. If they bank right hard and make a right, you have to whip your car to the right while jamming on the breaks to maintain a reasonable distance. What happens if you lose sight of the other vehicle? The simple version of this scenario is: you lose sight of the car and become lost in an area you're unfamiliar with, and you don't know which side street they went down or how they're getting to that destination. After all, if you knew how to get there, you wouldn't have been following them. Then you pause and realize you have other options. You can call them and reset their position. They mention they're waiting at the small café on Gordon Street, and you race over and continue to follow them until you reach the destination.

Following a friend in a car is similar to how businesses imitate the competition. What if you were unable to locate the car and then received a call that said the car was in Massachusetts? You'd likely quickly head to Massachusetts. But then you receive another call and learn that the car is in Florida. You'd then race down to Florida. However, if more and more reports started coming in saying the car was in South Carolina, Tennessee, Texas, and Illinois, you'd realize you can't get to all those places. Let's assume that each spotting of the car in this example was your awareness of a competitor's strategy. For example, if they launched a new product, service, or interaction, your organization could imitate it, but you have no idea of their "real" strategy. Chasing innovation doesn't work.

Sun Tzu, the famous Chinese military strategist, stated 3,000 years ago: "All men can see the tactics whereby I conquer. But what none can see is the strategy out of which great victory is evolved." When we look at companies, what we observe is where they've been or the level of success of their latest tactic, not the future strategy.

Original ideas aren't born from assumptions made in the past. They arise from the strategic and calculated alignment of ideas into seemingly abnormal combinations, creating new causes. Leading organizations use first-principle thinking to maintain a competitive advantage. These are foundational propositions or assumptions that can't be deduced from any other proposition or assumption. In short, you can't just read and connect the lines. There are no lines to connect.

Whether you're building the corporate innovation capability or driving results for a department, ask these questions to validate you're using first principles and not imitating:

233

1. Does most of your innovation come from inside the organization and not from merely asking customers what they want?
2. When a problem arises, is the first thought to apply approaches the organization has already leveraged or to deconstruct the problem to determine new causes?
3. Are new ideas suggested based on successful strategies of the past? Alternatively, are new ideas decomposed into the most fundamental components and evaluated for new value potential?
4. When you ask your leadership team what new strategies should be explored, do you first hear about what your competitors are doing, or do you hear new, original ideas?
5. Can your competitors link together your current tactics to determine your real strategy?

Solving complex problems? Emergent strategies address complex problems. If you first hear about what the competitors are doing, it's probable that you're following that car, waiting for a call that will never come. Build a team that can create new ideas that are not necessarily linked to what was done in the past. Emergent innovation isn't linear.

Strategic Alignment Drives Change

Forget about IT maturity curves. Focus on strategic alignment. A quick search for "IT maturity models" on Google produces over 4 million results. Finding the right maturity model is about as useful as searching through millions of records looking for a single actionable process to achieve IT maturity.

IT maturity models, maturity curves, and capability models all attempt to find your location on a map. The models do identify your location, but the effectiveness of these models is akin to a waypoint or dot placed on a white piece of paper. The model's methodology is, of course, proven by increased corporate adoption. However, this doesn't prove or qualify fitness for purpose and more closely resembles website clicks, not engagement. Sure, it's good to know 1,000 companies clicked on that link—but how does that really matter?

Our challenge as executives is to outline steps to improve strategic alignment, which we define as the process and result of linking an organization's structure and resources to its strategy and environment.

STRATEGIC ALIGNMENT

The MIT Center for Information Systems Research published a strategic-alignment model (SAM) titled, The Strategic Alignment: A Framework for Strategic Information Technology Management.

In its simplest form, the strategic-alignment model has four components (abridged for brevity):

1. Business strategy
2. Information-technology strategy
3. Organizational processes
4. Information systems and infrastructure processes

These components can be summarized as the finite resources of every organization: time, people, finance, and individual and organizational capabilities. Strategic alignment doesn't care about IT-to-business alignment or IT maturity curves. Alignment is about reducing uncertainly regarding the future. It helps leaders grasp challenges and opportunities for the future business environment. Successful leaders leverage organizational strengths against external threats. To do this efficiently, we must have internal agreement on our strategy.

WHO'S DRIVING CHANGE

The essence of strategic alignment can be condensed into a single question: "Is the organization following a business strategy or an IT strategy?" We have dual polarities that need to converge. On one side, we have technologies that aren't involved in business strategy and, on the other, we have business leaders who aren't participating in the technological strategy. Both roles need to integrate decision making for more effective outcomes.

Four criteria make up the levers of strategic alignment:

1. Communications
2. Partnership
3. Skills
4. Governance

Communication broadcasts transformation across the organization to establish a mutual understanding among stakeholders. IT has an obligation to make the criticality of IT decisions more transparent and digestible for business partners. Likewise, business partners must help improve the understanding of businesses by IT.

Partnerships establish shared goals and objectives for measuring outcomes. This mutual understanding increases business awareness of IT and pulls IT into more of the strategic business-planning processes.

Skills are defined competencies that are individually and organizationally required for achieving outcomes. This perspective isn't only retrospective or focused on today's requirements but also prospective, asking what future skills are necessary.

Governance integrates business and IT planning. We move the needle from the cost-containment aspect of IT to the revenue-generating entity. By involving IT in business planning, IT can prepare for future capabilities that currently aren't supported.

ALIGNING YOUR STRATEGY

When you think of strategic alignment, what comes to mind? Do you find yourself looking at a recent PowerPoint deck with an illustration of the future business model? Do you think about a vision communicated by a single leader? If you do, you're not alone.

What if, when the words "strategic alignment" are mentioned, you envision a dynamic discussion among leaders with a combination of business and IT capability knowledge working together to define a future state? After all, that's what we're driving toward—a unified model for change that ensures adoption and maximizes customer value.

Leaders must be aligned with strategic change in an organization. Strategic alignment removes common barriers to transformation. Achieving strategic alignment defines your processes to ensure the greatest customer benefit from organizational knowledge. Successful adoption of strategic alignment begins at the top. Forget about dots on a maturity map and concentrate instead on fostering communication, building partnerships, growing skills, and establishing governance.

Conclusion

Strategy is critical. Even more useful is to understand what a strategy is not. This is why I feel this section is vital for the innovation mindset.

I shared my definition of strategy. You might have a different or expanded version, and that's fine. Strategy is a broad concept. As you formulate your strategy, make a deliberate effort to determine if you're leveraging an emergency strategy. Also, consider what problem you're solving. Aligning your strategy with the organization is critical to securing buy-in, funding, and generating momentum for your innovation. Here's an outline of the steps from creating a vision to developing measurements.

1. Vision
2. Mission
3. Goals

4. Objectives
5. Critical success factors
6. Key performance indicators
7. Metrics
8. Measurements

CHAPTER 13

INNOVATION ON A DATA PLAYGROUND

"The world is one big data problem."

— ANDREW MCAFEE

Chapter Objectives

After reading this chapter, readers will be able to:

- Explain why architecting innovation is a game changer.
- Discover business-process models in play.
- Prevent your team from falling off the organizational cliff.
- Understand why designing a data strategy is crucial.
- Build an actionable data strategy.
- Understand the foundation of data science.
- Explain why teams need both types of skills for innovation and results.

Architecting Innovation

Success isn't random—it's architected into the process. There's a reason business-capability models resonate with executives. They transform businesses, box-by-box.

Business-capability models, business-process models, and business-organizational models define the foundation of your business partner's business. We've all seen them. Some look amazingly complex, and others you wonder if they were stopped halfway through the process. Together, these models are the cornerstone for tomorrow's success, as they define the present and future state of a company.

- Business-capability models: define the what
- Business-process models: describe the how
- Business-organizational models: frame the who.

Identifying business capabilities, processes, and organizations establishes the starting point to begin the design of your business and technology architecture.

BUSINESS-CAPABILITY MODELS

We can look to W. Edwards Deming for insights about business-capability models: "Learning is not compulsory…neither is survival." A business-capability model (BCM) defines the complete set of capabilities an organization requires to execute its business model. The model articulates a common language for change. This common language connects executive intent with specific operational activities to realize that change. The concepts and capabilities are no longer theoretical. Each capability is actionable. This transparency provides a framework for assessment and prioritization of capabilities.

Business-capability models answer these questions:

1. Which capabilities are our strongest, and which are our weakest?

2. Which capabilities facilitate operational vs. strategic efficiencies?
3. Are we investing in the right resources?
4. Do opportunities to lower costs exist by removing duplicate capabilities?
5. Can technology enable capabilities realization?

Business-capability models can be hierarchical and provide multiple levels of abstraction depending on the level being represented. Each level has more detail than the basic elements of a strategy but doesn't dive into the business processes. The process of visualizing a strategy sequence highlights missing capabilities or capabilities that are no longer needed for business operations.

Business capabilities are free from the constraints of how they'll be realized; e.g., whether they'll be done manually or by automation. This freedom allows stakeholders to focus on what's required to achieve the desired business outcomes.

BUSINESS-PROCESS MODELS

Einstein nailed the insight about business process models: "Everything should be made as simple as possible, but not one bit simpler."

Business-process modeling (BPM) is the activity of representing processes of a company so we can study, recognize, analyze, optimize, monitor, and automate them. Accurate business-process models decrease waste and re-work and enhance alignment within a company through improved efficiencies.

Interested in how drone operations can improve your business? Have you explored blockchain as an approach to improve provenance? What about the impacts of machine learning or cognitive intelligence on automating existing business processes for improved customer delivery? Start with business-process models. Each exploratory step into the world of innovation demands a clear understanding of your enterprise business process and its interactions. Business-process models are the building blocks of innovation.

Business-process models answer these questions:

1. Which process is our first step toward change?
2. How would we implement a given change to impact our processes?
3. Where could automation have the biggest impact?
4. Do we model business process from a human-centric or system-centric perspective?
5. How do we roll out policies, standards, guidelines, and procedures most effectively for minimal business disruption?

BUSINESS-ORGANIZATIONAL MODELS

Lewis Carroll may have unwittingly reflected on business-organizational models when he said: "If you don't know where you are going, any road will get you there."

Business-organizational models or structures are patterns of business organizations. Patterns illustrate how an organization creates, delivers, and captures values. Businesses follow patterns for five reasons. First, businesses have similar external influences. Second, businesses have common internal influences and goals. Third, pattern reuse encourages and reinforces consistency. Fourth, interoperability among systems offers benefits for better outcomes. And, fifth, patterns account for the ability to deviate from a normal pattern for competitive advantages. For example, having a selection of patterns to choose from allows variation from the usual pattern.

A pattern's characteristics of being adequately general, adaptable, and worthy of imitation frame the degree of abstraction required for an effective business-organizational model.

Business-organizational models or structures provide value by defining lines of authority, responsibilities, communications, and organizational alignment. The base of the organizational structure sets the framework for how the organization will operate and perform.

Business-organizational models answer these questions:

1. Which individuals participate in decision making?
2. How do roles fit into the overall system?
3. How will information flow within our organization?
4. How was agility designed into the organization?
5. How are responsibilities delegated, controlled, and coordinated?

THE ORGANIZATIONAL CLIFF

The disaggregation of business capabilities, processes, and organizations has made constructing business models extremely difficult. The increasing relevance of technology has made conventional business or technology towers an ineffective approach to business design.

Optimal organizations factor in which business capabilities are required, how business process creates a baseline for process improvements, and who business organizational models identify as role-essential for tomorrow. Success isn't random; it's architected into forward-looking companies.

Designing a Data Strategy

Every company is talking about analytics, but only a handful have a simple data-analytics strategy.

Big-data analytics, actionable insights, and powerful outcomes are the de facto expectations for data-analytics programs. Is your data strategy aligned to deliver those results?

Organizations are seeking sophisticated analytical techniques and tools to gain more profound insights into how they can capitalize on the blue ocean of data analytics. Listen this week at your office, and you'll undoubtedly hear whisperings about harnessing the power of analytics. It might not be called data management or big-data analytics, and the questions might be more subtle, such as:

- How do we discover new insights into our products?
- Which operational capabilities will deliver the highest ROI?
- How do we leverage our data to generate better strategies and execute with improved confidence?

Managers and leaders alike are searching for approaches to tap into the value of big-data analytics. What exactly is a big-data analytics strategy?

BUILD A COMPREHENSIVE DATA-ANALYSIS FOUNDATION

Set the frame mentally of the building blocks of a world-class data-analytics program. It doesn't need to be perfect. Identify the critical components that make up a data-analytics foundation:

- **Presentation layer**: where the dashboards and workflows live
- **Big–data processing and analytics layer**: the base for pattern matching, mining, predictive modeling, classification engines, and optimization
- **Data-storage and management layer**: relational data systems, scalable NoSQL data storage, and cloud-based storage
- **Data-connection layer**: data sensing, data extraction, and data integration

The analytics framework can also be segmented into four phases: descriptive, diagnostic, predictive, and prescriptive. The descriptive phase defines what happened. The diagnostic phase determines why it happened. The predictive phase forecasts what will happen. The prescriptive phase identifies what action to take. Together, these phases help leaders classify the types of questions they're receiving. These can also highlight capability deficiencies.

BIG-DATA ANALYTICS FRAMEWORKS

Frameworks—in data analytics—provide an essential supporting structure for building ideas and delivering the full value of big-data analytics.

Does it matter whether your framework is bulletproof? No, it doesn't. It's important that the framework provide a set of guiding principles to ground thinking. Establishing common principles prevents revisiting the same topics.

Think of a data-analytics framework as an ontological approach to big-data analytics. There's one framework that's particularly useful—the annual Big Data Analytics World Championships for Business and Enterprise—which stresses the following:

- **Practical concepts**: predict future outcomes, understand risk and uncertainty, embrace complexity, identify the unusual, think big
- **Functions**: decide, acquire, analyze, organize, create, and communicate
- **Analytics applications** business insights, sentiment analysis, risk modeling, marketing-campaign analysis, cross-selling, data integration, price optimization, performance optimization, recommendation engines, fraud detection, customer-experience analytics, customer-churn analytics, stratified sampling, geo/location-based analysis, inventory management, and network analysis
- **Skills and technical understanding**: data mining, statistics, machine learning, software engineering, Hadoop, MapReduce, HBase, Hive, Pig, Python, C/C+, SQL, computational linear algebra, metrics analysis, and analytics tools (SAS, R, MATLAB)

- **Machine learning**: machine-learning tools, supervised learning, Monte Carlo techniques, text mining, NLP, text analysis, clustering techniques, tagging, and regression analysis
- **Programming**: Python basics, R basics, R setup, vectors, variables, factors, expressions, arrays, lists, and IBM SPSS
- **Data visualization**: histogram, treemap, scatter plot, list charts, spatial charts, survey plots, decision trees, data exploration in R, and multivariate and bivariate analyses
- **Fundamentals**: matrices and linear algebra, relationship algebra, DB basics, OLAP, CAP theorem, tabular data, data frames and series, multidimensional data models, ETL, and reporting vs. BI vs. analytics
- **Data techniques**: data fusion, data integration, transformation and enrichment, data discovery, data formats, data sources and acquisition, unbiased estimators, data scrubbing, normalization, and handling missing values
- **Big data**: Setup Hadoop (IBM, Cloudera, Hortonworks), data replication principles, name and data nodes, Hadoop components, MapReduce fundamentals, Cassandra, and MongoDB
- **Statistics**: ANOVA, Skewness, continuous distributions (normal, Poisson, Gaussian), random variables, Bayes theorem, probability distributions, percentiles and outliers, histograms, and exploratory data analysis

Use these eleven lenses to define your data-analytics strategy. Unfortunately, the framework won't replace a great leader who understands how to execute these programs successfully. It will, however, help steer the conversations in the right direction.

If your team is less familiar with the principles of big-data analytics, use these questions as a guide:

1. **Practical concepts:** What future outcomes do we want to predict?
2. **Functions:** Do we have a methodology or process to mature data analytical requests?
3. **Analytics applications:** Which insights are we seeking to generate?
4. **Skills and technical understanding:** What skills and competencies are critical for producing new organizational insights?
5. **Machine learning:** Which business capabilities would benefit from enhanced machine-learned capabilities?
6. **Programming:** What are the most important technical programming skills to mature within the organization?
7. **Data visualization:** Which visual representations lead to the best decisions?
8. **Fundamentals:** What layer has the greatest potential for transformation—how we make decisions involving presentation, big-data processing, data storage, or the data-connection layer?
9. **Data techniques:** Which data-transformation techniques are essential to move us from data to information?
10. **Big data:** Based on our business architecture, which technology components are foundational to providing intelligent data analytics?
11. **Statistics:** How do we envision data being categorized and analyzed?

MAKE YOUR DATA STRATEGY ACTIONABLE

There are thousands of ways to develop a big-data program but only one method to measure success: Did we achieve the outcomes desired?

Leveraging top-down and bottom-up interaction models helps to lock in value and prevent leakage. Use the categories below to group ideas in your process of forming an actionable plan. Once this exercise is complete, place each interaction on the y-axis.

1. **Overarching strategy**: defines the value and categories of results
2. **Tactics**: articulates how value will be created
3. Measurement plan: identifies program success metrics, KPIs, and tracking mechanisms for tracking the plan
4. **Analytics**: captures predictive modeling to forecast experiments—largely to perform correlation analysis— leading to specific actions
5. **Optimization opportunities**: maximizes investments for the agenda with the highest probability to achieve the greatest outcome

Then list the three-tiered approach against the x-axis:

1. **Quick wins**: under 30 days
2. **Intermediate wins**: 31 to 90 days
3. **Long-term wins**: greater than 90 days

The result is a graphical view of your data strategy. This approach will help your team generate ideas and determine a general sequence of delivery, weighted by the idea that will most significantly impact the organization.

THE SECRET OF SUCCESSFUL BIG-DATA ANALYTICS PROGRAMS

Different stakeholders will be using your organization's data for different reasons. Perspectives matter. Data analytics is changing the way company decisions are being made. Data engineering, domain expertise, and statistics each can play a role in the discipline of data science for your organization. Understanding concepts such as mathematical techniques is increasingly more important for extracting the maximum information from large data sets. Roles we hired for—even two years ago—don't have the raw skills required to communicate the salient features of data succinctly.

Using a combination of "big" data and "little" data creates the foundation for quick wins. Sure, after reading an entire book on a particular subject, you'd gain more insights, but often even reading a chapter or two can offer substantial perspectives. Start small with little data and build strategically to achieve big-data analytics success.

Building a World-class Data-Science Team

Data science isn't about special people in special places. It's about teams.

We've all witnessed the wave of innovations that has washed over business models of late. These innovations didn't surface as the ideas of individuals. The architecture of businesses, business interactions, data collections, and the use of information is so complex that a single individual in a mid- or large-size company wouldn't have the knowledge to understand all elements required to make the idea a practical reality.

Also, it's long been proven that heterogeneity enhances group brainstorming. More diverse groups produce better ideas. This concept is especially important when we're designing data-science teams.

A PART OF THE WHOLE

You've probably been told you need to hire one of two individuals. The first is an astute data developer with a grounded understanding of Python, SQL and data storage, PostgreSQL, Unix and Linux command-line knowledge (mainly to run and schedule cron jobs); Python data libraries (Pandas, Scrapy, Keras, Matplotlib, TensorFlow, Bokeh, Scikit-learn, etc.); Flask, Bottle, and Django to host the analysis of the database as a RESTful API, AWS, or Azure-hosting framework; and, of course, AngularJS for presentation results and DS.js to create data visualizations.

If, for some reason, you botch the hiring of the astute data developer, you only have one other alternative—to hire a data academic. This is a theorist who pontificates about changing the world with data but whose experience rarely ventures outside the educational setting and has few practical applications. The data academic understands core statistics, categorical data analysis, applying statistics with R (multiple linear regressions, qualitative predictors, linear discriminant analysis, resampling methods like k-fold cross-validation, hyperplanes, hierarchical clustering), sequential data models (Markov models, hidden Markov models, linear dynamical systems), Bayesian model averaging, and machine-learning probabilistic theory. You hope some of this learning is connected to causality.

Are these two roles important for a data-science team? Of course. If you, by chance, hire both these roles, do you have a data-science team? No, you do not.

Let's begin with the origins of data science and, from there, we'll move into the critical capabilities required to build a world-class data-science team.

FROM THERE TO HERE
The foundation of data science originated with five key areas:

1. **Computer science**: the study of computation and information
2. **Data technology**: data generated by humans and machines
3. **Visualizations**: graphical representation of information and data
4. **Statistics**: methodologies to gather, review, analyze, and draw conclusions from data
5. **Mathematics**: the science of the logic of shape, quantity, and arrangement

In the 1900s, computer science evolved from Turing machines to cybernetics and information theory. Tree-based methods and graph algorithms surfaced in the 1960s. By the 1970s, computer programming and text or string searches popped up. Data mining, data classification, and similar methods pushed us into the early 2000s.

Data technology began before the 1800s with binary logic and Boolean algebra with punch cards. IBM introduced the first computers in the 1940s as DBMS matured. Removable disks with relational DBMS followed into the 1960s. By the mid-1970s, desktop computers, SQL, and objective-oriented programming was the norm. In early 2001, statistical modeling started to emerge, balancing the stochastic data model by using algorithmic models and treating data mechanisms as unknowns.

Visualizations arose prior to the 1800s with cartography and the mapping of astronomical charts. Line and bar charts came out in the 1800s, and statistical graphics were depicted by the mid-1800s. The box plot was created in the 1970s, and word or tag clouds started to form in 1992.

Statistics entered the 1800s with theories of correlation, probability, and Bayes Theorem. In the 1900s the concept of regression, times series, and least-squares made the rounds. The 1900s introduced the foundation of modern statistics with the hypothesis and design of experiments. By the mid-1960s, we had Bayesian methods, stochastic methods, and more complex time-series methods such as survival analysis and grouping time-series data. Through the 1980s, more developments occurred in Markov simulation and computational statistics, allowing us to better understand the interface between statistics and computer science. By the late 1990s, decision science, pattern recognition, and machine learning were starting to take shape.

Mathematics entered the 1800s with calculus and logarithms. Next, Newton-Raphson introduced optimization methods. By the 1930s, the military had started to adopt theories for manufacturing and communications. The 1960s were booming with networks, automation, scheduling, and assignment problems, which have only matured in recent years.

Understanding the origins of data science helps demystify it and allows you to develop a concrete capability in your company.

DATA SCIENCE CAPABILITIES

Finding success with data science comes down to four factors: people, data, tools, and security.

The most important elements of your data-science team are the people and the capabilities they enable. Next, to get insights—even with the best people—we ultimately need data and access to data. Usually, data is siloed across teams, departments, and systems, making gaining access difficult. Assuming we have the people and access to the data, next, we need tools. Performing analytics necessitates computational and data-storage resources. Fortunately, today we have many open-source options that are more than adequate. Lastly, data security and privacy protection are crucial as data becomes more centralized. With this convenience comes access—which, in the wrong hands, creates risk.

With this understanding of the origins of data science, it's fascinating to see the mix of conventional capabilities aligned with the less traditional data-science skills that are required for success. Let's cover examples of data-science capabilities and complementary data-science team skills that are found within world-class data-science teams. First, the data-science capabilities.

- **Statistics**: R, SPSS, Excel, Minitab
- **Mathematics**: MATLAB, Theano, Octave, NumPy,
- **Pattern recognition**: Scala, Google Cloud, Twilio, narrative science, cogito, PoluAI, smartling

- **Data mining**: SAS, Talend, Teradata, board, Dundas, orange, KNIME, Alteryx
- **Machine learning**: BigML, NET, XGBoost, DL4J, H2O
- **Artificial intelligence**: CNTK, Numenta, OSARO, Affectiva, Cognitive Scale
- **Neural networks**: Keras, Caffe2, Chainer, PyTorch,
- **Data visualizations**: js, Tableau, ggplot2, Matplotlib, Bokeh, Spotfire
- **Hypothesis testing**: Datameer, incorta, switchboard, Starburst, Pentaho
- **Data modeling**: QlikView, RapidMiner, Vertabelo, Lucidchart, Erwin, HeidiSQL
- **Big-data solution engineering**: Jupyter, Apache Spark, R Shiny, Databricks
- **Exploratory data analytics**: pandas, Hadoop, Hive, Pig, Flume
- **Modeling and prescriptive analytics**: SigOpt, TensorFlow

Second, we have the data-science team skills.

- **Stakeholder management**: business-relationships management, project management
- **Storytelling ability**: executive presence, presentation skills
- **Business communications**: clear and timely communication, governance
- **Consulting**: need analysis, solutions aligned to goals
- **Problem-solving**: Lean Six-Sigma, agile
- **Topical analytics techniques**: statistics, root-cause analysis, statistical-process control, value-stream mapping, flows
- **Domain expertise**: knowledge of the data, who's using it, and for what purpose

- **Business analysis**: experience evaluating and modeling business cases

The ultimate success of a data-science team depends on how well expectations are managed. When expectations are met, the data-science team will be viewed as impactful. Inversely, a weak perception of delivery is a significant reason why data-science teams eventually get disbanded—they focus on what's cool, not what's most impactful for the business.

THE HIDDEN ART OF STORYTELLING

It's idealistic to believe data-science teams can find value in data from day 1, but, eventually, they'll connect data to new insights. However, often that data is layered across hundreds or thousands of sources, and the team might be months or years away from collecting it all. Most data-science teams begin with a simple set of questions. These questions are challenging but tangible to answer. This approach also limits the data set required to be integrated into an initial proof of concept. Sample questions might include some of the following:

- Which applications in our portfolio have the most significant security risk?
- Why is the Durham, NC location the most profitable?
- What type of patient visit will be the costliest next quarter?
- Is antibody A or antibody B more likely to achieve FDA approval?
- Which drone should we bring in first for preventive maintenance?

Building a world-class data-science capability isn't about individuals; it's about assembling your team. It's crucial to ensure that essential data-science capabilities and data-science skills are part of your team design. To tap into the power of data science, we require teams to not only extract insights from data but also tell a compelling story. Quite often, we're left with a lot of data, confusing insights, and no story. Make sure the team you build can tell a story.

Conclusion

Innovation is a process. Innovation is also architected in or out of your process. It's wise to validate that innovation is, in fact, architected in.

Let me be so bold as to state that anything of value involves data. If you're creating an interaction, and it doesn't use data, it's utility will be quite limited. This makes designing a data strategy all the more important for innovators to consider from the beginning.

How are consumers going to access the data? Which data is useful for our customers? How can we utilize data to offer better insights and answer questions we couldn't even ask yesterday? The trend from data swamps to data lakes makes it clear that if we don't have an intentional approach to manage data, we'll be spending all our time wrangling and massaging it.

Be proactive, and take control of your data before it takes control of you.

CHAPTER 14

THE HUMOR OF INNOVATION

"Look at a day when you are supremely satisfied at the end. It's not a day when you lounge around doing nothing; it's a day you've had everything to do and you've done it."

— MARGARET THATCHER

Chapter Objectives

After reading this chapter, readers will be able to:

- Talk through the five behaviors essential for innovation development.
- Ask yourself if you have the seven competencies for innovators.
- Explore ideas that yesterday were impossible and today are status-quo.
- Understand why crazy ideas win.

Development Paths for Innovators

What's the career path for an innovator? Project managers have clear career paths: project administrator, project coordinator, project manager, senior project manager, program manager, and program director. The path for scientists is paved as well: research associate, scientist, research scientist, and principle research scientist. IT's challenged to define the career path of innovators as they take on myriad forms.

First, the role of an innovator can take various equivalent forms depending on the organization—chief strategy officer, vice president, or manager of innovation.

Second, there are crazy stories of how innovators became successful. Airbnb secured initial funding by selling its own brand of cereal.[97] Reddit had 1.2 billion unique visitors in March 2017, and the founders started by creating tons of fake accounts, embracing the good old, "fake it 'til you make it" principle. Warby Parker cofounder Dave Gilboa lost his $700 pair of glasses on a backpack trip and thought there must be a better way. This inspired Gilboa to buy a used school bus and travel across the country with his "mobile store" called "The Warby Parker Class Trip." Founders of PayPal gave out free money and, today, over $712 billion is paid through PayPal annually. The stories are endless.

Should we hire fake protesters to disrupt competitors as Marc Benioff, CEO of Salesforce, has done? Do we need to write to potential users, sending 7,000 letters like Pinterest cofounder Ben Silberman did to generate interest in our new platform? There's no single answer. As with the best and more complicated things in life—it just depends.

It's not effective to focus on the path to innovation enlightenment. If we're concentrating on each brick required to get us to our destination, we miss the broader picture. We must focus not on competencies but rather on behaviors.

THE INNOVATION LADDER

Are you thinking in terms of climbing a ladder—placing one foot in front of the other, each rung slightly elevated from the previous, which represents a progression into the next phase of the world of an innovator? As an innovator you're not always climbing vertically. Often the ideas with the most potential need to go sideways for a while before they have vertical trajectory. Look upward, and stop focusing on the bricks.

Our ladder is horizontal not vertical. We don't climb, we balance, and there's a difference. The reason for this is, there are no absolutes. We'll use principles and behaviors to shape and measure our effectiveness as a leader and innovator.

There are five behaviors that are essential for innovation development:

1. **Read**: understand the paths of those who came before you
2. **Observe**: absorb positive and negative aspects of your environment
3. **Micronize**: establish micro-habits
4. **Measure**: assess your effectiveness and adherence to your behaviors
5. **Refactor**: before you fall into a rut, reset the behavior

Think of each of these five behaviors as a rung on our horizontal ladder. At some point, to balance, you'll need to step on a rung. If you put all your effort there, the rung will break. As a result, you must divide your focus among each of these five behaviors.

Reading ensures that the information you're using to make decisions is current. Apply the "10 Percent Rule." Many of the most successful innovations only improved existing designs by 10 percent. They weren't revolutionary; they were evolutionary. You don't need to radically transform your reading schedule if you don't read daily today. Simply start today by reading one page. Don't read 20 pages, just one.

Start with a target that's only 10 percent of what you think you can do. Ensure the habit is attainable and maintainable.

Observing involves each of your senses. Have you ever tried to predict when it will rain? It requires some basic understanding of weather, patience, and the ability to adjust or invalidate previous assumptions. Predicting the weather is similar to predicting innovation events, trends, and patterns. It's not a requirement to be an expert, but everyone who successfully predicts is extremely observant.

Micronizing moves away from goals and toward systems. This approach helps to achieve long-term sustainability. These systems eventually become habits.

Measuring sharpens your reality to clarify what you're achieving. How are you doing on those New Year's resolutions? I thought so. Goals don't work. You either achieved your New Year's resolutions or you didn't. It's much easier to measure habits. Using iPhone applications such as Way of Life, you can measure and chart your process daily, measuring your adherence to your micro habits.

Refactoring is the tuning based on a broad awareness of place. Are you where you want to be? If you are, that's super. If you're not, refactor and change where you are today to be someplace different tomorrow.

By reading, observing, micronizing, measuring, and refactoring, you can build your path to innovation success.

Innovation

Innovators walk on the edges. They explore where others might have thought of looking but didn't. This curiosity is infectious, and it can be extremely powerful

Before innovators can venture out on that ledge and explore, they must have earned trust. The ability to earn the confidence of leaders is built on reliability, truth, or strength in a believer. Being honest and driven with purpose isn't enough to sway leaders to invest or walk down a path that may end abruptly.

Everything we do depends on trust. Besides building teams, creating value, and designing new experiences, innovators must master the seven competencies:

1. Capability
2. Character
3. Cognition
4. Commitment
5. Compassion
6. Confidence
7. Connection

#1 CAPABILITY

Surprisingly, innovators don't need to individually have the capability to innovate, but they do need access to it.

The resource-based view (RBV) is a theory of competitive advantage that states the advantage of a firm relies on the collection of tangible or intangible resources at the firm's disposal. The classic RBV theory was first contributed by Edith Elura Tilton Penrose in 1959, who suggested that the enterprise was more than an administrative hub.[98] Modern RBV theory states that each firm's strategy is determined by a collection of key resources and capabilities.[99],[100],[101]

Innovation today requires extending value beyond the firm's border and designing dynamic capability models that can adapt to changing business environments.

While it's true that innovators don't need the skills themselves, they do need to understand what value is, where value is found, and how value is captured.

#2 CHARACTER

To build loyalty, innovators embrace more than an awareness of the thin and often gray line between right and wrong. Leaders are born with an intangible moral compass. This call-

261

ing doesn't always lead to the greatest profit or the most elaborate levels of success. This approach to achieve innovation success does, however, do one thing extremely well—it breeds loyalty like rabbits.

The mental and moral qualities distinctive to you, as an innovator, must be unwavering. This unquestionable character is the foundation of trust. Your key leaders and your entire team should feel your support is absolute.

There's almost always a way to move forward against all odds. The challenge might be unlocking tightly controlled funding or gaining agreement on the framework architecture. Compromise is part of business; compromising on ethics is not. Achieving success means reaching adoption and scale embracing corporate social responsibility. Corporate financial responsibility must be measured in conjunction with corporate social responsibility and corporate environmental responsibility to determine corporate social performance [102]

#3 COGNITION

Have you ever been in the back seat of a car only to realize the driver missed a turn because he or she wasn't paying attention? This is an example of poor cognition.

Innovators need to pay attention to the road and watch much farther down the road than the driver (or team). This ability to acquire knowledge and understanding from thought, experience, and the senses reinforces trust in leadership.

This is the type of trust that can't be purchased. A temporary leader can't step in and keep a team moving once the ability to perceive begins to fade in the leadership.

While a fully vetted strategy and future path is, of course, ideal, it's not mandatory. What is mandatory is that you stay five or more steps ahead of the team. Anticipation is essential to proving to yourself and your team that you're not only in control but that you're thinking about the next big thing.

This adaptive and anticipatory approach to problem solving helps innovators discover solutions not found by others.

The reason innovators find solutions previously unheard of is that they explore in dark and sometimes remote areas such as blockchain technology, 4D printing, etc.

#4 COMMITMENT

The commitment to innovation is a commitment to sustainability. Innovation is a process, not an event. Breakthrough innovations and breakthrough events do occur. But they only occur within the structure and process of innovation. Without a process, the ability to repeat earlier transformative and breakthrough events would be impossible. Sure, they'd occur eventually. As innovators, we'd like these moments to occur with more frequency than a lottery win.

If I asked you to think of three significant innovations, what comes to mind? The iPhone, the personal computer, and the optical lens would be good choices. Undoubtedly, there were times during the process of innovation of these products that were point-in-time breakthroughs—single events that had a substantial effect on the outcome. These events were chained together in the process and likely wouldn't have occurred without it.

Define your commitment to innovation by applying a process to each of those innovative peaks.

#5 COMPASSION

Empathy isn't compassion. Empathy is simply the ability to understand the emotions of another person. Compassion epands empathy through understanding and feelings, including a desire to help.

It's easy to apply pressure to your team to perform. We're all under pressure, and each team member should be carrying their share of the stress. The challenge is that too much stress isn't productive. Where's that line between excessive and insufficient incentive to produce? Every great leader and innovator asks that of themselves every day. There's no one right answer. It depends on the team.

You should create incentive and design a high-performance culture. The best innovators first understand the situation of each of their team members. These innovators aren't shouting orders. They're asking questions and listening to better understand how they can remove those roadblocks and tackle how to improve the velocity of the team. Once these innovators are empathic, they act. Leading compassionately builds trust.

#6 CONFIDENCE

Failure isn't the end. Failure is an answer. It tells you not to continue down that path and to start another. An innovator's mindset is about creating ideas, not fixating on individual ideas. Oh sure, you'll have ideas that you think are more feasible than others, but you must let them go if they become less viable.

Whether you're a scientist in a lab, an engineer in a plant, or a leader of a data-science team, people often won't agree with you. It's not necessarily that they're trying to disagree. Rather, it's that they don't see what you see. The normal state of balance for an innovator is one in which others are in a state of disbelief. They can't see it. They don't understand it. They don't believe it.

That's okay. You need the confidence to keep generating ideas that support your ideology.

The lack of acceptance—most often—doesn't have any relevance to the credibility of the idea.

#7 CONNECTION

The last—and maybe the most important—innovation mindset competency is connection. No one needs to think your idea is the best idea ever or that it's the only path forward. However, not much will happen without support. This is the focus of this competency—external support.

Who else can you engage to support the materialization of your idea? It could be a peer, colleague, or supervisor that can add empowerment around your idea. Many times, when sitting on a board or governance committee, leaders agree to ideas that aren't exactly what they had in mind to garner the support they may need in the future for their idea. The result is you're able to build logical alliances. These colleagues are equally important to colleagues that fully buy into the idea.

Begin by forming a coalition to build support around the idea and develop a forum to help educate folks on the benefits of adoption. The ability to influence without authority is essential for an innovator's mindset.

The Humor of Bad Predictions

The pitted history of innovation is fraught with bad information, poor advice, and unstable experts—the overly enthusiastic to the sorely pessimistic. Listen for a balanced tone.

One expert is right. One expert is wrong.

SWIMSUITS OR RAINCOATS

How accurate are predictions? Every day, we have plans, even if that plan is to do nothing. At some point, understanding the weather often becomes a factor in the decision of what to do, where to go, or what to wear. A product manager at Minitab answered a question we've wondered about: How accurate are those weather forecasters?

There are three main forecast periods: 10-day, five-day, and next-day. The experiment recorded 10-day, five-day, and next-day weather forecasts. Over 30 days, the rolling forecast and the actual weather was recorded. The forecasts on some days were more accurate than others. Not surprising, the 10-day forecast was less accurate than the five-day forecast, and the five-day was less accurate than the next-day forecast.

As the prediction date moved closer to the actual date, less variability was observed in the prediction. Usually, we're talking about the standard deviation of defects, whether in the technological or manufacturer space. However, in our case, we're talking about the extent to which one weather forecaster would agree with another. Do experts mostly agree or mostly disagree? A low standard deviation isn't always good, and a high isn't always bad. Standard deviation is a factor of the observation data spread—in this case, how close one weather forecaster was to another in their predictions of the actual forecast.

The standard deviations varied based on the forecast period. The 10-day forecast had a standard deviation of 6.2 degrees, with the high temp off by as much as 8 degrees and the low temp off by as much as 17 degrees. The standard deviations of the five-day (4.3 degrees) and the next-day (2.1 degrees) forecasts were less pronounced.

Does any of this even matter? What if we weren't talking about weather forecasters? What if we were talking about experts predicting the lack of impact of blockchain on business or the impact of new innovative technologies? Think about the business impact of blockchain in 10 years, five years, and one year.

BRILLIANT INNOVATIONS OR DREADFUL EMBARRASSMENTS?

The answer to this question depends on which expert you ask. Television, radio, telephone, transportation, computers, space exploration, and medicine are riddled with renowned experts who offered horrible predictions. The most humorous were the most pessimistic. Keep that in mind as experts offer ridiculously pessimistic outlooks on the impact of blockchain technologies on the business, the economy, and the world.

TELEVISION

*"Television won't be able to hold on to any market it
captures after the first six months. People will soon
get tired of staring at a plywood box every night."*

— DARRYL F. ZANUCK,
HEAD OF 20TH CENTURY-FOX, 1946.

20th Century-Fox started in 1949 with shows on ABC and
CBS and later evolved into the Fox Television Network.

. . . .

RADIO

"Radio has no future."

— LORD KELVIN,
BRITISH MATHEMATICIAN AND PHYSICIST, CA. 1897

As of Nov. 1, 2020, the market capitalization of Sirius XM
Holdings was $24.4 billion.

. . . .

TELEPHONE

*"This 'telephone' has too many shortcomings to
be seriously considered as a practical form of
communication. The device is inherently of no value
to us."*

— WESTERN UNION INTERNAL MEMO, 1878

Verizon, the largest player in the wireless market, saw an
operating income margin of 12.% for FY 2019 on revenues
of $31.4 billion—not bad for a market that's of "no value."

TRANSPORTATION

"What can be more palpably absurd than the prospect held out of locomotives traveling twice as fast as stagecoaches?"

— *THE QUARTERLY REVIEW*, ENGLAND, 1825

Yahoo Finance reported the market capitalization of the railway industry at $68.1 billion in 2020.

. . . .

COMPUTERS

"There is no reason anyone would want a computer in their home."

— KEN OLSON, PRESIDENT, CHAIRMAN, AND FOUNDER OF DIGITAL EQUIPMENT CORP., 1977

The personal computer industry is about $688 billion—not bad considering that smartphones have shifted the PC market. Adding smartphones (iPhone, Android) dramatically raises this growth estimate. Global revenue from smartphones exceeded $404.6 billion in 2019.

SPACE EXPLORATION

*"There is no hope for the fanciful idea of reaching
the moon because of insurmountable barriers to
escaping the Earth's gravity."*

— DR. FOREST RAY MOULTON,
UNIVERSITY OF CHICAGO ASTRONOMER, 1932

In 1959, the Soviet Union made the first spacecraft landings
on the lunar surface with Luna 2 and Luna 3. The United
States reached the moon in 1964 and 1965 with Ranger 7
and Ranger 8.

. . . .

MEDICINE

*"The abdomen, the chest and the brain will forever
be shut from the intrusion of the wise and humane
surgeon."*

— SIR JOHN ERIC ERICSON,
SURGEON TO QUEEN VICTORIA, 1873

In 1967, a South African physician, Dr. Christiaan Barnard,
performed the world's first human-to-human heart trans-
plant at Groote Schuur Hospital, Cape Town.

What did each of these individuals have in common? They
all were among the most renowned industry experts of their
times, and each offered horrible advice. It's comical to think
about big innovations ignored by experts occurring 100 or
200 years ago.

What are the innovations in operation or experimentation
today that experts dismissed? Tesla? Airbnb? Next-generation
sequencing (NGS)? VR headsets for shopping? Blockchain?

Conclusion

Weather forecasters are often wrong. They also can be correct. In reality, no one knows what the next iPhone-like product or Netflix-type experience will be. A lot of people hope, invest, and make bets one way or another. But they don't know.

It's easy to get discouraged when you have an innovative mindset. It's not as easy as it is with the weather, which will let you know tomorrow whether your prediction was right or wrong. You may find out in weeks, months, or years, or you may die not knowing.

There's one common element in an innovator's mindset—you'll always be in the minority. You'll never hold the popular opinion, and it will be easy for others to reference the status-quo to defend why your vision will never materialize.

Learn to love that position. You have an idea, and you believe it will materialize—a new product offering, a radical new customer experience, or a process to create an outcome never tried. It only takes one to believe. One manager, one investor, one person that sees the potential that you see. The innovation mindset isn't black or white, right or wrong. It's nestled into the gray area.

This is where you'll find the innovator's mindset. It's resting comfortably on the fringe. Innovators push boundaries.

PUBLISHED PAPER 1

Citation

Nichol, P. B. (2020). *Assessing Project Management Capabilities Using Demonstrated Competencies*, 11. http://doi.org/10.13140/RG.2.2.20014.95041.

Abstract

This paper aims to present a practitioner approach to assessing project- and program-management capabilities across individuals, teams, and organizations. Executives must deliver value to business partners to stay relevant, engaged, and employed. Often, the value created doesn't equate to the net organizational investment. This situation creates challenges for the entire organization. Value isn't generated at a rate that sustains demand. When delivery is impacted, the expected project and initiative results aren't achieved, and value isn't realized. Many leaders blame individuals, focusing on the loudest but not necessarily the most critical areas. By applying a systematic approach to assess the management of an individual project or program, capabilities, the deficiencies within the team become self-evident. As a result, fixing the problem becomes quite straightforward. This paper will explain the method, approach, and technique to analyze and assess a team for demonstrated competency. Executive leaders will have a blueprint of what's required to effectively assess individuals, teams, and organizational capabilities to align with future business demands.

PUBLISHED PAPER 2

Citation

Nichol, P. B. (2020). *Quantifying Outcomes for Project Management in a Value Management Office*, 9. http://doi.org/10.13140/RG.2.2.34781.03046.

Abstract

This paper aims to present a practitioner approach to applying project-management principles of value realization within a value-management office. Portfolio leaders and program and project managers are confused about how to apply value management in the real world. Project-management offices are being shut down, because they've not delivered on the promise to add value to the business. What has emerged to fill this void is the concept of a value-management office. This new organizational construct is narrowly focused on maximizing value for the company's strategic initiatives. The result is a huge divergence from the traditional project-management office, which has been viewed organizationally as a cost center that provides little if any value to the company. To optimize the value-management office, new techniques need to be applied and integrated into the existing processes and procedures to deliver projects and quantify results. By using a general-structure portfolio, program and project managers can deliver impactful and quantified value to business partners. In this paper, we'll explore an example of how to achieve value realization. Leaders, by using this model, have a roadmap for achieving quantified outcomes for their value-management office.

PUBLISHED PAPER 3

Citation

Nichol, P. B. (2020). *Service Catalogs: Blueprint for the Future of Value Management*, 10. http://doi.org/10.13140/RG.2.2.20972.59525.

Abstract

This paper aims to present a unique approach to implementing a project-management-office service catalog for organizations focused on continuous value delivery. Business information executives and officers must validate investment decisions and demonstrate value achieved. The process of gaining additional organizational and cross-functional executive buy-in is especially difficult when team members, leaders, and executives don't understand what services the organization's project-management office provides. The traditional project-management office—centered around processes and templates—is being transformed into a new-age, value-management office that's hyper-focused on the value realized. Innovators understand and appreciate that if the services the project-management office provides are vague, business partners won't consume them. The act of creating a service catalog allows for a tailored or agile approach to delivery. This model accepts that not all projects are created equal. More specifically, leveraging a value-management service catalog refocuses the organization. Core capabilities are provided through the catalog, and investments in these areas are doubled down. Alternatively, capabilities that fall outside the core capabilities of the value-management office are evaluated for outsourcing. This shifts the traditional project-management office from a cost center to a value center and makes services offered transparent to downstream consumers.

PUBLISHED PAPER 4

Citation

Nichol, P. B. (2020). *Value Management as an Organizational Capability*, 11. http://doi.org/10.13140/RG.2.2.34402.56002.

Abstract

This paper aims to present a practical approach to institutionalizing business value realization as an organizational capability. Business and technology executives are under continuous pressure to justify investments and validate business outcomes. When executives are asked to explain the value generated by their team, department, or company, only then do they realize they lack the in-house expertise to produce the level of quantifiable outcomes expected. Progressive leaders know that the process of discovering, realizing, and optimizing value is an essential organizational capability. This paper presents a practitioner approach offering multiple value management frameworks to assist executives in making informed decisions when building a value-management office. Traditional project-management offices maintain project-management standards, establish best practices, define common languages, develop a resource-management view, and create and maintain project artifacts and tools. Unfortunately, the heavy burden of these core project-management office activities results in no time for strategic planning. The value-management office oversees the execution of all the company's strategic programs. The company's hyper-focus on connecting strategy to execution ensures the value maximization of its strategic initiatives.

PUBLISHED PAPER 5

Citation

Nichol, P. B. (2020). *Applying Six Sigma to Quantify Outcomes in Portfolio Delivery*, 10. http://doi.org/10.13140/RG.2.2.11880.49924.

Abstract

This paper aims to present a practical approach to applying principles of Six Sigma to statistically control portfolio delivery within a program-management office. Portfolio executives are continuously charged with transforming a low-performing team into a high-performance team. Often, the methods of transformation are based on experience, and these imprecise methods frequently produce inconsistent results. The transformation from a low-performing team to a high-performing team can be accelerated by using a quantified methodology to define, measure, analyze, improve, and control desired outcomes. This paper presents a practitioner approach to maximizing the organizational outputs from an agile program-management office by leveraging statistics and mathematical principles to tighten process variance. By applying a fit-for-purpose approach to corporate and operational excellence, portfolio executives can dial in and remediate the root causes of portfolio inefficiencies for maximum agility and value realization.

CITING THE BOOK

APA
Nichol, P. B. (2021). *Think, Lead, Disrupt: How Innovative Minds Connect Strategy To Execution* (1st ed.). Newington, CT USA: OROCA Innovations.

CHICAGO
Nichol, Peter B. *Think, Lead, Disrupt: How Innovative Minds Connect Strategy To Execution* (1st ed.). Newington, CT USA: OROCA Innovations, 2021.

ELSEVIER HARVARD
Nichol, P.B., 2021 *Think, Lead, Disrupt: How Innovative Minds Connect Strategy To Execution*, 1st ed. OROCA Innovations, Newington, CT USA.

IEEE
P. B. Nichol, *Think, Lead, Disrupt: How Innovative Minds Connect Strategy To Execution*, 1st ed. Newington, CT USA: OROCA Innovations, 2021.

ENDNOTES

CHAPTER 1

1. Powers, A. (2014). Understanding First Principles. http://fromfiction.com/understanding-first-principles/

2. Gunkel, P. (1997). *The Science of Ideas: An Introduction to Ideonomy.* http://ideonomy.mit.edu/pemail.html

3. Gunkel, P. (1997). *The Science of Ideas: An Introduction to Ideonomy.* http://ideonomy.mit.edu/pemail.html

4. Gunkel, P. (1997). *The Science of Ideas: An Introduction to Ideonomy.* http://ideonomy.mit.edu/pemail.html

CHAPTER 2

1. Godin, B. (2015). *Models of innovation: Why models of innovation are models, or what work is being done in calling them models?* Social Studies of Science, 45(4), 570–596. https://doi.org/10.1177/0306312715596852

2. Jennings, J., & Haughton, L. (2002). *It's Not the Big That Eat the Small...It's the Fast That Eat the Slow: How to Use Speed as a Competitive Tool in Business* (1st edition). New York: HarperBusiness.

3. Hagel, J., Brown, J. S., & Samoylova, T. (2013). From exponential technologies to exponential innovation. Retrieved January 16, 2017, from https://dupress.deloitte.com/dup-us-en/industry/technology/from-exponential-technologies-to-exponential-innovation.html

4. Wikipedia. (2014). Chain-linked model. In Wikipedia. Retrieved from https://en.wikipedia.org/w/index.php?title=Chain-linked_model&oldid=593993668

5. Gomory, R. E. (1989). From the "Ladder of Science" to the Product Development Cycle. Retrieved January 16, 2017, from https://hbr.org/1989/11/from-the-ladder-of-science-to-the-product-development-cycle

6. Mahdjoubi, D. (1997). Non-Linear Models of Technological Innovation. Retrieved from https://www.ischool.utexas.edu/~darius/05-Non-Linear_Models.pdf

7. Berkhout, A. J. (2015). CYCLIC INNOVATION MODEL (CIM). Retrieved January 17, 2017, from http://www.aj-berkhout.com/Cyclic%20Innovation%20Model/

8. Gomory, R. E. (1989). From the "Ladder of Science" to the Product Development Cycle. Retrieved January 16, 2017, from https://hbr.org/1989/11/from-the-ladder-of-science-to-the-product-development-cycle

9. Alic, J. A., Branscomb, L. M., Brooks, H., Carter, A. B., & Epstein, G. L. (1992). Beyond Spinoff: Military and Commercial Technologies in a Changing World (First edition). Boston, Mass: Harvard Business School Pr.

10. Branscomb, L. M. (Ed.). (1993). Empowering Technology: Implementing a U.S. Strategy. Cambridge, Mass: The MIT Press.

11. Alic, J. A., Branscomb, L. M., Brooks, H., Carter, A. B., & Epstein, G. L. (1992). Beyond Spinoff: Military and Commercial Technologies in a Changing World (First edition). Boston, Mass: Harvard Business School Pr.

12. OECD/Eurostat (2005), Oslo Manual: Guidelines for Collecting and Interpreting Innovation Data, 3rd Edition, OECD Publishing, Paris. DOI: http://dx.doi.org/10.1787/9789264013100-en

13. Wikipedia. (2017). Artificial neural network. In Wikipedia. Retrieved from https://en.wikipedia.org/w/index.php?title=Artificial_neural_network&oldid=760173488

14. Ziman, J. (1991). A neural net model of innovation. Science and Public Policy, 18(1), 65–75. https://doi.org/10.1093/spp/18.1.65

CHAPTER 3

1. Munger, Charlie. (1995). *Charlie Munger On the Physchology of Human Misjudgement: Speed at Harvard University*. Retrieved from http://www.rbcpa.com/mungerspeech_june_95.pdf

2. Munger, Charlie (1995). Charlie Munger On the Physchology of Human Misjudgement: Speech at Harvard University. (1995). Retrieved from https://buffettmungerwisdom.files.wordpress.com/2013/01/mungerspeech_june_95.pdf

3. 25cognitivebiases, C. (2000). *25 Cognitive Biases*. Retrieved January 18, 2017, from http://25cognitivebiases.com/

4. Miranda, P. (2015). Is there a written version of Charlie Munger's USC commencement speech? - Quora. Retrieved January 18, 2017,

from https://www.quora.com/Is-there-a-written-version-of-Charlie-Mungers-USC-commencement-speech

5. Tate, W. (2009). The Search for Leadership: An Organisational Perspective. Axminster: Triarchy Press Ltd.

6. Higgins, J. P. T., & Green, S. (2008). 9.7 Sensitivity analyses. Retrieved January 18, 2017, from http://handbook.cochrane.org/chapter_9/9_7_sensitivity_analyses.htm

7. Wikipedia. (2016). Critical mass (disambiguation). In Wikipedia. Retrieved from https://en.wikipedia.org/w/index.php?title=Critical_mass_(disambiguation)&oldid=726798208

8. Ramadan, A., Peterson, D., Lochhead, C., & Jones, K. (2016). Play Bigger: How Pirates, Dreamers, and Innovators Create and Dominate Markets.

9. Wikipedia. (2017). Paradigm shift. In Wikipedia. Retrieved from https://en.wikipedia.org/w/index.php?title=Paradigm_shift&oldid=766506627

10. Wikipedia. (2020). Philosophiæ Naturalis Principia Mathematica. In Wikipedia. https://en.wikipedia.org/w/index.php?title=Philosophi%C3%A6_Naturalis_Principia_Mathematica&oldid=979956140

11. American Cancer Society, Inc. (2017). Key Statistics for Melanoma Skin Cancer. Retrieved March 11, 2017, from https://www.cancer.org/cancer/melanoma-skin-cancer/about/key-statistics.html

12. Andale. (n.d.). Bayes' Theorem Problems, Definition and Examples. Retrieved March 11, 2017, from http://www.statisticshowto.com/bayes-theorem-problems/

13. Silver, N. (2015). *The Signal and the Noise: Why So Many Predictions Fail--but Some Don't* (1 edition). New York, NY: Penguin Books.

14. Vudalb. (2014). Simpson's Paradox. Retrieved March 11, 2017, from http://vudlab.com/simpsons/

15. Vudalb. (2014). Simpson's Paradox. Retrieved March 11, 2017, from http://vudlab.com/simpsons/

16. Urban, Ph.D., R. G. (2016). The Time-Tested Value of Optionality. Retrieved from https://whatsinnovation.com/2016/06/06/the-time-tested-value-of-optionality/

17. Wikipedia. (2017). Pygmalion effect. In Wikipedia. Retrieved from https://en.wikipedia.org/w/index.php?title=Pygmalion_effect&oldid=763517981

18. Purves, D., Cabeza, R., Huettel, S. A., LaBar, K. S., Platt, M. L., & Woldorff, M. G. (2012). Principles of Cognitive Neuroscience, Second Edition (2nd New edition edition). Sunderland, Mass: Sinauer Associates, Inc.

19. Dunbar, R. (1988). Grooming, Gossip, and the Evolution of Language. Cambridge, Mass.: Harvard University Press.

20. Cialdini, R. B. (2006). Influence: The Psychology of Persuasion, Revised Edition (Revised edition). New York, NY: Harper Business.

21. Wikipedia. (2016). Flypaper theory (strategy). In Wikipedia. Retrieved from https://en.wikipedia.org/w/index.php?title=Flypaper_theory_(strategy)&oldid=700606843

22. Rumsfeld, D. (2013). *Rumsfeld's Rules: Leadership Lessons in Business, Politics, War, and Life* (1 edition). New York, NY: Broadside Books.

23. Janz, C. (2014). Five ways to build a $100 million business. Retrieved from https://medium.com/point-nine-news/five-ways-to-build-a-100-million-business-82ac6ea8ffd9#.ut6i3txa6

CHAPTER 4

1. Rouse, M. (2016). What is incremental innovation? - Definition from WhatIs.com. Retrieved January 16, 2017, from http://searchcio.techtarget.com/definition/incremental-innovation

2. Wikipedia. (2017). History of Gmail. In Wikipedia. Retrieved from https://en.wikipedia.org/w/index.php?title=History_of_Gmail&oldid=748932573

3. Verganti, R. (2009). Design Driven Innovation: Changing the Rules of Competition by Radically Innovating What Things Mean (Pocket Mentor edition). Boston, Mass: Harvard Business Press.

4. Kadareja, A. (2013). Risks of Incremental, Differential, Radical, and Breakthrough Innovation Projects. Retrieved January 16, 2017, from http://www.innovationmanagement.se/2013/07/29/risks-of-incremental-differential-radical-and-breakthrough-innovation-projects/

5. Diamandis, P. H., & Kotler, S. (2014). Abundance: The Future Is Better Than You Think (Reprint edition). New York: Free Press.

6. Kotler, S. (2014). Steven Kotler's Six D's of Exponential Technology | Big Think. Retrieved January 17, 2017, from http://bigthink.com/think-tank/steven-kotlers-six-ds-of-exponential-entrepreneurship

7. Kotler, S. (2014b). The Rise of Superman: Decoding the Science of Ultimate Human Performance (1 edition). Boston: New Harvest.

8. Investopedia. (2003). Moore's Law. Retrieved January 17, 2017, from http://www.investopedia.com/terms/m/mooreslaw.asp

9. Ramirez, V. B. (2016). The 6 Ds of Tech Disruption: A Guide to the Digital Economy. Retrieved from https://singularityhub.com/2016/11/22/the-6-ds-of-tech-disruption-a-guide-to-the-digital-economy/

10. Wikipedia. (2017). Democratization of technology. Retrieved January 17, 2017, from https://en.wikipedia.org/wiki/Democratization_of_technology

11. Deloitte. (2015). Smart Cities: How rapid advances in technology are reshaping our economy and society. Retrieved from https://www2.deloitte.com/content/dam/Deloitte/tr/Documents/public-sector/deloitte-nl-ps-smart-cities-report.pdf

CHAPTER 5

1. Keeley, L., Walters, H., Pikkel, R., & Quinn, B. (2013). Ten Types of Innovation: The Discipline of Building Breakthroughs (1 edition). Wiley.

2. Govindarajan, V., & Trimble, C. (2010). The Other Side of Innovation: Solving the Execution Challenge (1 edition). Boston, Mass: Harvard Business Review Press.

3. Govindarajan, V. (2010). Innovation is Not Creativity. Retrieved April 9, 2017, from https://hbr.org/2010/08/innovation-is-not-creativity

4. Ulwick, A. W. (2002). Turn Customer Input into Innovation. Retrieved April 9, 2017, from https://hbr.org/2002/01/turn-customer-input-into-innovation

5. Ulwick, A. W. (n.d.). What is Outcome-Driven Innovation® (ODI)? (p. 19). Retrieved from http://grababyte.com/storage/Outcome-Driven-Innovation_.pdf

6. Russo, X. (2016). A step-by-step guide to.using Outcome Driven Innovation (ODI). Retrieved April 9, 2017, from https://medium.com/@xavierrusso/a-step-by-step-guide-to-using-outcome-driven-innovation-odi-for-a-new-product-ded320f49acb

7. Roberts, E. B., & Eesley, C. E. (2011). *Entrepreneurial Impact: The Role of MIT. Foundations and Trends® in Entrepreneurship*, 7(1–2), 1–149. https://doi.org/10.1561/0300000030

8. Acharya, N. (2016). *How MIT Is Teaching Regions Around The World To Unlock Their Entrepreneurial Potential.* Retrieved April 9, 2017, from http://www.forbes.com/sites/nishacharya/2016/05/17/how-mit-is-teaching-regions-around-the-world-to-unlock-their-entrepreneurial-potential/

9. Brandenburger, A. M., & Nalebuff, B. J. (1997). Co-Opetition (1 edition). New York: Currency Doubleday.

10. Blystone, D. (2015). Understanding Alibaba's Business Model. Retrieved April 9, 2017, from http://www.investopedia.com/articles/investing/062315/understanding-alibabas-business-model.asp

11. McKinney, P. (2011). The 7 Immutable Laws of Innovation – Follow them or risk the consequences. Retrieved April 9, 2017, from http://philmckinney.com/the-7-immutable-laws-of-innovation-follow-them-or-risk-the-consequences/

12. Maxwell, J. C. (2007). The 21 Irrefutable Laws of Leadership Workbook: Revised and Updated (10 Rev Upd edition). Nashville, Tenn: Thomas Nelson.

13. Kelley, T., Littman, J., & Peters, T. (2001). The Art of Innovation: Lessons in Creativity from IDEO, America's Leading Design Firm (1 edition). New York: Crown Business.

14. Schrage, M. (2001). Playing Around with Brainstorming. Retrieved April 10, 2017, from https://hbr.org/2001/03/playing-around-with-brainstorming

15. `Wikipedia. (2017). *Diffusion of innovations* - Wikipedia. Retrieved April 10, 2017, from https://en.wikipedia.org/wiki/Diffusion_of_innovations

16. Rogers, E. M. (2003). Diffusion of Innovations, 5th Edition (5th edition). New York: Free Press.

17. Thorndike, EL (1920), "A constant error in psychological ratings", Journal of Applied Psychology, 4 (1): 25–29, doi:10.1037/h0071663.

18. Salkind, N. J. (2008). Encyclopedia of Educational Psychology (1 edition). Thousand Oaks, Calif: SAGE Publications, Inc.

19. Rodgers, M. (2016). Create your own halo effect. Retrieved April 12, 2017, from http://www.thinkadvisor.com/2016/11/08/create-your-own-halo-effect

20. Cialdini, R. B. (2006). Influence: The Psychology of Persuasion, Revised Edition (Revised edition). New York, NY: Harper Business

21. Knox, R. E., & Inkster, J. A. (1968). Postdecision Dissonance at Post Time. Journal of Personality and Social Psychology, 8(4), 319–323.

22. Milgram, S. (1963). Behavior Study of Obedience. Journal of Abnormal Social Psychology, 64(4), 371–378. https://doi.org/http://dx.doi.org/10.1037/h0040525

23. Cialdini, R. C. (2016). *Pre-Suasion: A Revolutionary Way to Influence and Persuade*. New York: Simon & Schuster.

CHAPTER 6

1. Taleb, N. N. (2010). The Black Swan: Second Edition: The Im-pact of the Highly Improbable: With a new section: "On Robustness and Fragility" (2 edition). New York: Ran-dom House Trade Paperbacks.

2. Taleb, N. N. (2010). The Black Swan: Second Edition: The Im-pact of the Highly Improbable: With a new section: "On Robustness and Fragility" (2 edition). New York: Ran-dom House Trade Paperbacks.

CHAPTER 8

1. TechCrunch. (2016). *Groupon is buying LivingSocial, plans to downsize business to 15 markets from 27*. TechCrunch. https://social.techcrunch.com/2016/10/26/groupon-is-buying-livingsocial-plans-to-downsize-business-to-15-markets-from-27/

2. Byung-Choel, K., Jeongsik, L., & Park, H. (2013). Dynamic Platform Competition in a Two-Sided Market: Evidence from the Online Daily Deals Promotion Industry, 1–44.

3. Crunchbase. (2014). *Groupon – Acquisitions*. Retrieved from https://www.crunchbase.com/organization/groupon/acquisitions

4. Boomerang commerce. (2015). *Fast-growing boomerang commerce adds office depot, sears, and groupon as customers, makes key executive hires to fuel growth*. (2015). Marketing Weekly News, 48.

5. Eisenmann, T. R., Parker, G. G., & Alstyne, M. W. V. (2006, October 1). *Strategies for Two-Sided Markets*. https://hbr.org/2006/10/strategies-for-two-sided-markets

CHAPTER 9

1. Yucht, A. (1997). Flip It!: An Information Skills Strategy for Student Researchers. Retrieved April 13, 2017, from http://www.barnesandnoble.com/w/flip-it-alice-yucht/1111911468

2. du Preez, N. D., & Louw, L. (2008). A framework for managing the innovation process (pp. 546–558). IEEE. https://doi.org/10.1109/PICMET.2008.4599663

3. Eveleens, C. (2015). Innovation management; a literature review of innovation process models and their implications. Retrieved April 28, 2017, from https://www.researchgate.net/publication/265422944_Innovation_management_a_literature_review_of_innovation_process_models_and_their_implications

4. Roy Rothwell, (1994) "Towards the Fifth generation Innovation Process", International Marketing Review, Vol. 11 Issue: 1, pp.7-31, doi: 10.1108/02651339410057491

5. Keeley, L., Walters, H., Pikkel, R., & Quinn, B. (2013). Ten Types of Innovation: The Discipline of Building Breakthroughs (1 edition). Wiley.

6. Furr, N., & Dyer, J. (2014). Choose the Right Innovation Method at the Right Time. Retrieved April 16, 2017, from https://hbr.org/2014/12/choose-the-right-innovation-method-at-the-right-time

7. Furr, N., Dyer, J., & Christensen, C. M. (2014). *The Innovator's Method: Bringing the Lean Start-up into Your Organization*. Boston: Harvard Business Review Press.

8. W. Edwards Deming. (2017). In Wikipedia. Retrieved from https://en.wikipedia.org/w/index.php?title=W._Edwards_Deming&oldid=772513343

9. Pritchett, P., & Pound, R. (2014). *Business as Unusual: The Handbook for Leading and Managing Organizational Change.* Dallas, Tex: Pritchett, LP.

10. Handy, C. (1984). *The Future of Work.* Oxford: John Wiley & Sons.

11. Handy, C. (1991). *The Age of Unreason* (1st edition). Boston, Mass: Harvard Business Review Press.

12. Handy, C. (1995). *The Empty Raincoat: Making Sense of the Future.* (New edition). London: Arrow Books.

13. Sheldrake, J. (2015). Charles Handy's *The Future of Work* Revisited. London, England. Retrieved from http://www.gpilondon.com/wp-content/uploads/Sheldrake-Policy-Paper_Jan15.pdf

14. Cheang, H. (2014). The Sigmoid Curve: A Model for Constant Business Growth and Innovation. Retrieved May 18, 2017, from http://blog.cimpl.com/the-sigmoid-curve-a-model-for-constant-business-growth-and-innovation

CHAPTER 14

1. Zhang, M. (2014). 9 Of the Craziest Things Founders Have Done To Make Their Startups Successful. Retrieved May 19, 2017, from http://www.businessinsider.com/crazy-things-founders-have-done-to-make-their-startups-successful-2014-7

2. Penrose, E.T. (1959). *The Theory of the Growth of the Firm*, UK: Basil Blackwell, Oxford

3. Dierickx, I. and Cool, K. (1989). Asset Stock Accumulation and Sustainability of Competitive Advantage. *Management Science*, 35: 1504-1511.

4. Barney, J. B. (1986). Strategic Factor Markets: Expectations, Luck, and Business Strategy. *Management Science*, 32, 1512-1514

5. Barney, J.B. (1991). Firm Resources and Sustained Competitive Advantage. *Journal of Management*, 17, 1, 99-120

6. Manning, L. (2013). Corporate and consumer social responsibility in the food supply chain. *British Food Journal*, 115(1), 9-29.

INDEX

From OROCA Innovations: Author Peter B. Nichol, the first globally certified Masters Business Relationship Management (MBRM®) by the BRM Institute, 4x author, and an MIT Sloan School of Management-recognized CIO and award-winning innovation leader, is your guide to effectively communicate business value with *Leading with Value*.

"Learn how to speak the language of business value! Leading with Value is the solution that every business relationship partner has been looking for— the complete guide to effectively communicating business value!"

GLENN REMORERAS,

CHIEF INFORMATION OFFICER, MARK ANTHONY GROUP

Recently from OROCA Innovations: Author Peter B. Nichol, an MIT Sloan School of Management-recognized CIO and award-winning innovation lead-er, explores how blockchain transform the patient experience—in the book entitled, *The Power of Block-chain for Healthcare.*

"*The Power of Blockchain for Healthcare* provides a compelling argument for the transformative impact that blockchain will have on the patience experience. Nichol Magnificently articu-lates a future vision of health, a vision every executive should experience."

SAN BANERJEE,
HEAD OF CONSUMER DIGITAL SOLUTIONS, HUMANA

From OROCA Innovations: Author Peter B. Nichol, an MIT Sloan School of Management-recognized CIO and award-winning innovation leader, explores the for-gotten world of learning—the ability to learn—in the book entitled, *Learning Intelligence.*

"Peter dives into unexplored, valuable territory in Learning Intelligence. A must-read for any leader wanting to compete in the innovation-powered landscape of today."

MARSHALL GOLDSMITH,

THE AUTHOR OF THE #1 NEW YORK TIMES BESTSELLER,

TRIGGERS.